POLICELESS:

How Policing Lost Its Soul

By Al Robinson

This book is dedicated to everybody who has ever worked for the police service, still works for the police service or ever will work for the police service with the greatest gratitude.

Be strong, be brave, be proud.

Take good care of yourselves, you are loved.

Table of Contents

INTROEY THINGY

Please be kind enough to read these few words before you begin

In October 2017, I was very poorly. As a patrol sergeant I was meant to be in charge of a shift of police officers in Oxford. But the police service had constantly given me a quarter of the officers I needed to keep the community and my officers safe. Up until that point I had considered myself a capable person and a capable police officer, but it'd fried me. The constant stress of having to go into work knowing that there were nowhere near enough officers to deal with the amount of work was too much. And then I had to cope with the stress of the officers who had to deal with the strain of having to try and deliver some sort of service; it was horrendous, it turned my brain into a grey mushy mess.

The catalyst that sparked the *reloveution* was when the Resource Management Department had forgotten to give us sufficient resources for the New Year's Eve celebration in Oxford.

I fully appreciate that modern organisations are stifled by bureaucracy, hierarchies, promotion chasers, and statistic junkies and that those people in the Resource Management Department (and elsewhere) all probably started out with good intentions but ended up being swallowed up by the job, but there is never an excuse to treat a colleague badly, without love and kindness and without apologising when things go wrong. But, in an organisation that has to love and care for the public, we couldn't even love and care for each other. I noticed the *reloveution* was needed everywhere within the police service, except amongst the frontline officers–they loved and looked after each other. So, I decided to write a book. I'd keep a diary and write about 250 words a day and recall some notable events and bung it all together.

For twenty-five years I was a very ordinary police officer, so I'll be a very ordinary author. I don't say that to prompt the comment, "Oh no, Al, you weren't an ordinary police officer, at all, you were exceptional, the best copper I ever had the privilege to serve alongside.' I was awful, I was the very model of ordinariness, both as a person and as a police officer. No-one would ever give me a second glance. For my whole time in the police service, I didn't even know if I even existed.

But what I do have is honesty. It's all I've got.

Truth trumps everything.

Even love and compassion.

Obviously, the characters Nutt, Wyng, and PieChartMan are completely and utterly, what us authors (because that's what I am, an author) call composite characters or character types. Yep, character types. I mean, come on, obviously. They are made up of numerous characters that we've all encountered during our careers. The types of people who make an incredibly stressful job even more stressful. I've used character types to prevent the needless tittle-tattle of who these character types could possibly be.

These composite characters Nutt, Wyng, and PieChartman, transcend gender, rank, sexuality, locations, time and space, in much the same way that they transcend, love, compassion, kindness, and understanding.

Nutt is the character composite of someone who is quite likeable, who, in their own unique way is trying to help, but whatever you've done, they've already done it, but better. If you've been to Tenerife, they've been to Elevenerife, I think you get the picture.

Wyng is a character type who will stop at nothing to get to where he wants to be. You know the sort.

And PieChartMan is a compilation of people who put far too much emphasis on statistics, blissfully oblivious to the obvious human cost.

They just couldn't help themselves. And I just couldn't help myself.

No one person could possibly be as bad as each of these character types, so, I've decided to lump them altogether under those pseudonyms.

A lot of what is said is said with my tongue so firmly in my cheek, so much so, 'at I 'nd up 'alk'n' 'ike 'is

I'm really sorry but there are occasions when I've had to use the term "they". I have to say "they" because I don't know who "they" are, I don't think anyone knows who "they" are, I don't think even "they" know who "they" are. "They" are the unaccountable anonymous people who make huge decisions, that have huge consequences. "They" are like the Wizard of Oz, hiding behind a curtain of invisibility and invincibility, cloaked in anonymity and completely unaccountable for completely fucking up the police service. Anyway, that's who "they" are.

I use a tiny bit, alright, some, yes, yes, quite a lot, okay, you got me, nearly all exaggeration. This is what us authors, that's me that is, call satire. I think of it as an underused form of comedy to make a point. It's all based on the truth. I use the truth and make a joke out of it, in a desperate bid to make you laugh. I believe that this makes the book more entertaining and more enjoyable to read. It's satire. Nothing to get all eggy about. Nothing to be afraid of. I'm sure you've said far worse things about me – and if you haven't, you will now.

I'm not the Dalai Lama, although in a certain light you could be forgiven for thinking that, and I haven't reached a level of self-actualisation, I let myself down very badly on occasions, and some of the time that could be due to the pressure placed on me from the likes of Nutt, Wyng, and PieChartMan. But, then again, it might just be because I can be an arse.

There's a fair amount of *esprit d'escalier*, and on occasions I go into the realms of fantasy. I'm pretty confident that you're clever enough to know where this happens, I mean, come on, obviously. The spirit and the soul of what I'm trying to say is absolutely pure. I hope that when I'm making a serious point, it's game face, and I'm sure you'll get it. You're not silly.

Please give it a good go, bear with me, it's a bit raw and raggedy-rawny around the edges but I think it's worth persevering with.

I knew that I had to self-publish because no publishing house would want to touch this. So, I self-published.

If I say something that upsets you, I don't think that's a good enough reason to dislike me. When we have a difference of opinion, it should be the starting point of discussion, not the end, it doesn't mean we can't be friends, we can still have a hug and go for a pint. Lively discussion and debate never hurt anyone. I've given it all a lot of consideration, I'll stand by it, and up for it. And if you can persuade me to see things your way then I'll stand corrected, as the boy in his new orthopaedic shoes would say.

There is even a very remote chance that you may find yourself wanting to laugh at something very inappropriate and very politically incorrect. If this highly unlikely scenario should occur, please just go with it, have a good ol' laugh, I won't tell anyone; it'll be our dirty little secret, promise.

Please don't give up, please try and read it all. You don't look at the Mona Lisa and say, 'The way Da Vinci painted her left eye is a bit shit.' Although, apparently, he can paint a pretty mean smirk, or whatever it is. Ooh 'ark at me, comparing myself to Da Vinci but this is my little vanity project, and I really would appreciate it if you read it all, or at least gave it a good go.

I don't want to decry anyone else's book about serving in the police service, but I didn't want it to be about me, how and why I joined, and my meteoric rise to sergeant (and it really was truly meteoric). In these strange times where it's more important to be nice than right, out of the fear of causing offence, I just wanted to give my version of events; other people may've seen it all differently, but this is my account, and I'm very happy to listen to your side of it without being offended.

Unlike Da Vinci (oh no, there I go again) I'm a broad brushstroke kinda guy and I didn't want to get too bogged down in irrelevant (to this book) details like times and dates; it isn't ever going to be heard in a court of law as evidence. (But I hope it doesn't detract from the overall content and your enjoyment.)

In 1977, the Oxford Local Policing Area (LPA) was split between two police stations, one in Cowley and the other in St Aldates, Oxford.

At Cowley, every shift (team of officers) had an inspector, two patrol sergeants, a station sergeant, a civilian switchboard operator, two Station Duty Officers (SDOs), and an absolute minimum of seven single-crewed cars. Two or three Area Beat Officers (ABOs, now called Neighbourhood Officers) would be attached to each shift and work similar hours (apart from nights). In reality, at Cowley, they would normally parade eight to ten, what would now be called response officers.

At Oxford each shift would also have an inspector, two patrol sergeants, a station sergeant, a civilian switchboard operator and a Station Duty Officer (SDO) and an absolute minimum of of four single-crewed cars and a couple of foot beats. Again, in reality they would normally parade eight to ten, what would now be called response officers.

So, Oxford LPA, EVERY shift would have two inspectors, four patrol sergeants and about 13 officers per shift, minimum. With a full complement this could increase to about twenty officers and that's excluding, the wonderful officers, on CID, Traffic, ABOs etc.

This is vital for the context of this book, please bear this in mind when I write about five response officers, obviously, times change, and progress has to be made, and those changes are that the population of the City of Oxford has increased (I think it is about 160000 now, I've tried to look it up on The Google what the population was in 1977, I would think it would be about 120000) and the remit of the officers is far broader.

Progress has to be built on the truth.

Healthy communities and happy people are a product of good decision making, good decision making can only come from the truth, the truth is stifled by political correctness, political correctness suffocates good decision making, which leads to unhealthy communities and unhappy people.

If you remember just one thing from this book, please, stand up for your truth. That's all I ask, please just, stand up for your truth.

The *reloveution* is needed everywhere, absolutely everywhere: within the police service and outside of it. We've forgotten how to love each other properly. We're living in a society that needs the police service more than ever. But it's cultural to take the piss out of the police service and a police officer. It's cultural because it's so flippin' cool and so fuckin' groovy to take the piss out of the good ol' girls and boys, who work so hard to try and glue together a fucked-up society. You never get a cool celebrity sticking up for the police, you never get anyone sticking up for the police, the police don't even stick up for the police. But I will. These wonderful people weave miracles every day. They beat any alternative.

There's no longer the thin blue line, the line resembles Morse Code, with far more dots than dashes. Dot, dot, dot, dash, dash, dash, dot and we're so stretched we can't even finish with the last two dots. But that is what we call … life.

When I joined the police service, I fully expected the rudeness and violence from people outside the organisation.

I didn't expect to be told what to think, as well as what to do.

I didn't expect to not be allowed to use my initiative.

I didn't expect to see insidious 'yes' people go up the greasy pole.

I didn't expect some of my colleagues to treat me so badly.

I didn't expect to sell my soul to accommodate the latest diktat from the government, instead of serving the public.

To challenge this appalling behaviour is the real challenge within the job, and this is why the job grows you.

Lastly, and just as important, I'm not a psychopath, probably a bit bipolar, I'll give you that, but I'm definitely not a psychopath nor a sociopath. I care deeply and love everyone. Obviously, I'm profoundly upset when someone is harmed due to police action or inaction, or someone is murdered, raped, suffering domestic violence, burgled, or in any way wronged. Or wants to take their own life. Obviously, this has to be a given, but I joined the police service because I love people, I care deeply about society and community, I'm passionate, deeply compassionate, I feel empathy, and I'm honest.

Viva la *reloveution*.

Please enjoy, take good care of yourself.

With love,

Al Rob

THE FERKIN' MERKIN

SOME THINGS YOU NEED TO KNOW ABOUT SOMETHING CALLED 'THE NEW OPERATING MODEL' (AKA THE FERKIN' MERKIN') BEFORE WE GO ON …

What are the five things the New Operating Model has in common with a merkin?

1. It is far worse than what it replaced.

2. It is far more expensive than originally thought.

3. It doesn't get you off on time.

4. It irritates and stresses out anyone who comes in to contact with it. And

5. If it is applied properly it will make us all look like pussies (Mrs R wouldn't allow me to put the proper word!)

Let's not beat about the bush (if you can pardon the expression under these circumstances) the Non-Operating Merkin is set up to fail. Only under a penny-pinching Conservative Government wanting to privatise the Police Service; and a career-minded senior management could such a ridiculous system ever be entertained.

Cruelly the Non-Operating Merkin has turned colleague against colleague, has led to huge amounts of duty changes and great officers feeling stressed and anxious about the level of service that we are providing.

It was pure stupidity to place so much emphasis on a computer programme which could show demand times for police attendance– without accounting for how long it would take to investigate. The few remaining officers are stressed, they can't get leave, and are leaving.

The Ferkin› Merkin just ain›t ferkin workin›.

THIS IS RELEVANT FOR THE REST OF THE BOOK.

THANK YOU FOR YOUR TIME.

JANUARY

The Resource Management Department and the Dropped Bollocks

31 December 2017/1 January 2018

It's New Year's Eve and I can't stop asking myself and anyone daft enough to listen, 'How has it come to this?'

I appreciate that the police service has only been in existence for about 170 years and we're going to have some teething problems in the early days but, by only having seven additional officers on duty on New Year's Eve in Oxford, its blatantly obvious that the Didn'tKnowItWasNewYear'sEve Department had dropped a bit of a bollock. Simple mistake to make when it doesn't affect you, when you don't know what you're doing, and you don't give a fuck.

For some unknown reason it had completely slipped the minds of the Didn'tKnowItWasNewYear'sEve Department or the Resource Management Department (as they liked to be called – but I won't, if I can piss them off half as much as they've pissed me off, I'll be very happy) that they needed to get additional resources for New Year's Eve – by far the busiest night of the year. We all know the reason: it's not because their numerous office pot-plants are in need of some urgent attention, it's because they have to save money. And it wasn't even that they got in additional officers, all they'd done was rob officers from areas that were already struggling to be above the minimum resourcing level and stuck them on policing the pubs and clubs of Oxford.

They'd robbed Peter to pay Paul, but neither Peter nor Paul ever get paid.

As I said in my Introey Thingy that modern organisations are stifled with bureaucracy, hierarchies, etc, I have to say that through this The Culture has been allowed to devour this amazing institution. My opinion is that the Resource Management Department have lost the human touch, that every duty change has a massive impact on the officer, if they thought of them as people and not just numbers, I'm sure there would be a far clearer definition of what 'exigency' means. It wouldn't serve the organisation to define 'exigency', so it remains undefined.

So, either the Didn'tKnowItWasNewYearsEve Department didn't know it was New Year's Eve or they forgot they were messing with officer's lives. In a desperate bid to reconcile this in my own mind, I have to believe that no-one would be cruel enough to deliberately mess about with another person's life, so I prefer to believe that the Didn'tKnowItWasNewYearsEve Department, didn't know it was New Year's Eve. Easy mistake to make, when it doesn't affect you, when you don't know what you're doing, and you don't give a fuck.

As an organisation, the frontline officer is on the receiving end of disrespect and discourtesy almost daily and it's all rather unpleasant. This is what I will refer to as The Culture.

It's subtle.

And, it's why officers won't and don't stay too long on the frontline.

It's far more difficult to prove disrespect through omission than through an act.

Anyway, it dunt ma"er this is supposed to be a light-hearted romp through my last year as a police officer; it's not supposed to be about The Culture and the unpleasant disrespect and lack of courtesy towards frontline officers. I'll really endeavour not to mention The Culture again.

Somewhere along the way we've lost our way. We've forgotten that the most important thing in the police service is the officer. If the officers aren't looked after there's absolutely no way that we can deliver any kind of meaningful service to the people we're supposed to serve.

It makes me angry and sad to think of what has happened to this amazing organisation.

In the good old days, we had one person in Abingdon Police Station who'd look after all of us. Great big good old Sergeant Roger

Mills, the station sergeant. He loved his officers and we all loved him. He cared, he cared passionately about his officers. He got it. If you look after the officers who serve the people, they can go out and look after the people.

Big old great good Sergeant Roger Mills would ask me if I minded having a duty change to ensure we had enough officers and because it was old great big good Sergeant Roger Mills asking, I wouldn't mind one tiny bit, and because I was dealing with old good great big Sergeant Roger Mills I knew damn fine that if ever I needed time off, he would move heaven and earth to accommodate it.

It was 'give and take', reciprocal, and it all worked beautifully, because he loved and cared for his officers did great old big good Sergeant Roger Mills. I loved him to bits.

He was everything a police officer should be: compassionate, kind, proud, honest, intelligent, courageous, respectful, he used his common sense and discretion. He did everything for the good of everyone else and not for himself. He was great, and he was also big and old and good and a sergeant, but mostly he was great.

My real hero was Inspector Graham Sutherland. Our paths criss-crossed throughout my career, he bailed me out when a few tossers tried to kick me out in my early days and he helped when I was struggling as a sergeant. He taught me that great policing comes from love. Love for your colleagues, love of the people you serve, and love for the people I had to arrest. A lot of them had had awful lives. I loved them all. I loved Graham for looking after me. I did my best to pass his message on (I didn't get it right every time, but at least I tried). I'd like to think that it was my default position to love everyone, until I knew they were out to hurt me.

Like the Didn'tKnowItWasNewYear'sEve Department – they couldn't give a fuck. Not even an incy-wincy fuck for the community and certainly not a tincy-incy-wincy fuck for their colleagues. They just take and take. Oops, there it is, sorry I did say that I'd endeavour not to mention The Culture again.

Now, it's become a mightily thin blue, Morse Code-like, line: fourteen officers, seven for the pubs and seven, including myself, a patrol sergeant, for the rest of Oxford. On New Year's Eve in Oxford we had fourteen officers looking after at least 150,000 predominantly drunk people dealing with all the nonsense that occurs when people and alcohol collide.

If only the public knew. 'How has it come to this?' I thought to myself as I looked at the resources available and the state of the city.

I just had to write my book.

Early doors there were thirty travellers in urgent need of being ejected from the St Aldates Tavern; elsewhere there were people wanting to kill people and people wanting to kill themselves and everything in between. It was horrendous and stressful and bewildering, but the dangerously few officers rolled their sleeves up and got stuck in.

Cutbacks have led to the closure of a custody suite at Oxford (good decision to make when the decision doesn't affect you, when you don't know what you're doing, and you don't give a fuck), so police officers have to tootle the eight miles down the A34 to the custody suite (or Hotel Babylon as my good friend and colleague, the brilliant Phil Gardiner calls it) in Abingdon, and then blast back warp-factor greased weasel to bail out their colleagues when they're getting a shoeing outside the Atik nightclub.

(And it's far worse for all my colleagues dotted around the rural parts of Oxfordshire, Buckinghamshire and Berkshire, who have to drive over thirty miles to their nearest custody suite, often single crewed, because their senior officers think that they'll increase the visibility of the police by adopting such an horrendously unsafe policy. Oops, there it is. But it's a fairly easy decision to make when it doesn't affect you, you don't know what you're doing, and you don't give a fuck.)

Inevitably, people were arrested and off the officers would tootle to accompany them to the cells, leaving the ever-decreasing number of officers to deal with the ever-increasing drunkenness of the people of Oxford.

While I think of it, every Friday and Saturday night Oxford Local Police Area (LPA) work Operation Nightsafe – when we try to cobble together about fourteen officers from other LPAs and Neighbourhood Teams to try to prevent and detect crime caused by people going to the pubs and clubs. We call this the Night-Time Economy (NTE). If we should have fourteen for an ordinary Nightsafe, seven ain't gonna cut it for a New Year's Eve … obviously. With some very notable exceptions (Littlelegs and Kelly and a few others), the officers from other LPAs would find something more important to do like watering the station cactus, or summut like that, summut they'd been meaning to do for the last few years, and Nightsafe night seems as good a night as any. The officers from the Neighbourhood Teams would work extremely hard to rearrange their duty to avoid doing Nightsafe (my God, if they put a fraction of the amount effort into doing Nightsafe as they did into getting out of it, it would've been a doddle), they'd invent some sort of community engagement event – that Battenberg ain't gonna eat itself y'know. There was no limit to their ingenuity in getting out of doing Nightsafe.

Most of the time it was just down to the good old local response officers to police Nightsafe.

At 0200hrs on New Year's Day, after four hours of being run ragged, without any chance of having a break, me and my colleague attended an incident where a lad had been stabbed. We didn't have any officers to take victim and witness statements, seize exhibits, preserve the scene, or even to look for the suspects and that's without worrying about cross-contamination issues. (This kind of minor detail was overlooked by the people who devised and implemented the New Operating Model: every big incident requires at least six officers, simple mistake to make when it doesn't affect you, when you don't know what you're doing and you don't give a fuck, but more of that in a bit). All of my officers were either dealing with equally serious incidents or balls-deep in some other drunken dipshittery eight miles away.

13

It was only because some good old boys and girls from the Special Constabulary giving up their time free of charge, that we stood a fighting chance. And that's why I'll always be eternally grateful to the Specials – if it wasn't for them, we wouldn't have had a cat in hell's chance. I hope these wonderful people know who they are, they're too numerous to list, but they are truly incredible people and should be very proud of what they do.

While all of this was kicking off in Oxford, four young men were stabbed to death on New Year's Day in London. Knife crime is out of control. More about that in a bit.

About two months ago on Channel 4 News, a black youth leader, a Conservative MP and a Labour MP were discussing the legalities of stop and search. They discussed it from the 'victim's perspective' but they all completely missed the point: every time a police officer challenges someone who they believe to have a knife, the officer puts their life on offer. That police officer is someone's brother, sister, mother, daughter, father, son, loved one and friend, and is brave enough to challenge someone with a knife. That officer does not have a forum to tell the public of the reality of what they have to go through on a daily basis because no one in the media talks about the realities of modern policing from a police officer's point of view.

Now, I just so happen to love these great old girls and great old boys. A lot.

These are amongst the compassionate, respectful, dignified, polite, proud, courageous, wonderful, kind, considerate people you could ever meet. I'm not, but they are.

These officers work extremely long and difficult hours and get very little respect, appreciation or understanding of what they do. Both from the public and from senior officers who've become detached from the realities of policing. And even from some of their colleagues (oops, there it is!!)

Back in the good great big old Sergeant Roger Mills days, Abingdon, which is about a fifth of the size of Oxford, had at least fourteen officers on each shift/party. The officers dealt with crime –

its detection and prevention but so much of the work we do now is safeguarding, something that used to be the responsibility of Social Services but due to the cutbacks caused by austerity, it's left to the police to deal with. The police have become the default backstop, left to pick up the pieces of all of our social ills. We hardly deal with crime any more.

And crime and time waits for no-one: it's a 24/7/365 thing, and in an effort to police the 24/7/365 demand frontline, policing is split into 'shifts', 'teams' or 'parties'; all the same thing. On Oxford Local Police Area (LPA) we have five parties to cater for the 24-hour demand. I'm on Party 3 at Cowley – Oxford LPA is split between St Aldates (in the centre of Oxford) and Cowley.

Before the introduction of the New Operating Model (the Ferkin Merkin–more about that in a bit), policing revolved around a team of officers. We used to have twelve officers all at Cowley, of which two would have to attend appointments – where a witness or victim would give a statement of a non-urgent nature and one of which would attempt to find the missing persons (mispers). That left nine officers to respond to the incidents coming in and progress their investigations and the numerous other bits of bureaucracy that needed to be tickled along.

We all started at the same time and all went through the Briefing Site together. I always enjoyed the briefing it gave us a chance to be together and have a bit of a laugh.

I had wonderful officers: Stanstead, TeeTee, EM, Paddy, Sophie, Ryan, Davey V, Beard, Becca, Oz, Luke and a few others you'll meet as we go along; they loved people, they were my kind of people, they were all incredible people.

I'd go through the previous day's incidents and the Briefing Site, which told us about any officer safety information, the most important part, because all that matters is that the officers get home safely to their loved ones. I also told the officers about the people who were wanted. There was something called ID Sought where we'd try and identify someone from a still photograph. I'd hand out incidents that needed to be attended. We'd be aware of who was wanted on the rolling arrests, who needed to be checked on curfew and where the tasking area was (a location which had been identified as likely to be subjected to crime). I'd have to allocate officers to do the arrests, do the curfew checks and to ensure the tasking areas were patrolled. Now, I've only got a CSE (grade 3) in maths but even I could work out there was nowhere near enough officers.

But I loved briefings, it gave us a chance to be together, bond together, and have a bit of a laugh together.

Since the introduction of the New Operating Model, it's all become incredibly fragmented. On Party 3 we've got two sergeants, me and the amazing Ash, trying to look after the response team – usually only about five officers. And down at St Aldates we've got the wonderful Triff looking after the five (if we're lucky) officers in the I(nvestigation)Hub who dealt with volume crime, which is almost any crime not deemed to be too serious, such as murder, rape, robbery and burglary, and kidnapping which would be passed to wonderful people in CID. This involves gathering the evidence to try and bring offenders to justice. They'd interview the prisoners and attend the appointments for the less urgent incidents. They also had to resource scene-watches and cell-watches but because they were so horrifically resource-short in the IHub it was passed to the horrifically resource-short response team (someone forgot that scene and cell-watches had to be resourced –a simple mistake to make, when it doesn't affect you, when you don't know what you're doing and you don't give a fuck). There's a fourth sergeant, the wonderful Ali who'd deal with the more complex cases (this was not the case back in the day but due to the cutbacks they decided to stick these cases on to the shift instead of CID), and Ali bailed me out when I didn't know what I was doing … which was, like, all the time. This crazy arrangement was due to the introduction in June 2017 of the New Operating Model (NOM). ('The Ferkin Merkin' as I so wittily called it and made my incredibly witty poster at the beginning of my book.)

So, now we only have a briefing with four or five officers, and the IHub officers start at different times to the response officers, just to add to the drama and the lack of cohesion, and the lack of co-ordination and the lack of co-operation.

And all this to satisfy the egos of senior managers and consultants who didn't consult.

'There won't be as much demand on response teams'

In April 2017, just before the New Operating Model was introduced, loads of us had to go to a presentation at Headquarters South, organised by one of the very few people who had their, (I've got to use a gender neutral pronoun, crikey, there are so many to choose from, zie, xem, ver, etc, I'll just plump for good ol' fashioned them and their, if that's all right with you) high potential identified and developed on the High Potential Development Scheme (in fact, they may be the only one), Chief Inspector Poto'PinkPaint. Now, here's someone suffering from a severe case of the good ol' Dunning-Kruger Effect. The vast majority of the Senior Management are amazing people, they really are.

This should be good for a laugh.

'Okay, what d'you know about the New Operating Model?' they asked.

And I thought, nothing, no nothing at all, you've got me on that one, I hope the questions are gonna get a lot easier.

'Okay, what's going to happen is that we are going to split the response teams in half, one half will stay responding, and the other half will pick up all the investigation and that will be known as the IHub.'

And I thought, well, that ain't gonna work, the response teams can't respond to all the jobs they've got to attend at the mo, so half of them will only be able to respond to only half as many, and the IHub won't be able to handle twice the number of investigations that will be dumped on them from response. And the response team will spend most of their time writing handovers for the IHub, instead of just cracking on and dealing and building a rapport with the prisoners. I will spend all my time reviewing the handovers, instead of serving the public. And you may have people who want to be on response and people who want to investigate in the early days, you might very well have square pegs in square holes but what happens when they all have to swap round in a year's time, you'll have some mightily pissed off dodecagons being hammered into triangular holes, and people will want to leave.'

I mean, it was pretty bloody obvious really.

'Okay, and if there aren't enough response officers to respond the control room will be told to escalate the problem which means that they'll go to the 'outers' (officers from neighbouring areas), or call upon the Force Roamers, officers on roads policing and suchlike, or the IHub, or the Neighbourhood Team, there will be an officer somewhere within the Happy Valley or Hampshire. There will be a spare officer somewhere to respond.'

And I thought, well, that ain't gonna work, if we're going to be short in Oxford then they'll be short everywhere, and by the time someone responds from another area the whole flippin' incident will be long over and the offender long gone

I mean, it was pretty bloody obvious really.

'Okay, and anyway, we will get the Domestic Abuse Unit to attend domestics, and the Burglary Initiatives (Op Basil) to attend burglaries, so there won't be as much demand on the response teams, which will be called the Emergency Response Team because they will only be responding to emergencies, and incredibly busy, so all the other departments, such as Op Basil, will be supporting them.'

And I thought, well, that ain't gonna work, we tried that years ago with Op Quest which was an initiative where the whole idea was to get the burglary team (Op Basil) to, hey, attend a burglary, the robbery team to attend a, erm, a robbery, the Domestic Abuse Unit to attend er, yep, I think you get the idea. (It just didn't happen, in fact it got worse, it resulted in the response officer attending more incidents than the departments that had been set up to deal with that specific incident. No amount of lube, talc, or WD40 could budge the officers in any of the departments out into the scary world.) But, anyway, at least they were going to try and take something away from response team, and this, to me, was completely and utterly and wholly and entirely what the New Operating Model was all about, because everything else was going to be dumped on them.

The belief in the other departments, is that the response teams should support everyone and do all the arrests (oops, there it is). Domestic Abuse Unit attend a domestic? Not on your Nelly, you've got more of a chance of going a whole day without the Littlemore Hospital reporting someone missing, it just ain't gonna happen.

. This is cultural. No other department will ever support the response team, it's unheard of, and I know everyone here is thinking the same.

I mean, it was pretty bloody obvious really.

'Okay, and we'll be introducing the Contact Management Platform, which will be turning off the tap of demand.' (And made a wanky hand gesture of turning off a tap), subsequently anyone who ever talks about the Contact Management Platform has to make that wanky bloody hand gesture, and it got right on my bloody nerves.'

And I thought, well, that ain't gonna work, we haven't got a Contact Management Platform, and I don't think we ever will have, and if we ever do have, we will employ people on a very low wage who will have absolutely no idea of how the police service operates and will spend most of their time asking me how the police service operates, and so the demand on me will be greater (and I'd make a wanky hand gesture of turning a tap on). Come on, guys, let's think about this. I'm sure everyone here is thinking exactly the same as me.

I mean, it was pretty bloody obvious really.

'Okay, and we'll be introducing the Problem-Solving Team, who will be beavering away on all those long-term problems that police officers do not have time to deal with. Like the missing people from the Littlemore or the constant and persistent anti-social problems.'

And I thought, well, that ain't gonna work, you're going to employ police officers to do the job that a civilian should do, and those officers will become massively de-skilled and be no use to man nor beast. And I could bet my mortgage money that they'll be working Monday to Friday 8 to 4 with a cheeky little flyer on Friday, precisely at the time when the problems are occurring. Come on guys, am I the only silly sod in 'ere thinking this?

I mean, it was pretty bloody obvious really.

'Okay, and the Neighbourhood Teams, they will be cut from four officers to two and about four Police Community Support Officers (PCSOs), and they will be ring-fenced from doing police work, because they've been propping up the response teams, and they'll be thought of as Engagement Officers, who will go out and identify the hard to reach and vulnerable people within the community because they will be working on longer term issues within their community.'

And I thought, well, that ain't gonna work, why would people join the police to be engagement officers? Not support their colleagues and go home at midnight, that is not why people join the police service, they'll become massively de-skilled and about as much use as a bucket under a bull. Come on, guys, am I the only one in 'ere thinking these things? Someone please tell this person that they're making a huge mistake.

I mean, it was pretty bloody obvious really.

'It has failed in almost every force where it's been implemented,' they said.

And I thought, oh wow, why didn't you say that in the first place, you've convinced me, I dunno what everyone was chatting about, this is gonna work

I mean, it was pretty bloody obvious really.

They'd only gone and reinvented the square wheel. At a time of austerity, it would've made far more sense to put all available officers on the frontline.

And the funny thing about it is, I can see no logical reason for it, unless they're thinking about civilianising and then privatising the investigation part of policing, and that's the funny thing about it.

The NOM had piggybacked the idea of demand-led policing. An anonymous person who is not accountable for their decision noticed that there wasn't much demand for policing between two and seven o'clock in the morning and decided police officers weren't needed between two and seven in the morning. This showed a tremendous lack of understanding of policing – if these consultants had liaised with frontline officers, the officers would've told them that between two and seven in the morning was the opportunity to go out and patrol to prevent crime, and to reduce the chance of receiving the seven o'clock phone call, saying that some tools had been stolen; that it was the time for officers to complete the never ending online pointless training packages which only had to be completed to cover their collective arses; to yawn and delete without ever reading, the numerous crappy e-mails from PieChartMan, Wyng, and Nutt, sent out purely to cover their own arse (yawn, delete, repeat), complete and compile their Court files, and to do the myriad of other things that they have had to put off because they had been so bloody busy they didn't have a snowball's chance in hell of doing it whilst responding to the incredible number of jobs they have to respond to throughout the day. This was also a chance to bond and get to know your colleagues without all the relentless pressure that occurs before two o'clock in the morning.

But, anyway, the consultants didn't know that officers needed time to investigate crime – at any time. Easy mistake to make when it doesn't affect you, when you don't know what you're doing, and you don't give a fuck.

You don't need me, to tell you, that it was Albert Maysles who said, 'Tyranny is the deliberate removal of nuance' and it is the deliberate removal of nuance that has allowed the removal of canteens, and not understand the importance of handover times, nor understand that police officers are human beings and can, and do, make mistakes, just tiny little things like that.

Because these people have never been police officers, they cannot understand the idiosyncrasies and nuances of policing. Not so long ago a police officer had to learn their skill, craft, art; they all started as a police constable and had to learn to understand how incredibly difficult it was, so when they were promoted, they understood nuance. Good, sound decisions were made.

21

The last copper's copper to make it to the Chief Constable's Management Team was Mick Page, the New Operating Model wouldn't've happened on his watch.

Meaningless statistics

The biggest difference between the big old great sergeant days and now, obviously, is the drastic reduction in the number of frontline officers but also, we're no longer allowed to use our common sense and discretion, our judgement. Instead, everything has been reduced to a soulless process. By this I mean, if CCTV captures two lads fighting, we used to be able to say either shake hands or go your separate ways; now everything has to be recorded, all their details are recorded, and the officer is under pressure to get them charged or cautioned (this is called a 'detection' or a 'positive outcome' – much more about that in a bit). This is an appalling way for the police to behave, this is where we lost the public and the public lost their confidence in us. A lot of wonderful people who've committed some extremely minor misdemeanour ended up being criminalised for something that should've been resolved in seconds with the officer gaining the respect of all the people involved.

We've disappeared behind meaningless statistics, that people neither care about nor trust. 'I don't need no weatherman to tell me which way the wind blows,' as good ol' Bobby D sang all those years ago. If officers could use their judgement, the change in society would be tangible and you wouldn't need any pointless statistics to prove it. And, come on, let's be brutally honest, nothing reduces the crime figures quite like a reclassification – a cheeky little attempted theft from a vehicle to a vehicle interference, ah, great stuff, great stuff that is.

That's the point

I joined the police service to take the fight to the criminals and to serve the public, but also, I joined to point.

Every police recruitment brochure or poster that has ever been and will ever be printed, has a picture of a police officer pointing. And I thought, if pointing is what they want, then pointing is what they'll get. I'll be the best pointer there has ever been. I practised long and hard, did the hard yards, and put my application form in, went for my three-day interview where they could not fail to recognise my pointing potential. And I got in.

One time, long ago, some old biddy sidled up to me and said, 'Excuse me, officer … ooh I say, don't the police officers look so young these days?'

(Get on with it, I haven't got all day, I've got crime to fight.)

'I was wondering if you could tell me where the police station is?'

I'd just come from there, so I was in with a fighting chance.

'Well, if you go up Ock Street...' I said, pointing with all my might, 'turn left on to Drayton Road...' With an enormous arm movement to my left.

'Yes, yes.'

'You will be going in completely the wrong direction. So, what you have to do is turn around go straight down here...' (Doing a cheeky little pinky point just for added drama) 'And turn off to your right.' Taking myself off my feet as my arm swung to the right. 'And then it's on your right, I think,' I said meekly.

'Oh, thank you so much, officer, have a nice day.'

A short time later I discovered what all the finger pointing was all about. Police officers love nothing more than to play a game of 'guess where my finger's been?' And present their finger to their colleague in a motion, that, to the untrained eye, would make you believe that they were pointing.

Years later this stood my good friend Tom in very good stead when investigating a serious sexual assault; he had no difficulty in correctly identifying that a young gentleman had, in fact, put his fingers where a young lady didn't want him to put them. And that young gentleman was arrested, charged and convicted.

And that's the point.

Concise instructions

Twice a year we get trained in self-defence, Officer Safety Training (OST), and once a year we have a fitness test. Today (4 January 2018) it was just OST.

'Okay then, er, handcuffing. We have our stooge, Al, over there. What you need to do is give loud, clear, concise instructions.'

'Ptyer'ands'nyer'eadslowl'urn'roun'go'o'yerknee'd'ye'derstan' doi 'NOOW.'

'I'm terribly sorry, I... ' I tried to have some clarity.

'Loud, clear, concise instructions. Ptyer'ands'nyer'eadslowl'urn' roun'go'o'yerknee'd'ye'derstan'doi'NOOW.'

'I'm ter...' Again, I sought clarity.

''E's not complying ... stop resisting ... stop resisting.'

'Aaaaghh fu...'

'Stop resisting ... stop resisting ... and double lock the cuffs, and that's what we call ... done.'

OST was one of the very few things that changed massively for the better (the other was the introduction of the wonderful mental health triage, incredible people), our instructors Jon and Rich were magnificent, absolutely magnificent. They made their training fun and informative, and put officer's welfare above everything else, they absolutely got it. They got that all that matters are that an officer gets home safely to their loved ones, everything else takes second place. It's such a novelty and refreshing to be amongst likeminded people, officers who care for other officers, instead of the usual bullying from Resource Management, some Senior Managers, some Control Room staff et al (the pies), which serves only to demoralise officers.

The CMM and NDM

Almost on a daily basis, a complete stranger, someone who I'd never seen before, would come up to me and say, 'Officer, are ... you ... on ... crack?'

And I'd say, 'Nah, mate, I'm alright, just working my way round the CMM and NDM. But thanks ever so much for askin'.'

And they'd say, 'Ah that's alright then, crack on.'

And I'd say, 'It's all in a day's work.'

We both walked away and respected the other's point of view, and that's the funny thing about it.

In my Introey Thingy I did warn you that you may get offended. I should've also warned you that there's also going to be times of high excitement, you're not ready for this, you're definitely not ready for this, the world ain't ready for this, so hold on to your hats, we're off on a mad one, scream if you wanna go faster, things are just about to get terribly lairy.

The CMM is the Conflict Management Model, used to resolve conflict and the NDM is the National Decision Model, used to make a decision. These are the vital tools police officers use to resolve conflict and make decisions. It might be an idea to put on your incontinence pants.

Here we go. On the CMM you have to imagine three entwined circles like the Olympic flag, which has five, but yours has three, so you need to get rid of two, because yours only needs three, so two have to go, so you have just your three entwined circles. Plonk, 'Offender's Behaviour' in one, plonk 'Reasonable Officer Response Options' in the second, and plonk 'Impact Factors' in the last.

Deep breaths, deep breaths.

Under 'Offender's Behaviour', think of six escalating behaviours:

1. Compliance
2. Verbal gestures, body language or saying they aren't going to comply
3. Passive resistance, they won't budge
4. Active resistance, they budge too much
5. Aggressive resistance, they budge far too much, and
6. Serious or aggravated resistance, they've got a knife, and/ or they're on a mad one.

(Come on, hang on in there, your eyes should've rolled to the back of your head by now.)

In the second circle under 'Reasonable Officer Response Options' there are six behaviours (so I'm sure you'll get the general idea that the officer's option should roughly mirror those of the person).

1. Officer presence, sometimes that is all that's needed.

2. Tactical communication, which is a posh way of saying talk to the person. (I think officers should always think of people as people and not offenders, however awful they're being – in their head they've got a pretty good reason for it, so it's always good to think of a potential offender as a person. And it's a pretty good rule for life.)

3. Primary Control Skills, unarmed skills, such as armlocks, and use of handcuffs.

4. Secondary Control Skills. This is where it all gets a bit fuzzy, the use of Taser is in there, with incapacitant sprays.

5. Defensive Tactics. An officer strikes the person and/or takes them to the ground. This is a Home Office ruling and is an option after taser.

6. Deadly Force, even you, in your overexcited, hyperactive state should know what that is.

Be still your heavily beating heart, your whole body should be fizzing, this damn thing should come with a Government health warning. But wait, you've still got your Impact Factors to go, and then you'll still have to do your NDM. Pace yourselves.

In the third circle, obviously, you've got your 'Impact Factors'. Now this can be anything from the size, age, and sex of the person or the officer's knowledge of the individual, or absolutely anything that will have an impact on how the officer is going to resolve the situation with the minimum amount of force.

There you go, as your eyes roll round and round like a Las Vegas fruit machine and the four bells fall into place, you're through it. You may want to make yourself a nice mug of green tea, check your incontinence pants are up to the job, before we crack off to the NDM.

The CMM is an absolute rush of endorphins but the NDM makes the dopamine kick-in; it can be a lethal cocktail, better than methamphetamine. I couldn't get enough of the stuff, the CMM and NDM, not meth. Tape down your wigs. Or get a hat, and stick that on, and hang on to that.

The National Decision Model works in an ongoing cycle.

The incident comes in, the officer is presented with the information; based on the information received the officer should conduct a Risk Assessment identifying any threat, harm, opportunity and risk (THOR). The officer needs to know the policy and procedure (and law, I tended not to get too bogged down in this kinda thing) that applies to their decision. They should then consider any tactical options such as whether to deploy a Taser Trained Officer (TTO) or more accurately whether an officer is needed at all and make the decision and boom, that's it, another one done, what a doddle, piece o' piss, gimme summut difficult to do. But not quite, obviously because the officer has to keep reviewing the decision as the situation evolves.

Sometimes I worked my way around it so fast I gave meself a nosebleed.

And that's it. I told you we'd be off on a mad one. I hope no hats or wigs have been blown off or damaged while we went through that. It's a flippin' rollercoaster ride I tell ya. And all the time I've got to be thinking about the Code of Ethics. I'm sorry, you've had far too much excitement for one day, you just can't have instant gratification all the time, it'll wait for another day, if you can get to sleep with all that dopamine coursing through your veins, it's only about three sleeps to go. It might be an idea to sit in a dimly lit room and get some green tea down ya. It works for me.

I genuinely and seriously love the NDM and CMM – they're my meth.

This policing lark isn't all just safeguarding and engaging, you know, sometimes you actually have to make a decision, and on extremely rare occasions we actually go out and do a bit of police work.

Killed by the river

For two days in the first week of January 2018 I had to supervise nine officers who were trying to secure and preserve the evidence following a lad being killed by the river. Well he wasn't actually killed by the river, he was killed by someone stabbing him, by the river.

On the third day I had to cover the South and Vale, an area I didn't know very well, with officers I do not know very well, and problems I do not know at all.

South and Vale covers a massive area including Abingdon, Didcot, Wantage, Faringdon, Henley, Wallingford and Thame. I only had seven Response officers to sort out any problems that arose in that vast area with a total population of 116,000. When I first joined Thames Valley Police or the 'Happy Valley' as we called it, there was absolutely no way in this world that I thought that Abingdon, Didcot, Wantage, Faringdon, Wallingford, Thame and Henley and all points in between would be policed by seven officers. This is Crazy McCrazyface off her tits on acid because I know that back in the Roger great big good old old good Mills sergeant days, each one of those towns had its own police station with its own officers, so there would have been at least twenty-four officers on patrol.

Today, 6th January 2018, there were two officers for Abingdon, one of whom was on a cell-watch for the female suspect in the murder investigation and was going to have to go to Court with her to ask the magistrate for an extension of twenty-six hours to secure the evidence to enable the custody sergeant to remand the suspects in custody. The other was scurrying around to all the incidents that needed attending. There was a very real and imminent danger of me having to do some work. I'm joking, I'm joking, I worked extremely hard, there's absolutely no hiding place when you've got your radio on, you have to respond to everything. It was a choice between responding to incidents or going to Court with my mate Dringo … so I went to Court with my mate Dringo.

Dringo took quite a shine to one of the female barristers and asked, 'How would you like that bobbing up and down on your cock with that wig on?' I had a good ol' think about it, because these things call for a lot of deliberation and a good ol' think, and replied, 'My cock 'ud look very silly with that wig on.'

I was one of the four officers who were required to ensure that the two suspects (one male and one female) didn't escape or call the magistrate, or anyone else in the Court for that matter, all the names under the sun. The two defendants, four police officers and two security guards were shoe-horned into a tiny dock, designed for about three people.

The detective inspector (DI) outlined the reasons why the suspects should stay in custody for a further twenty-six hours.

He explained that the offence occurred in a drug dealing hotspot. I could see the magistrate thinking 'if it is a drug dealing hotspot, how come there was no CCTV or police patrolling the area?'

I was trying to say 'There ain't any police officers, bruv, there are more police officers cooped up in this tiny box than there is in the whole of South Oxfordshire. Bro, we don't stick a fucking chance. Brother, we haven't even got a fighting chance, my friend, we're fucked, mate.'

The magistrate, my new best mate, couldn't hear me, I was being teabagged by the male defendant, much to Dringo's amusement. We were all unwilling participants in the most gratuitous game of Court Room Twister ever. I've arrested people for sexual assault for doing far less.

After hearing all the evidence, I came to the conclusion that definitely, definitely, definitely, 100%, beyond any shadow of doubt, definitely, definitely, I'd stake my reputation on it, they won't be charged.

They were charged.

Xkclunt

Ah no, what are we getting treated to here?

One day, a long, long, time ago. When I was extremely young in service.

Some lad was trying to commit a misdemeanour. I jumped out of the police car, immediately recognised him as Biggsy, the glue-sniffing burglar of the parish. You didn't have to be in his company for too long to come to the conclusion that for all intents and purposes you were in the company of someone who was as daft as arseholes.

'Oh hi, Biggsy, you glue-sniffing burglar of the parish, I didn't recognise you without your bag of glue stuck on the end of your nose, have you given that the ol' Evo?' I arrested him on suspicion of the misdemeanour, handcuffed him (I didn't fuck about) but as I was trying to put him in the back of the car he squirmed away and ran off down a lane.

'Run, run as fast as fast as you can, you can't catch me, I'm Biggsy, the glue sniffin' man, and, you can't catch me. '

I was struggling a bit. ''Ere, I want a word with you,' as I chased after him, with his hands handcuffed behind his back.

'Run, run as fast as you can, you can't catch me, I'm Biggsy the glue sniffin' maaaa'—. As he face-planted with only his jaw to break his fall.

'I fuckin' well can and I fuckin' well have,' I said as I helped him to his feet and led him back down the lane where a large crowd had gathered.

'Fuckin' police brutality,' one of them said.

'No, no, no, honestly, I know you're not going to believe me, but he just ran away with his hands handcuffed behind his back and went flying and fell over with only his jaw to break his fall.'

'Fuck off, you've beaten him up.'

'No, honestly, I didn't. Ask him.'

'E'sclch fuckclchin well beatclchin me up,' garbled Biggsy.

What the fuck had happened to him? He was doing a pretty mean impersonation of John Merrick.

'Honestly, please, you've got to believe me, he ran off, with the handcuffs on and went a pearler. Please, I'm not that kind of person.'

'Wait a fuckin' minute, you're the cunt who robbed my house. Well done, mate, he's a cunt.'

'Yeah, well, shucks, just doing my job.'

'What happened?'

'He tried to throw a haymaker, but I caught him with an upper cut, just one punch, he went down like a sack of shit, stuck the handcuffs on, and that's it basically. I don't want to boast about it or anything, it was just one punch straight on his jaw, like Tyson but a bit better, his legs just buckled. I don't like talking about it, but it was a magnificent punch, just one, yeah, just one punch, that was it,' I said, playing along with them (we all knew he'd fallen over when he tried to run away with his handcuffs behind his back).

'Fuckin legend.'

'Yes, well, you know, shucks.'

'Xkclunt.'

His face was a right mess. He'd broken his jaw and needed a plate inserted and lost a lot of movement in his neck.

I still see him around from time to time, and we both know what happened, and we're on nodding terms, well, I'm sure we would be if he had a bit more movement in his neck.

Cycle of respect

Back in the Roger Mills great sergeant big good old good old days, everyone in the policing family had huge respect and appreciation for each other. It didn't matter if you'd gone up the greasy pole, from constable, to sergeant, to inspector, to chief inspector, to superintendent, to chief super and eventually to God, everyone had an understanding of the other's role and appreciated how incredibly difficult it was. There was no such thing as Accelerated Promotion schemes, or High Potential Development schemes, or Direct Entry to God schemes, everybody had got their rank on merit and were massively respected for it. There was a cycle of respect. Some people call it a two-way handshake, but whatever it's called, it's sadly missing today.

Now, with the exception of our wonderful superintendent, our Senior Management Team (SMT) aren't around when the grafting is getting done so they've got no appreciation of what it entails but even so, aren't slow in criticising. Because they get promoted so bloody quickly, they do not understand the blood, sweat and tears required to get the job done by the sergeants and constables.

Back in the day, the respect and understanding spread across the departments in the police. There was great respect to the officer who had the courage to put the big hat on and the bravery to be on the frontline. This went through the CID, all the undercover officers, the burglary, auto crime, and assaults initiatives – everyone respected that the frontline officer's role was the toughest, and it was their job to help and support the frontline officer. Now, it's all reversed: as soon as someone moves away from the frontline, they believe that it is the frontline officer's job to support them; they consider themselves to be superior, they lose their power of arrest and forget the 'caution', so they constantly spam the hardest working officers with the arrests they're more than capable of making. It's a dreadful way to behave and only serves to create a silo mentality and the making of the most goddamn awful policing decisions. (Oops, there it is).

23 January 2018

Today the crime figures for England and Wales were released and there's been a 20% rise in violent crime, a 29% increase in robbery, a 21% rise in knife crime and a 21% rise in gun crime. Somehow the Senior Management within the Happy Valley are proud to announce that they were one of only two Constabularies who were graded 'Outstanding' in (pause) efficiency.

This was a masterpiece of misdirection of which Derren Brown would be proud. While pointing their grubby little fingers over there, no-one notices their disgusting behaviour over here. Coming from an organisation that never hesitates to shake their shitty stick of statistics to prove that the officers should be more focussed on their priorities, they've somehow managed to ignore the obvious: the cuts to the police service have had disastrous effects on policing, resulting in far more victims of serious crime. But what they want us to focus on is that a meaningless organisation, Her Majesty's Inspectorate of Constabulary Fire and Rescue Service (HMICFRS), led by an even more meaningless Special Kinda Guy (much more about the Special Kinda Guy in a bit), have awarded the Happy Valley outstanding in (pause) efficiency.

The senior officers just don't get it.

The figures speak for themselves, but they're swept under the carpet and the officers soldier on.

Stick my signature

I take it all back, I never thought I'd see the day when the Senior Management Team would admit that they had made an awful mistake with the New Operating Model.

Oh, wait, hang on, they've admitted they've made a mistake … but it's all my fault. They've made an awful mistake in having two sergeants (Ash and I) on response and now one of us will have to go to St Aldates, permanently, to try and stave off the tsunami of wanky bureaucracy in the IHub. It was decided that I'd have to go. I didn't want to go.

This is The Culture at work. As an organisation they seem to take great delight in messing officers about.

Because they can.

The organisation (you can never get to the bottom of who actually is accountable) seems to thrive on moving people from where their skillsets can be utilised to the fullest and giving them a menial task to perform. Absolutely soul-destroying for the officer.

What a terrible end to a wonderful career, I was so proud to have served my whole career on the frontline and now I'm going to languish in some shitty IHub office amongst those flippin' awful dick-swingers on the middle floor at St Aldates. I didn't join to do this shit, and I despise anyone who does.

I've got to spend my last few months quality-assuring files. I was gutted, absolutely fucking gutted. Fucking well quality-fucking assuring fucking files. That's not a police officer's job, they shouldn't have that skillset, that should be done by a civilian who should have that skillset. This is another problem within the police service: we've got too many police officers doing jobs that could be done better by civilians and too many civilians messing up jobs that could be messed up far better by police officers. More about that in a bit.

My idea of quality-assuring files is asking an officer where they want me to stick my signature and boom, that's another one done, piece o' piss, gimme summut difficult to do.

And how will Ash cope on his own with all the incidents and all the issues with his officers?

Another incredibly stupid decision had been made by someone who hasn't done any policing for a very long time, if ever at all. Easy mistake to make when it doesn't affect you, when you don't know what you're doing, and you don't give a fuck

So, in May, good old AlRob will be in St Aldates trying desperately to stick his signature somewhere (anywhere, actually).

Every weekday morning

Oh, hello. What are we getting treated to here?

Oh, look here they come, the professional meeting-goers of St Aldates.

At half past eight every weekday morning they begin to assemble. Ash and I have a sweepstake as to how many will be there and how many will have a police radio. The first answer is anywhere between fifteen and twenty-five, the second is easy, it's always two, me and Ash. And on a Monday morning these people sit in judgement of how we've policed the last sixty-six and a half hours.

How on earth have we managed without them for the last sixty-six and a half hours? The busiest sixty-six and a half hours of the week. Honestly, all the frontline officers should be on some sort of Enterprise Allowance Scheme for keeping all these people in a job. Seriously, if these people left, it might take, two, three, four, maybe five years, for the frontline officers to notice.

Just imagine what they'd do if there was a terrorist attack, across the road at Tesco, during the Daily Morning Meeting (DMM).

'Oh oh oh, my radio? I've only just put it down … a couple of years ago.' The lack of wearing a police radio is a status symbol, it's been the in-thing not to wear one for quite a few years now. Nothing says, 'I don't care too much about serving the public' and nothing screams in the face of your colleagues quite as loudly, 'And I care even fucking less about you' than the absence of your police radio. It says it with every sinew of their being. You're an absolute nobody in St Aldates Police Station until you've gone the whole hog and not been bothered in the slightest about the welfare of your colleagues. The number of hours wasted by these wasters trying to find the bloody things must be astronomical.

'Tell the horrible terrorist to calm down. I'll be with him in a minute, I'm having a bit of trouble doing up my stabby, I last wore a couple of stone ago.'

Only joking, only joking.

Some of the people in the meeting, were from outside agencies and just thought it would be a bit of a hoot and a nice place to pop in and have their latte from Café Loco and it was a rather nice way to spend half an hour, watching me get my nuts gently roasted and made to look a completely incompetent twat. They never said a bloody word, they just sat there, watching my lovely nuts getting gently roasted. Ricky Gervais would pay good money for a One Liner or No Liner like that.

And somehow, from somewhere, I have to summon up some diplomacy to be nice to these people. It's cruel.

With the notable exception of the superintendent and Inspector Axe, it was just an excuse to bully and dick-swing.

I get the heebeegeebees just thinking about it, the whole idea is to reassure the Senior Officer that all the incidents are in hand and no bollocks have been dropped; and, of course, their cock won't be on the block. That's all they're interested in, really. We had to go through the incidents of note: assaults, burglaries, missing people and domestic incidents. I had to have my finger on the pulse on all the incidents that were going to be brought up. And know why the curfew checks, rolling arrests and tasking areas hadn't been done.

It was just an excuse to grill the response sergeant or IHub sergeant who had to contend with the incidents that just kept on coming in during the meeting, which everyone else were blissfully unaware of because none of them would have their bloody radios on. I usually ended up medium rare and saved a fortune on tanning products.

And we're off.

'Right, Al, what are the incidents of note over the weekend?'

'Oh Sir, it was an absolute nightmare, two officers have been injured, and we didn't have enough officers to attend to a lot of serious incidents and give any kind of service. It was incredibly stressful, there were two high-risk mispers, thankfully they were found, and three suicidal people have been taken to hospital, it was absolutely horrif—'

'Yeah, well whatever, if we can just crack on, we've got a lot to get through. Right, Al, what can you tell us about the six assaults last night?'

I'd beautifully go through each one in turn, saying whether there was a suspect or not and if there was, whether they'd been arrested or whether there was a plan for them to be arrested and whether or not the victim was being safeguarded.

What I should've said was, 'I've got no idea, I'm busy running a high risk misper, and you've got more than enough sick, lame and lazy officers, or officers who've far less to do than me, who'd be better able to answer your question. 'Right, Al, what can you tell me about the three burglaries?'

I'd reply, 'There's a detective sergeant there, maybe she could answer that one.'

"Ah yes, just force of habit, I expect you to know everything.' And the detective sergeant would beautifully go through the three burglaries, and say if there was a suspect and if there was, whether or not they've been arrested or if there is a plan to arrest them, which was a doddle because all they'd have to do was tell me to arrest them and whether or not the necessary safeguards had been put in place for the victim.

Ah that's good stuff, good stuff that is.

'Right, Al, what can you tell me about six mispers?'

I would reply, 'I'm very worried about the high risk one, and the other five are either from the Warneford or Littlemore Mental Health Hospitals. I've allocated an officer and dedicated them to do nothing but look for these mispers. They've been fully risk assessed and I've prioritised them so there is a very real focus to find the one who poses the greatest risk, it's all in hand, ma'am.'

What I should've said was, 'I'm shitting myself over the high risk one and I'm wasting valuable time being here, and I really couldn't give the steam off two tiny turds about the other five. If the Warneford and Littlemore are stupid enough to let them out, they should be stupid enough to have to find them. My five officers have got far too much to do, so I haven't even bothered them with this crap. The mispers will all return after they've had their crack or heroin, and the hospitals will take ages to let us know. Now if you don't mind, I've got a high risk misper to find.'

'Right, Al, what can you tell us about the seven domestics?'

I would beautifully go through each one in turn, there was always a suspect, such is the nature of a domestic, whether or not they've been arrested and if they haven't, whether two of my hard-pressed officers will somehow bust their balls to arrest and bimble the eight miles along the A34 and whether or not the necessary safeguards had been put in place for the victim.

And then tell them the curfew checks and rolling arrests haven't been completed, because, in all likelihood, we didn't have enough officers.

What I should've said was, 'For the love of God, there are twenty people in this fucking charade and only three have spoken. It's the Al Fucking Robinson Show, what the fuck do the rest of you wankers do? You should be charged an entry fee to come and watch me get my lovely nuts roasted. You've got a fucking Domestic Abuse Unit, get those fuckers to come down here to answer your fucking questions. It's disgraceful for you to roast me over something I should know fuck

37

all about, and I've absolutely no fucking intention of knowing fucking anything about. I've been telling you for the last five fucking years to sort this fucking shit out, now fucking do it. And the fucking curfew fucking checks and the fucking rolling fuckin' arrests ain't been done because the Operating Model is shit. This would never've happened in the big old good old great Sergeant Roger Mills days, we would've had more respect for one another. Now if you don't mind, I've got a high risk misper to find. Have a nice day.'

It's enough to make a monkey want to eat its young.

None of it really mattered, because whatever had gone wrong, I'd do what any decent person would've done in the same circumstances and blamed it all on my ol' mate Bally, who was the off-going night turn sergeant.

In a compassionate, healthy and well-functioning, organisation the morning meeting would start by the chair asking if all the officers are fit and healthy and happy; if leave requests have been approved; if rest days have been cancelled; if support was in place for those suffering, and if we have enough officers. Anything and everything to ensure that the officers knew that they were valued.

Nothing could be further from their minds.

It sets the tone and mood for the day, all they're concerned about is themselves, and this behaviour is actively encouraged.

And that is just a tiny part of the reason of how it has come to this. And that's the point.

FEBRUARY

Threat, harm, opportunity and risk and the Code of Ethics

Hippopotamus

Miss Twoody Gooeyshoes has got herself all unnecessary because it's been reported that a taser had been drawn, aimed or fired fifty-eight times in mental health establishments in six months.

Twoody is involved in a debate on the radio. She doesn't realise that a police inspector is running rings around her.

'PK, who was suffering a mental health episode, was tasered when he was self-harming, and, eventually, conceded that the police officers saved his life by tasering him.'

In light of this amazing concession (which should surely have swung even the most entrenched beliefs), Twoody continued like it'd never been said, or if it had been said she wasn't going to acknowledge its existence. Like an old biddy when they let a fart go. Such poise. Everyone looks at each other with that 'did you just hear what I just heard' look, while the old biddy just biddies around pretending to be blissfully oblivious to the obvious and to all the consternation they'd just caused. It's one of life's little joys. The police inspector shows immense restraint by politely pointing out to Twoody that she is suffering from 'a theory/practicality gap'.

Twoody isn't the only one to suffer from the theory/practicality gap, it's exactly what we promote within the police service; this is precisely what Accelerated Promotion programmes promote (apart from my Boss). But, no, Twoody is having none of it, she's lived so long in her own echo chamber that she won't acknowledge the obvious. She waffles so badly that she could sedate a marauding hippopotamus.

We're so incredibly lucky to have these incredible men and women to act in these incredibly difficult situations. The pressure on them is immense, if they get it wrong the ramifications for them are unbearable, only to have what they had seconds to decide to be picked apart for months and years. What would Twoody do? Bore them into submission.

'I am Sergeant Al Robinson, I'm an NDM-trained supervisor and I'm authorising the deployment of taser, to minimise the threat, harm and risk to the public, officers, and the subject, and maximise the safety of everyone else.'

An officer would pipe up, 'I'm really sorry, Sarge, I don't think you've got a handle on this one. This bloke's on a proper mad one, taser ain't gonna cut it, we need you to authorise the use of Twoody.'

My officers would always have my back.

The police inspector did a magnificent job of calling Twoody out on this. All too often, the police capitulate to being nice instead of being right. We're a culmination of compounded bad decisions to the point of being impotent. But more about that in a bit.

If Twoody had seen the effects of a schizophrenic person killing a wonderful, husband, son and father as I did in the Trevor Joyce case, I'm sure she wouldn't be quite so quick to condemn those officers who have to make a huge judgement call in a split second. Of course, we get it wrong on odd occasions but to condemn it without offering any alternative is just plain crass.

Blow another copper (chance would be a fine thing)

In early February I have to work from 1500hrs to midnight. As usual I arrive about half an hour early to enable the off-going sergeant to give me a handover. I was good like that.

It isn't too bad, only one low-risk misper, and a one-person scene-watch on the tow path near Iffley. A large quantity of cannabis had been found. I had seven officers, including a student officer and a Special Constable (a great lad, who gives up his time to serve the public, support his colleagues, without getting paid). Sooner or later it will be Blow Another Copper Out Of My Arsehole (BACOOMA) Time, the time when we've run out of officers and I have no officers to respond to incidents that carry a tremendous amount of threat, harm, opportunity and risk (THOR). It usually happens within a couple of hours of the shift starting but sometimes we're out of officers before we even start. As I've already mentioned, the New Operating Model was sold to us with the promise that scene-watches and cell-watches (looking after suicidal people in their police cell) was going to be resourced by the IHub, the inevitable happened and this didn't materialise and just like everything else, it got plonked onto the response officers.

Nothing ever gets taken away from response.

Hold on to your hats, let's see how far we get.

Before we even start at 1500hrs, the first job comes in, it's a domestic incident, involving someone with a knife. It's an everyday occurrence, I've every confidence in my officers, they'll sort it. Using the NDM, I establish that there is a huge risk of harm, so I authorise a Taser Trained Officer (TTO) to minimise harm to the subject, the public and the officer and to maximise safety. No matter what we do someone, somewhere will complain.

At the same time there is a report of someone with a firearm near the river by the ice rink on Oxpens. Huge risk, I called for the circus: the helicopter, dog handler, and Armed Response officers to deploy, and it's BACOOMA Time. All available officers put their lives on the line, it's what we go to work for. Despite our best efforts the person reportedly with the knife was never found.

It's BACOOMA Time, every police officer, wherever they are, whatever they're doing, leaps up and sings:

It's BACOOMA Time, it's BACOOMA Time

Blow Another Copper Out Of My Arsehole Time

It's BACOOMA Time, it's BACOOMA Time

It's someone else's fault not mine,

It's BACOOMA Time, it's BACOOMA Time,

But I'll be the one to blame,

It's BACOOMA Time, it's BACOOMA Time,

We haven't even got a Thin Blue Line,

It's BACOOMA Time, it's BACOOMA Time.

Stick on their party hats, pop their poppers, and blow their party whistles, it happens so often there could be a national crisis of a shortage of party poppers.

The next job comes in – a drug deal going down on Western Road.Because it's a crime in progress we have to attend, 'Screech' in the Control Room tells me that she doesn't have any officers to deploy.

I compose myself and say, 'Yep, just use the escalation process as per the New Operating Model, well, it's not a New Operating Model anymore is it? It's been in for over eight months, and I think it's fair to say that the Control Room never really embraced it, I think they should just write this one off and try and join in on the next one. But in case you don't know what the escalation process is; ask if anyone is available in the IHub, they're probably all off sick, sick of coming into work; then go to the outers there won't be anyone because nowhere has got anyone; go to the Force Roamers (officers on Roads Policing, Dog Section, Armed Response Units). They've been cut so much that they won't be able to help, and as a last resort ask the Neighbourhood Team but they'll all be too busy eating Battenberg at some engagement event, so I guess I'll have to just carry all the threat, harm and risk, as always. Thanks.'

I'm not in the slightest bit interested, any risk has been created by themselves.

Next.

All this is before 1600hrs.

Then four jobs that I have even less interest in come in: a car parked at Redbridge without tax and MOT; a food caddy has been stolen; an iPhone has been found, and a report of a car parked on Bedford Road that hasn't moved for four weeks. There is no threat, harm, opportunity (to find out who the offender, or obtaining evidence which would help us to identify who the offender, is) nor risk. They can all be dealt with in slow time. A police officer or a Police Community

Support Officer (I think of them as the same, so when I talk about a police officer I also mean a Police Community Support Officer (PCSO); in fact, if I had my way I'd make all PCSOs police officers) will bimble along in a couple of days, be abused by the caller about why it has taken so long to attend, tell the caller that there aren't enough officers and leave. Huge potential for a complaint. So now we're on a roll, reports come in like a tsunami.

EVENT: On Elizabeth Jennings Way some kids are playing music and smoking on a bench that they have moved under the bridge.

'Have you asked them to turn it down?' someone within the police service bravely asks.

'No, that's the police's job,' the coward replies.

People have grown so used to the police sorting everything out for them that they are incapable of sorting out anything for themselves. As well as wasting my time, it eventually leads to a breakdown in communities as everyone avoids any kind of responsibility.

ACTION: I ignore it.

OUTCOME: When an officer tells the caller that they should sort out their own problems there is massive potential for a complaint.

EVENT: Someone reports a transit van at the traffic lights on London Road with someone in the back shouting for help. It turned out to be a GEOAmey prison transport van with a prisoner clowning around.

ACTION: Massively resource intensive, and massively funny.

OUTCOME: No possibility of a complaint. And I laughed a lot.

EVENT: Antisocial behaviour on Ryder Close.

'Have you asked them to stop whatever they're doing that is upsetting you?'

'No, that's the police's job, and anyway, if I didn't report it to you, I wouldn't have the chance to go and tell everyone how fucking useless you are, now hurry up.'

No threat, harm or risk.

ACTION: Ignore.

OUTCOME: Probably a complaint.

EVENT: Antisocial behaviour on Temple Road, neighbours throwing a grapefruit, yep, a grapefruit. I could understand it if it was a melon. Why would you even bother?

ACTION: Try and recover the grapefruit. I like grapefruit.

OUTCOME: They can complain if they like, I'll be getting stuck into my grapefruit.

EVENT: A Road Traffic Collision (RTC) involving a bus. Roads Policing can deal with that, but they've been cut so much, that they're probably already dealing with other incidents elsewhere.

ACTION: I haven't got any officers; I pray that things can be resolved without anyone getting hurt.

OUTCOME: I think Roads Policing attended and did a great job (as usual) the collision was recorded on a form known as TA1 (I think that's what it's called, I've never filled one in.)

EVENT: A car broken into on the Woodstock Road. Ah now, yes, a crime, this is what I joined the job for. There is no threat, harm or risk and the opportunity to find out who the offenders are lies with our Crime Scene Investigation (CSI) who may or may not bimble along. A police officer from the IHub may or may not bimble along in a couple of days' times, look remotely interested and leave.

In the good old days before the New Operating Model the Neighbourhood Team would attend. This is the perfect opportunity for Neighbourhood Officers to get to know the residents within the community and try and resolve issues by conducting house to house and CCTV enquiries. Neighbourhood Teams have become Engagement Officers, they've become deskilled, they focus on 'vulnerable' people within the community, most of them aren't vulnerable at all, somebody really should explain the difference between weakness and vulnerability, they are people who won't make a good decision, as opposed to someone who can't. They're just a culmination of all their own stupidity. I can see where this is going; instead of being 'a nice to do' this will metamorphisise into being 'the police's responsibility', just like it did with domestic incidents. Please bear with me, I've dedicated a chapter to domestic incidents, more about that in a bit.

ACTION: Nothing of any great significance.

OUTCOME: Aggrieved will lose what little faith they had left in the police service but probably won't complain.

EVENT: Robbery at Martin's newsagent on the Balfour Road.

ACTION: A gun in a bag was found at the scene and the newsagent was threatened with a machete. Officers had to redeploy from whatever they were dealing with (the domestic incident, the firearms incident, or the drug deal, or the kids playing music). There's a huge amount of threat, harm, opportunity and risk; the officers pull out all the stops including Taser Trained Officers (TTOs) and the Armed Response Vehicle (ARV); when it's a genuinely serious incident we do pull out all the stops.

OUTCOME: There is no potential for a complaint, a genuine victim of crime is always happy with our response.

EVENT: Someone playing knock and run on Woodlands Road. In what world would someone think that this is worthy of police time? Next.

ACTION: Didn't even have the thrill of using the NDM.

OUTCOME: I went and had a nice cup of Yorkshire Tea.

EVENT: Another RTC on Marston Road. By and large, RTCs are attended by the Roads Policing Department; they work incredibly hard, and I'm enormously grateful.

ACTION: I'm not in the slightest bit interested, I know they'll do a great job, and if they don't and there's a complaint, I will not be dealing with it. Such is the silo mentality that has engulfed the police service. If it's not going to impact on me, I'm not interested, no-one's interested in my problems, we've been divided and conquered.

OUTCOME: I dunk a Bourbon (they're my favourites) into my tea.

EVENT: Another drug deal in Jericho.

ACTION: Crack on, not interested.

OUTCOME: The only person who can complain is the caller, and I can handle that.

EVENT: I dealt with a paedophile who has to sign on annually.

ACTION: No-one had told him that Cowley Police Station had closed about a year ago.

OUTCOME: There will be no complaint. And my tea went cold.

EVENT: A lady had set off her domestic alarm in error in Jericho.

ACTION: Massively resource intensive. And not funny.

OUTCOME: At least there won't be a complaint. I have time to wonder whether it's time for another tea.

EVENT: Vehicle broken into on Chester Street.

ACTION: It's a crime but we're too busy dealing with threat, harm and risk to attend. CSI and police officers will have to get their bimbling boots on.

OUTCOME: Huge potential for a complaint, or at the very least the victim will have a good moan to his mates in the pub.

'My car was broken in to and the police officer phoned me up three days later to say that there is nothing they're going to do about it.'

Slurp. 'Sorry, what did you say, mate?'

We place far more importance on safeguarding than on preventing and solving crimes.

We have overcomplicated a very simple job. We just need to get an officer there, as soon as possible, don't record it as a crime until the officer makes their decision, let them use their discretion, and go on their merry way. And if it's a safeguarding issue get social services to attend. We love overcomplicating the simplest of jobs. Just get back to basics and get the bobby back on the beat.

EVENT: A peeping Tom on Warwick Street.

ACTION: I could not resource. We're too busy dealing with everything else that we attend too late. Massive threat, harm, risk and opportunity to catch an offender before he does something incredibly bad.

OUTCOME: And should be a massive complaint but there won't be, the aggrieved is just thankful for our help.

I'd like make a point. On this occasion we were dealing with a robbery and a firearms incident but usually we are dealing with so many people with mental health issues and safeguarding them that we can't get to the crime. We're like an under-8s football team chasing the ball – continually getting caught out of position, when the opposition lob one over the top.

EVENT: A man who is a huge drain on our resources is getting up to his usual tomfoolery in his home, close to the city centre, and not content with his usual nonsense, he also wants to make a complaint about the police. Glug, glug, glug. In the past he's phoned in to say that there's a dead person in his house, there wasn't. And this is why we are constantly out of position. M'Lord, I rest my case.

ACTION: Yep, it's definitely time to make a tea.

OUTCOME: Extremely enjoyable, I should have tea more often, and think of making another tea.

And all this before 1900hrs.

While all this is going on, I've received an e-mail from a Tip Staff member (I'm not quite sure who Tip Staff are, I was told that, they're people employed by the Court and if the Court decides that they want something done, and it's the Tip Staff's job to inform the police, and I was told that when the Tip Staff tell us to jump we don't jump we say 'How high?' well, I don't, I say 'Go fuck yourselves') from a Court in London demanding immediate action to locate a child. I have far too many things to be interested in and too many things not to be interested in, and too many complaints to deal with but I know I won't get any support from Senior Management if it's not resourced. Collective success, and individual failure. And I've no doubt that when it all does go wrong, and inevitably it will, there'll be no shortage of people willing to throw me under the bus.

EVENT: A broken down vehicle on Heyford Hill roundabout.

ACTION: Some risk and I pray that the situation is resolved without anyone getting hurt and the need for a police officer to attend.

OUTCOME: Little chance of a complaint.

EVENT: Someone acting suspiciously on Arnold Road.

ACTION: I am interested and hope and pray that the situation will be resolved without a crime occurring. Inevitably, someone will ask at the DMM why it wasn't resourced.

OUTCOME: Possibility of a complaint. And I wish I had a few more officers.

EVENT: A car broken into on Quarry Road.

ACTION: No risk. The bimblers may or may not bimble along. Another unsatisfied customer.

OUTCOME: There is a possibility of a complaint.

EVENT: A person has found his bike that was stolen two days previously.

ACTION: Huge opportunity to identify the offender. This will be allocated to an IHub officer, who will look at it in about a week's time, and by this time any CCTV or forensic potential will be lost. This is a crime and I'm interested.

OUTCOME: There should be a complaint. Now, where are those bloody Bourbons.

EVENT: An officer accidentally set off the alarm at St Aldates.

ACTION: I call him a silly twat.

OUTCOME: He laughs.

EVENT: Car damaged on Silkdale Close.

ACTION: There is no threat, harm or risk, and a small opportunity to identify the offender. An officer won't attend, it will be given to an IHub officer who will try and appear to be remotely interested and then file it.

OUTCOME: Probably there will be no complaint. Ahhh, there they are.

EVENT: A woman screaming on Christchurch Meadow.

ACTION: Unable to attend, I am interested and I do wonder from time to time what went on there but if it was something really bad, I would hope that people would've done something, and we would've had more calls. Very difficult to gauge threat, harm and risk.

OUTCOME: Caller may complain because of the lack of response. Will probably be mentioned in the DMM. I won't be there, so I don't care. My ol' mate Bally will be though, and I think it's extremely funny spamming him to explain something he knows nothing about. He's done it to me loads of times.

EVENT: Warneford Mental Health hospital reporting one of their patients is missing – she returned a short time later.

ACTION: Not in the slightest bit interested and couldn't care less if they complain. This is a huge issue, people go missing from the mental health hospitals ALL the time, it has a huge potential for risk, and the staff at the hospitals make no attempt to find them, they absolve themselves of all responsibility by just calling the police and dumping all the risk on us.

OUTCOME: Oh bugger, I really need to hone my dunking kills, my bloody Bourbon has only gone and broken into my tea.

EVENT: Someone has breached their bail conditions and needs arresting.

ACTION: No officers, and I will pass to the Party who will be taking over after Party 3, to resource but because the night turn has fewer officers (because of the New Operating Model) they won't be able to resource so I will come in tomorrow and will not be able to resource, and it will be brought up at the DMM.

OUTCOME: I have got to show that I'm remotely interested, no possibility of a complaint but massive potential for a massive bollocking in the morning meeting. I won't be there, Bally will, and that makes me chuckle. Right, I'm really going to concentrate this time, big time – Bourbon successfully dunked.

EVENT: A male peering in through windows on the Bartlemas Road.

ACTION: Unable to resource, I am immensely interested.

OUTCOME: The caller should complain.

We're at about 2030hrs now.

EVENT: A car broken into on St Clements.

ACTION: Err, I'm getting a little bit stressy now, this should be attended but the Neighbourhood Teams have tucked themselves up with engagements. It will be passed to some poor officer in the IHub, who has already amassed a massive workload, who is completely stressed out, will do nothing with it for a couple of weeks and will then try and file it. While the Neighbourhood Team are too engaged in engaging.

OUTCOME: Wouldn't blame the victim if they complained.

EVENT: A support worker reporting a client missing, she returned a short time later. Just passing all the risk to the police as per policy.

ACTION: Great, thanks. Okay, if ever you ever want to waste our time in the future, just give us a call. Not interested.

OUTCOME: Time for more dunking practice.

EVENT: Another missing person from the Warneford Mental Health hospital. ACTION: Massive risk. Not in the slightest bit interested.

OUTCOME: Don't care if there is a complaint. It might be time for salt and pepper chicken balls from Top Wok, where's Ash? He needs to know we've got a very hungry man on our hands here.

EVENT: An ex-police officer is suffering with mental health issues.

ACTION: I speak with him on the phone until the mental health nurse arrives with an officer. Because he had self-harmed with a knife earlier, a TTO had to attend.

OUTCOME: Strangely enough, he did complain. I pacify him and tell Ash I need some salt and pepper chicken balls from Top Wok.

EVENT: Homeless people playing loud music on Caroline Street.

ACTION: Not interested. What's the offence? If there is one, it should be dealt with by the council, but because of cuts to their budget, they can't, so it's another thing that's been plonked on the police.

OUTCOME: There won't be a complaint. I wonder if they'd like some salt and pepper chicken balls from Top Wok. I'm getting pretty desperate now.

EVENT: Swan and Castle asking for assistance with two drunken males.

ACTION: Unable to resource. They employ door people to deal with this, get them to do their job, stop expecting us to do their job for them. Not in the slightest bit interested.

OUTCOME: There won't be a complaint. Chicken balls arrive!

EVENT: A drunken male being a nuisance on Park End Street.

ACTION: Unable to resource. Am interested, but I can't do anything about it. I hope he doesn't do anything too silly.

OUTCOME: No possibility of complaint. The chicken balls are up to their usual standard, we've got a very happy AIRob on our hands.

Ah no.

EVENT: At last something I can get involved in, another missing person from the Warneford. By now I've just about had my fill of people going missing from either Warneford Mental Health hospital or Littlemore Mental Health hospital. A day couldn't possibly go by without someone going missing from one of our mental health hospitals.

ACTION: I decided to pull out all the stops and put in the same amount of effort to find him as the hospital staff. I looked to my left and then my right, I even looked behind me, which is probably a bit more than the hospital staff had done, and then I spun on my chair a full 360 degrees to celebrate. 'Area search, no trace.' Boom, gimme summut difficult to do. He was fine, he'd only gone to score some drugs, and returned to the hospital as happy as Larry. Like he does every couple of days, and like he's reported missing every couple of days. But as long as he's reported missing the hospital have passed their responsibility to the police service.

OUTCOME: Micper has returned to hospital off his tits on drugs, happy as Larry.

One day, inevitably, we'll get caught out with this, big time, it's absolutely inevitable, we fly by the seat of our pants every day.

And the poor old officers, working so incredibly hard just to hold it all together, come in at least half an hour early, most of the time go home late, never have a lunch break, and all people want to do is complain, and all we do is be stupid enough to take it.

When you see a documentary on telly, quite rightly highlighting the errors made by the police, you're never told about the vast number of other incidents officers had to deal with at the same time. It's never mentioned. We weave absolute miracles each and every second, of every minute, of every hour, of every day, 24/7/365, and the people who phone in to complain are blissfully unaware.

Also, there is a genuinely missing lady, for whom a risk assessment has been completed but I have not been able to find any resources to attempt to find her. BACOOMA. There is a slight risk of something bad happening to her, but there is nothing I can do about it, I hope that she's all right.

This is incredibly stressful, if something happens to her, there will be a huge investigation, and saying that we didn't have enough resources just won't cut it. Not only is there a possibility of a complaint, there is a possibility of a huge investigation probably lasting about a year and a huge chance of me suffering from stress. And that is the same with every single incident, there's always potential for every single job to go horrifically wrong.

And that's why the NDM – for all my moaning about the police service – alongside Officer Safety Training, are the big changes for the better. The NDM is so vital, and it's my high, and that's my buzz.

It's my meth.

And that's why my nose bleeds.

This is why it's so important to have experienced police officers: the more experience a police officer has the less chance there is of a huge mistake happening. Obviously, I made some absolute howlers, but I stand by what I say, the more experience an officer has the less chance of them making a bad call. Experience is crucial.

A short time ago, it was rumoured that the Government wanted officers to be on five-year contracts. They'd worked out that experienced officers were expensive. This was a very strong rumour and may very well still come to fruition. A consultant had worked out that in a thirty or thirty-five year career, the first five years were the most productive. Even I could work out, that if an officer was on a five-year contract, the first two years they'd be learning, so being carried by their colleagues, you might, if you're lucky have a good third year and the last two years they'd be about as much use as a chocolate ashtray on a motorbike because they're leaving. And then you'll have no experience to teach the young in service. But I digress.

Back to early February, there is an immensely tall homeless lad, who I know extremely well, saying that he would rather take an overdose than freeze to death as he doesn't have a sleeping bag. Thanks for that, fella, so you've absolved yourself of all personal responsibility and plonked it on me. Due to lack of resources all I can do is to ask officers and the CCTV operator to keep an eye out for him. Great isn't it? If anything happens to him, poor old AIRob and every other copper who has any slight involvement will be on the fizzer.

And, and, and, get a load o' this. A person wanted for an attempted murder came into Oxford, and when he was being chased by Roads Policing Officers he decamped and was running around off the Woodstock Road. This was at about 2100hrs and just like the firearm incident at the beginning of the shift, the whole circus came to town. The helicopter, armed units, dog units, roads policing units, they were all there. I don't think I had any response officers to attend, I'm not sure. Massive threat, harm, opportunity and risk, extreme chance that something can go wrong, huge chance that I'll be on the fizzer.

And all of this tells you why you never see a police officer. It's extremely difficult to know how many incidents were attended and how many couldn't be resourced, because it's so stressful and all I'm trying to do is stave off getting bitten on the arse. It's also very difficult to tell you the timings because the time that the incident came in will not be as the same time the Control Room inform me of it. I hope you can get a sense of how incredibly busy it was and why it was so important to have two sergeants there, me and Ash (to get my chicken balls from Top Wok – they were lush, oh come on, lighten up, I'm joking, he was tear-arsing around supporting officers at most of the incidents/jobs).

I would say that was a very typical day, in early February 2018.

And most of the callers couldn't possibly miss the golden opportunity to be obnoxious towards the call taker.

In addition, we'd also be dealing with issues with officers and various other things that crop up, like the tampon machine needing replenishing. And someone's nicked my blimmin' Bourbons. I bet it was those little buggers from Armed Response. Yeah, I remember now, that rascal APS Jon Lewis was deliberately distracting me, I thought he was overly interested in me explaining my dunking technique, bastards. It's a shame, I was really, really looking forward to dunking them.

I always loved it when the great old girls and lads from the Armed Response Vehicle, Roads Policing, and Dog Section (the Force Roamers) popped in, it was an honour and a privilege to serve with them, but it would've been nice if they'd brought a few more packets of Bourbons.

But with it being so incredibly busy, something has to give, and quite often the thing that has to give is the help and support to the blue-arsed officers. They just get their head down and get through, knowing full well that the sergeant just hasn't got time to give them the support and advice that they desperately need. And there is absolutely no chance of helping or developing their career. Every day is like survival (Ha, I've just reread this – I've only gone and turned into Boy George) for all of us who try to do police work. The blue line isn't thin, it's non-existent.

Superpower

At just gone one in the morning we receive a call from someone in one of the pubs on The Blabber saying that twenty people are fighting.

06 flick the switch. (My way of reminding me to turn on my BWV (Body Worn Video) when I arrive at an incident (bloody hell, I've surpassed myself, I've even got parentheses within parentheses)). (I really wish I'd thought of a really easy way of reminding myself, to turn the bloody thing off, I live in constant fear of somebody auditing my BWV and hearing me say "well, he was a right wanker wa'n"e" after nearly every incident.)

Boom and we're in. To be welcomed by L'ilOl'Poddymouth.

'What's fuckin' Babylon doin' here?'

Whatever have I ever done to you? I'm your lover not your rival.

'There's been a great big fight,' I stated.

'There ain't been no great big fuckin' fight,' L'ilOl'Poddymouth stated back.

'Do you kiss your mother with that mouth?' I politely enquired.

'I'll kiss your mother with this mouth,' she politely enquired back.

I was intrigued, I wanted to know if there was the slightest glimmer of humanity in there, so I said, 'My mother's dead, she died eighteen years ago, I miss her terribly'. Just to see her reaction.

And there was the slightest glimmer of humanity, but she soon composed herself to return to her drunken stupidity. She called me a wanker and walked off and kept coming back to abuse me more, she comes and goes, she comes and goes.

All of a horrible sudden, a girl being chased by another girl came bursting out from behind the bar, I heard a glass smash and could see the girl had sustained facial injuries.

L'ilOl'Poddymouth had got herself in to a horrible little vortex. 'Is it because I am black or is it because we are Muslim?'

Round and round she goes, where she stops nobody knows. (Like me on the NDM.) She was spinning off her jolly little tits. (Not like me on the NDM, mine are massive.) Loving would be easy if your colours were like my dreams, red, gold and green, red, gold and greeeeehen.

She thought I could tell what religion she was, and I was picking on her because of a dislike of that religion. Remarkable stuff. She had blessed me with the superpower of knowing someone's faith. And not only that, she believed that I was prejudiced against her faith. That's not what I'd choose to have as my superpower. If I had a superpower, I'd love to give everyone a sense of humour and to know what a joke is.

I'm a man without conviction which is pretty rare for a man on The Blabber, (only joking, the vast majority of them are the salt of the earth), I'm a man who doesn't know (nor care what race or religion you are).

Anyway, Ash had arrested the girl for assault, and the customers of the pub had a lovely time abusing the police officers, and I, for one, very much hope they enjoyed it. After an awful lot of police work, the aggrieved dropped the charges.

Karma, karma, karma, karma chameleon, she came and went, altogether now, she came and weeeeeent.

And therein lies another massive problem. The media love to say that we only detect fifteen per cent (or whatever it is, I have no idea; and I bet no-one really cares too much), as long as they get a police officer in their hour of need, no-one cares too much what the stupid detection rate is because the vast amount of time the reason why the crime isn't detected is because the aggrieved is unwilling to support proceedings, and a lot of the time that is after the poor old police officer has spent hours investigating it, been given numerous bollockings by all and sundry, usually the creatures of the corridor, for not investigating it quickly enough, only for the aggrieved to phone up and say they are no longer interested.

'That's all right, my love, any time you just want to waste thousands of pounds of taxpayers' money, and a helluva lot of my time, and cause me a helluva lot of stress, just give us a call.'

Seven foot by five foot

The next day was even worse, lots of incidents involving knives, and at least two young men wanting to take their own life, one by jumping off a roof in Littlemore and another behaving like the horse's arse because he had been caught having an affair. Eventually he told us where he was.

'The suicidal male is by the front doors at Tesco on Ambassador Avenue,' Screech screeched from the Control Room.

'Description, please?' Glorz, one of my wonderful officers and the most prolific of all prolific complaint's getters asked.

'Yeah, approximately seven foot by five foot, predominately made of glass,' I said, from the comfort of the Sergeants Office. I hope that helps.

I was good like that.

Death by a thousand cuts

In a speech to The Association of Chief Police officers and Association of Police Authorities at the National Conference on 29 June 2010, Mrs May said, 'I know that some officers like the Policing Pledge (oh my golly gosh, what a laugh that was, millions of pounds of taxpayers money down the toilet, on a pure whim, trying to impose unrealistic targets on stressed out officers), and some, I'm sure like the comfort of knowing they've ticked boxes. But targets don't fight against crime. In scrapping the confidence target and the Policing Pledge (oh, how we laughed), I couldn't be clearer about your mission: it isn't a thirty-point plan; it is to cut crime. No more, and no less.' And, I don't think we'll ever stop laughing at that one.

In reality, we spend twenty-five per cent of our time dealing with crime, and seventy-five per cent dealing with threat, harm and risk issues (safeguarding). The police are taking up the slack for the cuts to social services and mental health services.

And she has cut our budget. No more, and a lot less.

1,200 officers in England and Wales have left the service over the last six months – over six a day.

Previous Main Duty

This is how we get told that our duties have been changed.

Sent: 14 February 2018 14:48

To: Robinson Alan

Alan.Robinson@happyvalley.pnn.police.uk

Subject: Change of Duty Notification

Please do NOT reply to the above email address.

―――――――――――――――――――――――――-

Employee: P3630 PS Robinson, Alan Gordon User: 123

STN/Team: Oxford Police Station, Relief: Response Team

―――――――――――

11/05/2018 – 12/05/2018 inclusive.

―――――――――――――Previous Main Duty: 1200-2200

New Main Duty: 2100-0700

Main Duty Details:

New Breakdown Duty:

Breakdown Details:

Further Information:

There you go, brief and to the point.

The good people in the Didn'tKnowItWasNewYear'sEve Department don't fuck about, do they? Straight in there. No time to say, 'I'm extremely sorry if you had anything planned, but work really is far more important than your family, so tough luck Buster. ' Or, 'Sincere apologies, Al, I know you and Mrs R were looking forward to some hot and steamy porridge, you like yours with milk and honey, Mrs R likes hers as it comes; but you have to babysit the drunken folk of Oxford.' No, no, no, there you go, you thought you were finishing work at ten but now you have to start work at nine. It doesn't seem very fair to me. Every frontline officer gets tens of these bloody things every year. If only we had someone who could ensure fairness in the police service. Yep, that's what we need, someone who could ensure fairness, no doubt about that.

It dunt ma''er in December me and Party 3 are off to Amsterdam and we'll raise a glass to the good people in the Resource Management Department.

And the duty change will have been made because a Neighbourhood sergeant has cried off and got himself involved in some pointless engagement event or anything to get himself out of doing Nightsafe, and far more importantly to get himself a nice slice of Battenberg. It's hardly fair is it?

And this duty change will happen on the very first weekend after I go into the IHub. Those files ain't gonna check themselves you know.

Ben and Spen the Dogmen

A report comes in of a male running round with a knife and he has his girlfriend in a headlock.

Ah no, where is Twoody when you need her? It's BATOOMA Time. She's probably chatting shit somewhere. Fortunately, there are two officers from the Dog Section very close by. Obviously, they won't be as good as Twoody but they'll have to do.

They see him in his home throw a weapon out of his house window and go in and arrest him.

Instead of getting any kind of acknowledgement for their bravery, they're on the receiving end of a complaint from a relative of the offender, who is alleging that their loved one has sustained an injury during the arrest. I haven't got a clue what his problem is, a witness clearly heard one of the officer's shout, 'Ptyer'ands' nyer'eadslowl'urn'roun'go'o'yerknee'd'ye'derstan'doi'NOOW.'

Five times

Now, if only I could stop my wonderful colleague, PC TeeTee, (one of my amazing officers) from upsetting people.

Not satisfied with upsetting the Didn'tKnowItWasNewYear'sEve Department by pointing out that they didn't know it was New Year's

Eve on Facebook, he's broken the Golden Rule of Policing – 'There are no consequences for those who make appalling decisions, but massive consequences for those who criticise them. '

PC TeeTee, the silly little bugger, has only gone and done it again by telling someone that they were an obnoxious prick.

And the person in question was an obnoxious prick.

He had been arrested, and now he wants to make a complaint. He explained to me that 'I was perfectly reasonable until I was arrested and then I was a xkclunt' and now he can waste taxpayers' money and then everyone will know what a wonderful human being he is, and what a bunch of obnoxious pricks the police are, and then the whole world order will all be restored and the whole universe will be in equilibrium and everything will all be all right.

And that's the way it goes, we do something, somebody doesn't like what we've done, so they complain, and we waste more of our time and more of your money. And then I phone him and apologise and then I feel like shit, and then we go out and do it all over again.

Apologising to people because they're upset is a problem. It devalues every apology that I've ever made and will ever make. It just feeds into the recipient's condition of entitlement. And it shouldn't happen. We apologise because it's expedient, and because we can't be bothered to deal with more complaints – it takes up far too much of our time and it shows weakness. If we got these small things right the rest will fall into place. PC TeeTee showed tremendous courage to stand up to the obnoxious prick, only to be undermined by me, by apologising to the obnoxious prick.

It's really strange that an organisation who won't ever apologise to its officers for the appalling way it treats them, encourages them to apologise so readily to people who really don't deserve an apology.

This would never have happened back in the big old good old great Sergeant Roger Mills days, he would've told the obnoxious prick that he was an obnoxious prick an' all.

Why do we apologise to someone who's been obnoxious to someone who is working extremely hard for the community? It's wrong. We choose the path of least resistance. And it's dishonest. And it undermines us and destroys morale.

Truth trumps everything.

And that is why PC TeeTee is such a good ol' boy. He has the bottle to stand up for what he believes in, many officers would've ignored it, and that's where we've lost the respect of the public.

Yah

I'm on Nightsafe again – those engagement events won't attend themselves you know. I think you can tell I've got my teeth into the Neighbourhood Teams almost as much as they've got theirs into Battenberg.

Eleanor, a first-year student, has got a bit of a bee in her bonnet and simply must tell me and PC Beard all about it.

'You'll never guess what yah, I was talking to this homeless guy yah, Malcolm yah, really sweet guy yah, and he said yah, that you, Babylon, are constantly busting his balls yah, because you think he's a thief yah, he's a really sweet guy yah, had a tough life, yah, and you feds are busting his balls yah. Anyway, yah, I gave him a hundred quid yah, I've got to live on baked beans for the rest of the month yah, but what the fuck yah, he's had a terrible life yah, and he's a really sweet guy and everything yah. Anyway, yah, when I went to get in my taxi yah, I had lost my purse yah, or someone has stolen it yah…'

'No shit, yah.'

And one of my wonderful officers, Davey V, is on the receiving end of a minor assault. Party 3 all rally around him and he'll be all right.

This is all happening while Xavier Wyng is all nice and toasty in his bed.

Seven-point plan

Xavier Wyng wakes up, has a scratch of his immaculately coiffured nutsack and he's ready for the day.

Cheeky little latte from Cafe Loco and X Wyng is in, just in time for the morning meeting.

'Party 3 have knitted miracles last night, but, but, but look, AlRob has not followed the seven-point plan for assaults on police,' says the senior officer chairing the DMM.

X Wyng's immaculately coiffured nutsack is enormously stirred.

Don't do it, don't do it, just deny yourself that initial rush of pleasure.

But he recovers his composure to go into his well-honed monotone, staccato, robotic shit. He pipes up to say that he'd send an e-mail to me, telling me that a seven-point plan needs to be completed.

He couldn't help himself.

Bloody hell, Xavier, all that money that you've spent on CBT, er, Cognitive Behavioural Therapy, as opposed to the other CBT (no lady of easy virtue is going to get her grubby mitts on those dinky beauties) flushed down the toilet.

'Er, okay, Xavier, one volunteer is worth twenty pressed men.'

'Haha … haha … ha … er … haha.'

Every organisation has their own version of X Wyng: They're constantly point-scoring while constantly missing the point.

Point six of the seven-point plan reads: *Victims recover better and more quickly if they receive the right welfare and supervision.*

So, obviously, X Wyng has contacted the great Davey V to see that he's okay and offer a bit of support, right? Has he fuck. And that's the point about X Wyng.

Maybe he needs a seven-point plan on how to use the seven-point plan.

So, X Wyng sends me an e-mail telling me how useless I am by not completing the pointless seven pointless plan and I send him a nice little e-mail and make it clear that I know that he's missed the point, and he replies, *Come to my office … the next time you're on duty.*

Wow, he's a man of few words, isn't he? The strong silent type. Even his e-mails are monotone and staccato.

Gee-whizz, I'm on duty now, X Wyng will be waiting, and getting extremely animated, a miniscule raising of his left eyebrow, imperceptible to the human eye but it happens, it definitely happens. I don't want to make him angry.

'You … wouldn't like … me when I'm … angry.'

I don't like him at all. I think he's a xkclunt.

I bomb down to St Aldates and nip up the stairs, three at a time with the help of the brass rail. I'm late, I'm late, for a very important whoa, whoa, whoa, whoa, what's happened?

Where is the little twa…

Oh, I feel such a fool. Its 2230hrs. He only works eight till four.

The job was far too stressful without his silly shit, what we need is an independent body to preside over grievance procedures, all I've ever known is the organisation to support the higher-ranking officer or civilian; which perpetuates the bullying of the officer.

Half his face missing

A report comes over the radio to say that there' s a lad with half his face missing on Cuddesdon Road. When we arrived, the people of The Blabber (having had my incredibly cheap jibe at the people of The Blabber during the Li'l Ol'Poddymouth sketch, I want to make it absolutely clear that the vast majority of people on The Blabber were incredibly kind to me) were already administering first aid but the lad had been bottled and his ear and cheek were hanging off. He wasn't going to tell us who'd done it. But we had one massive crime scene, and one smaller scene where he had collapsed.

We didn't have enough officers to deal with the incident, even with the Neighbourhood Officers who'd put down their Battenberg to come and help.

We had two sergeants covering Oxford and it was stressful. What, in the name of all that is holy, is it going to be like in May when they cut it to two for the whole of Oxfordshire?

Just for your information, you may find it useful, you may not; whenever I was in charge of a big incident like this, I'd think of it as a piece of PISS.

P reserve life and limb – that is our first responsibility at all incidents.

I dentify the victim, suspect, and witnesses.

S eize all the evidence.

S cene preservation.

You may also find it useful, you may not, when things had died down a bit, I would think of catching the person responsible as a game of CHESS.

C CTV

H ouse to house enquiries.

E verything else. Be creative, think outside the box, how else are you going to solve this crime?

S tatements, from everyone: witnesses, victim and officers, and anyone else who could assist.

S cenes of crime – which are now called Crime Scene Investigation (CSI), they only changed their name to bugger up my wonderful mnemonic.

It really doesn't matter what a police officer does or doesn't do, because inevitably the victim won't support any police action, which is exactly what happened in this case.

This has a dramatic effect on our detection rate, more about that in a bit.

It's near Kent

I hope that you've calmed down after all the excitement of the NDM, but I did promise to tell you all about the Code of Ethics. And I'm good to my word so here it comes, get those incontinence pants on.

'Okay, what is or are ethics?' asks the chief inspector at the beginning of our Code of Ethics Training Day.

'Ith it a plathe near Thuthex? Pipes up some clown.

Bloody clown, everyone knows it's near Kent.

The Code of Ethics is the code that all officers have to abide by and covers nine themes: accountability, fairness, honesty, integrity, leadership, objectivity, openness, respect, and selflessness.

And the funny thing about it is, out of the nine, it's with honesty that the police service has the biggest difficulty.

I'm not talking about honesty at an evidential level, we do all right at that. I am talking about honesty at a really funny and funky level.

We're dishonest because we're too scared to offend anyone, some people are offended by our mere presence so we may as well be honest and make 'em be offended for all the right reasons.

We are dishonest at every level and in almost every communication. To improve, grow and evolve there has to be honesty. This calls for considerable effort, strength, determination and sacrifice. If the Code of Ethics has any chance of working EVERYONE has to buy in to it, not just those in the lower ranks.

Common sense, decency, and ethics go out the window as soon as money is involved.

We always choose the path of least resistance, the easy route, the expedient way, sometimes because we haven't got time, and sometimes because we can't deal with the stress that doing the right thing would cause. But this is the most important fight and it's a fight that has to be won and sometimes if you play with feathers, you're going to get your arse tickled, and sometimes, I rather like having my arse tickled.

By and large, apart from Officer Safety or First Aid, Training Days were just an excuse for an organisation or department to bundle more work onto the hard-pressed response officer, or tell them they were useless, or if at all possible, both.

We had an extremely insightful Training Day on Domestic Abuse, during which we were told about the plight of Slink, a young man who was being violently abused by his female partner. On video, the narrator, informed us that Slink and his female partner had a son, but, he was being repeatedly punched by her, and kicked by her, and stabbed by her, so they decided to have another baby. It was wonderful comedy timing. But we all sat there stoical. This is how police officers have the reputation of being dour. Having sat through so many training days with wonderful one-liners like that, one cannot help but become a pretty dab hand at keeping a straight-face.

In time-honoured Training Day stylee we were split into little groups and had to write down reasons why Slink stays in the violent relationship. Some clown in my group wrote down 'Soft lad ... duh'. I thought it was absolutely outrageous, so outrageous, in fact, that I ended up smelling of tinkle. I really tried to tell them how outraged I was, but I couldn't quite get the words out. Cooome ooooon, please, this is someone passing their responsibility to the police and we're supposed to not question their stupidity.

In a healthy and honest organisation, you wouldn't need to sell your soul to avoid a complaint; dick-swingers wouldn't get promoted; Resource Management would treat people fairly and with respect. That's just a very brief list as to how it's come to this. And that's the point. I'm pretty sure others may come to light as we work our way through the year. But it really dunt ma"er in December Party 3 are off to Amsterdam. Hey ho, ten months to go.

MARCH

PDR and the academics

Thankless

Hundreds of officers are leaving the job, a lot of them very young in service. This is a job that they'll've worked incredibly hard to get into, and they, and their families, were so proud to join. Now, I'm no expert and I stand to be corrected but my theory is that they soon become disenchanted with the crap they have to deal with from the public and from within the organisation.

The Chief Constable thinks everyone's leaving because of cheap house prices in other parts of the country. He's deluded. Predominantly, it's because of the Oops, there it is.

It's a thankless job, just dealing with other people's crap, and never getting to deal with crime.

The Police and Crime Commissioner (PCC), never one to waste an opportunity to get his name and gorgeous fizzog in the papers says, 'We are managing our response to the current situation in relation to the police officer numbers, looking at how we can improve our recruitment process and how we can make TVP a more attractive proposition without increasing the long-term cost.'

How about by you resigning?

They just don't get it.

Dem's de Rules of de Game

March is the month of high excitement for police officers because it's when we've got to complete our Talent Performance. Yep, even the title doesn't make any sense, so I'll refer to it by the name that all police officers know it by, the Personal Development Review (PDR). (Only it wasn't personal, it wasn't developmental, and I hadn't actually had a review for the last twelve years. I'd been bothered to do one – I could just about be bothered enough to copy and paste most of the previous years', into the current years' – but no-one could just about be bothered enough to talk to me about it.)

Frontline officers have got neither the time nor the inclination to do their PDR, which is my way of saying they can't be arsed, they're far too busy. However, Xavier's is fully up-to-date and immaculate. He knows dem's de rules of the game, be a 'yes' person and go along with the narrative coming from above, overdose on the corporate pill, implement an awful policy or Model that just thwarts an officers attempt to serve the community, take someone's legs, and get the Chief Constable a knighthood, Dem's de Rules of de Game.

Anyone foolish enough to swallow the corporate pill lacks logic and sense. These are the very real perils and pitfalls of hierarchy, it ensures the narrative, however ridiculous, is rammed down the throat of every hardworking officer, through the use of PDR, Work Based Assessments and 360 Reviews. There's no room for lively discussion and debate, or honesty.

The corpocracy is debilitating, as the senior managers wring every last ounce of creativity and character out of every wonderful officer. Leaving nothing but 'yes' people to shimmy up the greasy pole so bloody high that it's only their arse that anyone gets to see.

They simply don't get it; they think that a police officer should serve the senior management who in turn think they should serve the politicians. They've got it all wrong, the only people a police officer should serve is their public.

Officers who were passionate about serving the public suffered from stress when the Ferkin' Merkin' was introduced, because they knew that they couldn't possibly serve. Officers who couldn't give a shit about serving, flourished, because all they cared about was themselves.

I'm going to go out on a bit of a limb here, but I think the questions on the PDR may have been written by an academic. Have a close look at the kind of shite we've got to contend with. Police officers don't speak like this, they don't understand what the hell it's chatting about.

Only an academic would understand what it's chatting about. It's a great example of the disconnect between officers and the consultants and academics who've infiltrated this wonderful institution.

WE ARE EMOTIONALLY AWARE–I consider the perspectives of people from a wide range of backgrounds before taking action. I adapt my style and approach according to the needs of the people I am working with, using my own behaviour to achieve the best outcome. I promote a culture that values diversity and encourages challenge. I encourage reflective practice among others and take the time to support others to understand reactions and behaviours. I take responsibility for helping to ensure the emotional wellbeing of those in my teams. I take the responsibility to deal with any inappropriate behaviours.

When I joined the job all I wanted to do was get into work, do a good day's work and if I was being a bit of a twat, my colleagues would tell me, and it all worked swimmingly. I have to admit that I can't really be bothered to challenge inappropriate behaviours (especially those of senior officers), it's more trouble than it's worth, you never get any support and, in all likelihood, you'll be on the receiving end of a bollocking. But I do think ensuring the emotional wellbeing of those in my team is one of my strengths.

One day I could see that a young-in-service officer was completely demoralised. I had a pretty good idea of what was wrong, but I went through the motions anyway.

I said, 'How's it all going?'

He said, 'Sarge, I'm really sorry, it's the job, it's not what I thought it would be, I just deal with other people's shit, shit that they should sort out themselves, all day, every day. I'm really sorry, all I do is go from one domestic to another, all day, every day, day after day. I'm really sorry.'

I said, 'If you don't want to deal with another domestic, have you considered joining the Domestic Abuse Unit?' (Ha, only joking, only joking, they do a great job.)

He said, 'That's a great idea, Sarge, thank you ever so much.'

I said, 'It's all in a day's work.'

We both walked away respecting the other's point of view, and that's the funny thing about it.

WE ANALYSE CRITICALLY–I ensure that the best available evidence from a wide range of sources is taken into account when making decisions. I think about different perspectives and motivations when reviewing information and how this may influence key points. I ask incisive questions to test out facts and assumptions, questioning and challenging the information provided when necessary. I understand when to balance decisive action with due consideration. I recognise patterns, themes and connections between several and diverse sources of information and best available evidence. I identify when I need to take action on the basis of limited information and think about how to mitigate the risks in so doing. I challenge others to ensure that decisions are made in alignment with our mission, values and the Code of Ethics.

When I joined the job, all you had to do was roll your sleeves up, get stuck in, not let your colleagues down and just do the very best you could. That said, I do think balancing decisive action with due consideration is one of my very strongest of strengths.

One time, I was at the BP petrol station at Wolvercote roundabout, I'd just had a great old blether with the good old boys Victor and James, the workers in the shop, and was just getting back in the transit when a young officer drew my attention to James Corden who was getting into a car and was exiting the wrong way out of the station. I took decisive action and stopped the car (and an absolute catastrophe) and opened the door just as James was about to take the most almighty bite I'd ever seen anyone take, out of his sandwich. Honestly, I've never seen anything quite like it. I think he must've been hungry.

I said, 'How's it all going? I'm very sorry, James, but would you be kind enough to have a selfie with the team.'

He said, 'Absolutely, no problem.'

I said, 'Thank you very much.'

He was an absolute gent, exactly how you'd imagine him to be.

He said, 'Do you know the way to Soho Farmhouse?'

I said, 'I haven't got a clue.'

He said, 'Thank you, officer, take good care of yourself.'

I said, 'It's all in a day's work.'

We both walked away respecting each other's point of view and that's the funny thing about it.

WE ARE INNOVATIVE AND OPEN-MINDED–I explore a number of different sources of information and use a variety of tools when faced with a problem and look for good practice that is not always from policing. I am able to spot opportunities or threats which may influence how I go about my job in the future by using knowledge of trends, new thinking about policing and changing demographics in the population I am flexible in my approach, changing my plans to make sure that I have the best impact. I encourage others to be creative and take appropriate risks. I share my explorations and understanding of the wider internal and external environment.

I joined the job to use my common sense and discretion. I think 'new thinking about policing' has caused a tremendous amount of harm to the service that used to be the envy of the world. It's a load of old bollocks, and we all know it. There's absolutely no substitute for a police officer being on the beat – it's the most important part of the job. We've had a couple of generations growing up aware that there are no police on the streets, kids who've never even seen the lesser spotted po-po on the beat. Frankly, it's no wonder knife crime has gone into a different stratosphere: there's no-one out there to prevent it or gather information and intelligence. Please, no more 'new thinking about policing', let's stop the bollocks and get back to basics and get the bobby back on the beat. And if we do, I don't think we'd have to worry too much about changing demographics. But I do consider that spotting threats is one of my strongest of all my strong strengths.

One day there was a bloke on the briefing site with a rather rare haircut. He was a renegade from the 1980s with a massive fringe and mullet. I immediately spotted the threat from his barnet. My team, being quite young, were visibly stunned; I hadn't given them any warning, they'd never seen anything quite like it. I have to admit I was struggling to keep them calm.

They said, 'Oh my God, what is that?' They were shaking.

I said, 'It's a mullet and fringe.' There was no point in skirting around it, they had to be told.

They said, 'Are there any offences?'

I said, 'Consider being in possession of an offensive haircut or weapon. One flick of his forehead could take your eye out. Remember your reactionary gap, which ordinarily is six foot, but on this occasion, I would allow for at least nine, just to be on the safe side.'

They said, 'Do you think there is any chance of it making a comeback?'

I said, 'No, I don't, but please be aware that the ones that are remaining are Grade-2 listed.'

They said, 'Thank you, Sarge.'

I said, 'It's all in a day's work.'

We both walked away respecting each other's point of view, and that's the funny thing about it.

WE TAKE OWNERSHIP–I proactively create a culture of ownership within my areas of work and support others to display personal responsibility. I take responsibility for making improvements to policies, processes and procedures, actively encouraging others to contribute their ideas. I am accountable for the decisions my team make and the activities within our teams. I take personal responsibility for seeing events through to a satisfactory conclusion and for correcting any problems both promptly and openly. I actively encourage and support learning within my teams and colleagues.

When I joined the job all I wanted to do was to make a difference to people's lives, walk the beat and go home. Over the years I've made many suggestions to make improvements to policies, but no-one ever listens. I told senior officers that if you take the bobby off the beat, there will be generations of people who are not used to seeing the lesser-spotted po-po, so we won't be able to build trust within communities. I told them there are only ever three ways of catching offenders: by forensics, red-handed, and by information received. By taking the bobby off the beat we're severely hampering two ways of catching offenders but I was told that a bobby will only catch a burglar red-handed once in their thirty-year career, and on such dumb statistics and lack of understanding of what a police officer actually does, really poor decisions are made. I gave up trying to improve policies and procedures years ago. The only people that the organisation listens to are academics and consultants and almost anyone who has never done a moment of police work. But I do consider 'seeing things through to their conclusion' as my middle name.

One time, I was driving along the Cowley Road and I saw an old fragile lady of Afro-Caribbean heritage waiting on the pavement. I stopped my patrol car and got out, took her by the arm, and ensured her safe journey across the road.

She said, 'What d'you think you are doing? What d'you think you're doing?' And wriggled to get away. 'I was just waiting for my friend.'

I said, 'Never mind, you're here now.'

She was extremely angry and said, 'Take me back.'

I said, 'I'm very sorry but you've made me late for the DMM, tata.'

She said, 'Wanker.'

I said, 'It is all in a day's work.'

We both walked away respecting the other's point of view, and that's the funny thing about it.

WE ARE COLLABORATIVE–I manage relationships and partnerships for the long term, sharing information and building trust to find the best solutions. I help create joined-up solutions across organisational and geographical boundaries, partner organisations and those the police serve. I understand the local partnership context, helping me to use a range of tailored steps to build support. I work with our partners to decide who is best placed to take the lead on initiatives. I try to anticipate our partners' needs and take action to address these. I do not make assumptions. I check that our partners are getting what they need from the police service. I build commitment from others (including the public) to work together to deliver agreed outcomes.

I only joined the job to serve the community. I knew almost everybody on Saxton Road in Abingon, when I was on the beat there and almost everybody on Saxton Road knew me. I absolutely loved them, and I loved my job. It really doesn't take more than a couple of months to establish yourself on the beat when you're prepared to get out and about and talk to people and show an interest in what they're saying. I knew what was expected of me, and it all worked swimmingly.

I'm quite often seen walking around the mean streets of Witney sporting my 'I manage relationships and partnerships for the long term, sharing information and building trust to find the best solutions. I help create joined-up solutions across organisational and geographical boundaries, partner organisations and those the police serve. I understand the local partnership context, helping me to use a range of tailored steps to build support. I work with our partners to decide who is best placed to take the lead on initiatives (because our partners always spam us with taking the initiative – more about this in July). I try to anticipate our partners' needs and take action to address these. I do not make assumptions. I check that our partners are getting what they need from the police service (which means we're doing their job for them). I build commitment from others (including the public) to work together to deliver agreed outcomes', T-shirt.

One day, a senior officer walked into the Sergeants Office and noticed my phone was off the hook.

He said, 'Why is your phone off the hook?'

I said, 'I've noticed that if I don't answer the phone, I find that I improve the long-term relationship with our partners, because all they do is ask me to do their job for them, and ask me to find missing people that if they just did their job properly they wouldn't be missing.'

He said, 'But that means you can't build any trust.'

I said, 'I think I have a better chance of building trust with them if I don't speak to them at all, than if I do.'

He said, 'But then the police will not be able to take the lead on initiatives.'

I said, 'Well, you got me there, Sir, you got me there.'

I said, 'It's all in a day's work.'

We both walked away respecting the other's point of view, and that's the funny thing about it.

WE DELIVER, SUPPORT AND INSPIRE—I give clear directions and have explicit expectations, helping others to understand how their work operates in the wider context. I identify barriers that inhibit performance in my teams and take steps to resolve these thereby enabling others to perform. I lead the public and/or my colleagues, where appropriate, during incidents or through the provision of advice and support. I ensure the efficient use of resources to create the most value and to deliver the right impact within my areas. I keep track of changes in the external environment, anticipating both the short- and long-term implications for the police service.

When I joined the job, I worked alongside amazing people (Reesy, Leachy, Stevie E, Karen R, Little Ol' Johnny B, Terry D, Alan B, Jack in Property – obviously I've missed loads out, but nearly everyone was amazing) I had their back and I knew damn fine that they'd have mine. If we had an issue with each other we would hug it out and sort it out. It was bloody great, we worked incredibly hard, we had focus, and I loved every second of it. Every officer would wear their radio and back each other up, it's how we caught criminals.

So, when people see me, do they say? There goes Al Robinson, he fucks about.' No, they don't, they say, 'There goes Al Robinson, he leads the public and/or his colleagues, where appropriate, during incidents or through the provision of advice and support.' Yep, that's what they say.

One day Ash asked me to attend the scene of a very horrible road traffic collision (because he's completely useless and always asked me to bail him out, honestly, I'm going to have to have a knee operation when I leave, they've buckled due to having to carry him so much), where a bus had run over a boy. I had to take complete control of the incident, I led the public by putting on a crime scene, which meant that I cordoned off the scene to enable Roads Policing to measure the length that the bus skidded, ensured there was a sterile area for the paramedics to administer first aid to the boy, and led my colleagues by diverting traffic onto an alternative route. Ash informed me that a lady was not happy that she had to walk a long way around.

I went over to her and threw up the goofiest of all goofy salutes and stomped my right foot on the ground and said, 'Police Constable Sergeant soon to be Acting Inspector Al Robinson, here to serve.'

She said, 'Why do I have to walk all the way around there?'

I said, 'Because I want you to. And is that your child drinking from that massive family sized chocolate Frijj?'

She said, 'Yes.'

I said, 'I wouldn't let him do that, it's not good for his health.'

She said, 'It's none of your business what he drinks. You wanker.'

I said, 'You're absolutely right.'

She said, 'And thanks a fucking bunch for making me walk miles around there.'

I said, 'It's all in a day's work.'

We both walked away respecting the other's point of view, and that's the funny thing about it.

I think that the PDR was written by an academic, or a consultant, or someone who hasn't done a moment's police work, and in all probability, all three.

If you are going for promotion, the senior officers love to see evidence that you 'take responsibility to deal with any inappropriate behaviours' which includes 'not embracing change' which means any new political diktat is rammed home, unchallenged.

And, come on, let's be brutally honest, the only reason we have the PDR is for management to shake their shitty stick at the officer "If you don't embrace the target culture I'll put an entry in your PDR."

And that is yet another reason it has come to this.

Darts

The day has come, it's a weekday and I'm in work and so is Xavier.

I see him down the corridor, but he darts down the stairs, the keyboard warriorin' twat has no balls in his immaculately coiffured nutsack.

No doubt he's some urgent dick-swinging to do elsewhere.

Big Hat Back

'O's that twat?

'O's that twat?

'O's that twat?

'O got the big hat back

'O's that...?

'O's that...?

'O's that twat?

'O got the big hat back

'O's that...?

'O's that...?

Ummm, well it's none other than our very own Police and Crime Commissioner (PCC), of course. He tried to sell it to us by saying that it would increase police visibility, but the real reason is because he just didn't want us to look like a sack of shit in front of the eyes of the world at the Royal Wedding. He dropped a massive bollock when he, and his fellow cronies on the Police Authority, got rid of the big traditional helmets and replaced them with the crappy peaked cap.

'O's that twat?

'O's that twat?

'O's that twat

'O got the big hat back

'O's that...?

'O's that...?

'O's that twat?

'O got the big hat back

'O's that...?

'O's that...?

'E's a horrible little twat

And a Tory twat at that

'O's that...?

'O's that...?

I think it's fair to say that I didn't really agree with the PCC. It might've been something to do with him being a Conservative, but the PCC should not be aligned to any political party. I think it was more to do with him wanting police officers to throw up a salute when he walked into Newbury Police Station or that he said "Don't you know who I am?" when an officer asked him who he was, when he was trying to get into the backyard of Cowley nick. Such a complete and utter nob, not really my kinda person when he puts himself above the people who keep him in his job.

How about doing something to make the officer's life slightly easier, instead of a bloody Victims Contact Contract that just clogs up the investigation log, you can't see what investigation has been conducted because the log is littered with Victim Contracts and Seven Point Plans.

Butterfly

And I'm off to see the wizard, the wonderful Wizard of Oz.

In the middle of March, I'm off to our Training Centre, on a leadership workshop (fuckin' workshop, what will they think of next?)

Dofuckinwot? A leadership workshop. There ain't gonna be no leadership, not in the police service, as my mate Jonno would say. There just ain't. You can't be a leader in the police service. That's why good officers leave, if you have anything about you, you leave. You can't take risks, you can't be creative, you have to maintain the status quo, you cannot use your initiative, you can't have a vision. You definitely can't be a leader. And, I admire their honesty in calling themselves managers.

And they're extremely good managers.

They manage to get every weekend off.

Okay, they manage to get every evening and night off.

Okay, okay, I'll stop it now, but they manage to not wear their radios.

Yeah, yeah, okay, they manage to make me look like a complete twat in the morning meeting.

They managed to implement an Operating Model that caused so much stress and anxiety to their officers, and if anyone was to sue them for it, they'd have a pretty good chance of winning.

So, they're extremely good at managing.

The Chief Constable started the day. He was loving, compassionate, kind and understanding. An absolutely marvellous man.

He made a magnificent speech, in which his warmth shone through. It made me wonder where it all went wrong.

As The Academic started his lecture, little did I know that he was about to unleash his own unique brand of dipshittery on an unsuspecting world, with his own unique brand of political correctness. He wasn't a leader he was an academic. He kicked off by saying, 'I have to start this off with an apology, yep, yep, I have to apologise,

79

I'm used to giving this speech to a room full of academics who can understand what I'm saying.'

Oops, there it fuckin' is, right fuckin' there.

That's how to win friends and influence people.

Such grace.

Such humility.

Such a fuckin' fucker.

Crikey, go easy my good man, why would I want to go out and get insulted by the crazy cats of Oxford when I can be insulted in the comfort of my very own Training Centre?

Ah, nice one, chap, yep, I'm just a police officer, just go for it and I'll put my hand up when it all gets a bit lairy; I'm just someone the Recruitment Department has recruited, just to be a police officer, please be gentle with me, I'm a liiiiiiiittle bit sloooooow.

I just sat there and took it. Another little bit of me gets frazzled, shrivelled up, dies and lands on the ground next to me, leaving a dent in the floor and a hole in my soul. My spirit had been destroyed. And I wonder how many times this had happened to me. And I'd love to know how many times it's happened to you. Somebody who's not fit to lace yer boots has got the temerity to tell you how you should behave, that you ain't good enough, you've got to improve, and be more like the fuckin' fucker, I should've told the fuckin' fucker to go fuck himself, the fuckin' condescending cunt, but I can't, I would've twenty five years ago, but I'm a broken shadow of the person I once was, I don't recognise myself. I know I was never gonna set the world alight, but I'm not a bad ol' boy and this fuckin' fucker was having a pop. There's only so much of this shit that the good ol' boys and girls can take before they crack. And I'd cracked, somewhere along the way I'd lost my way. I was no longer the good ol' AlRob I once was. In exactly the same way that the police service had lost its identity, I'd lost mine.

He's an academic. As far as I know, he's never been a police officer.

He wasted no time in telling us how fuckin' marvellous he is, cos he's fuckin' worked on fuckin' organisational fuckin' justice and he had a fuckin' formula, yep a fuckin' formula, for fuckin' fairness, yes, him, fuckin' fairness. Fair fuckin' play. I'm looking forward to it starting. Fair recruitment, fair leave embargoes, fair grievance procedures, fair misconduct hearings, fair duty changes, fair resourcing levels, fair work distribution, fair shift pattern, fair promotions, fair appointments, fair etc, fair etc, I can't fuckin' wait, to be fair, I'll keep you fairly well updated. Fuck me fuckin' sideways, a fuckin' formula for fuckin' fairness.

Pure shit. He was having a laugh at my expense.

He had a fuckin' arrow going to the left, with two fuckin' arrows coming down, and I couldn't give two tiny turds about his fuckin' formula for fuckin' fairness. Ramming political correctness down my throat. This doesn't help the poor ol' boy who's had tools stolen from his van overnight and doesn't see a police officer. And it certainly doesn't help that poor ol' officer that doesn't get to see the poor ol' boy who's had his tools stolen. This ain't what I joined the job for, I thought I was going to be catching criminals, not listening to this shite, shove it right up yer fuckin' arse, I want to serve. This is how mumbo jumbo conquered the police service and me. We can't sustain this level of shit any longer, something has to give, and unfortunately what is giving is the police service and its officers.

He was followed by The Consultant, he wasn't a leader, he was a consultant. He had a couple of tasty one-liners. And then went on some kinda wankathon about critical, wicked, and tame problems.

He's a consultant. As far as I know, he's never been a police officer.

It was a masterclass on how good ol' horseshit devours good ol' sense. He'd over-intellectualised what the rest of us find incredibly easy. I've never thought of any of my problems as critical, wicked or tame, he's over-thought it, I'm too busy spinning off the NDM to worry about his shit. Then he started asking people to do press-ups. Yep, seriously, he wanted people to do press ups; the first person had to do five, the next ten, by the time it got to twenty the person refused to do it. The punchline was 'no-one can make you do anything'. Er, they can if the mortgage and bills have to be paid, bro. In fact, if they told me to wear a tutu and do the Dying Swan outside the O2 on a Saturday night, I'd do it.

In fact, the horrible truth of it all is, that too many of us have to sell our bloody soul just to make ends meet. Not least having to listen to this horseshit. He stressed that a good leader consults with their staff about change. I pointed out that we weren't consulted about the implementation of the New Operating Model. And he soon shut up. Some blimmin' unaccountable consultant hadn't consulted. It all needs to called out. Someone needs to call it out.

Blinded by the shite.

This means absolutely nothing to me. I don't care about his critical, wicked and tame problems, and I care even fuckin' less about that fuckin fuckers fuckin' formula for fuckin' fairness. All I care about is the officers, and how hard they bloody work for so little reward, it has to be lowest effort to reward ratio in the history of mankind, the actual blood, sweat and tears that these wonderful people put in, has to be seen to be believed. And then to be told by the very type of people who'd turned the vocation that I loved into a politically correct, pointless dropdown, ticky box exercise was all too much for me.

And then a funny little thought just fluttered into my head, honestly, some days I just don't know what goes on in this woolly head of mine. The police service doesn't benefit from this, the poor and vulnerable certainly don't benefit from it, and you certainly don't benefit from it. In fact, the whole system only serves the rich and powerful. They love the status-quo, it serves them well. Because while we're getting bogged down with this inconsequential claptrap, we're not dealing with the crimes of the rich and powerful. And then the funny little thought that had fluttered into this woolly head of mine, fluttered away, never to return.

Then there was a lecture by the Head of the Professional Standards Department (PSD), who came across (unfortunate expression under the circumstances) as a very reasonable and fair man (but they got it completely wrong when they dismissed the wonderful Ben H and

Dan G). He told us that they were inundated with complaints and that we should use local resolution instead, which means that wherever possible the sergeant should be able to use their discretion to give the officer a bit of bollocking or support instead of troubling PSD with some trifling matter.

Followed by some nonsense about coaching.

And then a Chief Superintendent who, for some inexplicable reason, showed us a video in which a boy was taught how to draw a butterfly.

Now, I have to be absolutely fair here (I knew that formula for fairness would come in handy one day, that's what I've been trying to tell you), this Chief Superintendent is an incredible man, police officer and leader, and I must've missed what he was trying to say. He really is a remarkable man, who despite being on the Accelerated Promotion Scheme, spent more time than he should in the lower ranks to get to know the nuance and idiosyncrasy. I love him to bits. I hope to goodness he gets to be Chief Constable, there'd be a radical change in culture. He could be the catalyst that sparks the reloveution.

This Chief Superintendent is a leader. Which is only right and proper, considering I'm on a leadership workshop.

Anyway, this Chief Superintendent is a true leader. He has a vision. He wants change and is not worried about upsetting the status quo, and I don't mean by doing a pretty awful rendition of "Rockin' all over the world". He'll take risks. He looks long term (some of 'em couldn't see the far end of a fart). He wants growth, both in himself and his officers and not stifling procedures which stifle creativity. He builds relationships with his officers and does not rely on soulless procedures. He coaches instead of bullies. He has people who look up to him and respect him.

Great person. I've already stated that the vast majority of Senior Officers are great, they really are amazing people and fully deserve their rank, but unfortunately there are a couple who get promoted purely for power, but this is very rare. I think that most get swallowed up because the diktat has to be obeyed. There is no room for anything else.

But I had no idea of why he was teaching us how to draw butterflies, I'd probably listened to far too much corporate horseshit for one day. I'd probably drifted off to my happy place, on The Maldives with Mrs R.

Six hours too late, the wankfest was over, spunk goggles off, and relax.

And in that tiny microcosm of life I could see how policing had completely lost its soul. This had no relevance to arresting a criminal or sorting out problems within a community. In fact, it was very difficult to see what it had any relevance to, apart from the self-gratification of The Academic and The Consultant.

So, there you have it, to be a great leader in the Happy Valley Police you have to:

1.   Surround yourself with wankers.
2.   Talk pure shit, and
3.   Learn to draw a butterfly.

Boss's Kebabs

Mathew was a lad going through a bit of a bad patch, he was going out nicking. He'd been arrested and as part of the Court bail conditions, he was to obey a curfew between 1900hrs and 0700hrs. His mum had got so fed up with the police going there that she was going to kick him out, so by default he was going to breach his bail conditions and had to be arrested. Now I'm not known for fucking about.

This is my arrest statement; this has to be read by the custody sergeant to establish the reason for the arrest and by the Court for them to understand why Mathew was arrested.

Witness Statement

Page 1 of 1

Criminal Procedure Rules, r 16.2; Criminal Justice Act 1967, s.9

Statement of: Alan Gordon ROBINSON

Age if under 18 (if over insert 'over 18'): Over 18

Occupation: Police Officer

This statement (consisting of ......1...... Pages(s) each signed by me) is true to the best of my knowledge and belief and I make it knowing that, if it is tendered in evidence, I shall be liable to prosecution if I have wilfully stated in it, anything which I know to be false, or do not believe to be true.

On Friday 16th March 2018 at 2100hrs I was in full police uniform on mobile patrol with PS6309 GARDNER.

Acting on information received, namely that Mathew was outside his mother's address, we proceeded to said location. I was aware that his mother was withdrawing her consent for him to stay there in keeping with his Court Bail Conditions. Outside the address I recognised Mathew, I said to him 'Mathew, I am arresting you because you have Breached your Court Bail Conditions, you do not have to say anything, but it may harm your defence if you do not mention when questioned something that you rely on in Court, do you understand?' to which he replied, 'Fuck me sergeant you don't fuck about do you?'

I replied, 'You're fucking right Mathew I fucking don't.' I went on to say that I have a chicken wrap waiting for me at Boss Kebabs on the Banbury Road and that I would appreciate it if he could get a move on, to which he replied 'Sergeant, I am terribly sorry to mess you around, please go and enjoy your chicken wrap they're lush from there.'

I said, 'Good old boy.'

Signed Alan Gordon ROBINSON   Date 16th March 2018

Worthy

And then there's Jake Nutt.

For reasons best known to the creatures of the corridor, Jake Nutt is going to have greater influence over my working life. He gets to sit in on any training or meeting where he can spout his endless bollocks. His record is almost unbelievable: he's arrested thirty-one murderers (it's incredibly rare for an officer to arrest a murderer, most officers go a whole career without arresting one, needless to say I didn't); he's exaggerated about it hundreds of times, or, as he'd say, 'I've exaggerated about it hundreds of times. You ask anybody.' Apparently, and slightly less impressive, but still worthy of note, is that he's already caught two burglars red-handed. 'I've caught two burglars red-handed hundreds of times. You ask anybody. '

On average in a twenty-five-year career, an officer will only catch one, needless to say, I didn't.

Oh my God, I'm not worthy.

Every five weeks our inspector and a sergeant (Ash and Triff usually go, I give it a massive body swerve whenever possible) have to attend a health check meeting. This is where the Detective Chief Inspector (DCI) flanked by Wyng and Nutt get to tell us how fucking great they are and how fucking useless the response and IHub officers are, and if we could only be as half as fucking great as the fucking great Jake Nutt and the even greater Xavier Wyng then the whole of the fucking Happy Valley Police would be fucking great.

What better place for Jake to sit in judgement and send a detailed report evidencing that we were fucking useless at a couple of burglaries and if we ever need any help or support to go and see him on Op Basil (the burglary initiative, not allowed to say burglary team). That won't be happening, and how about someone from Op Basil attending a burglary and showing us all how it should be done like it was promised when the New Operating Model was introduced.

28 March 2018

'You should have been here five minutes ago,' she screeched.

'Why, what happened?' I calmly replied.

'That fucking fat schizophrenic bitch has got herself pissed again and come and banged on my door,' she continued to screech.

'Oh dear, are you okay? All I care about is you.'

'Do I fucking look okay? She's always doing this, she did it a year ago.'

'Oh.' My face is one of great concern, I've honed it over the years, my well furrowed brow becomes even more furrowed and I have a good ol' go at the worried squint. My arms are crossed, my 'go-to' position of concern.

'Oh, oh, is that all you can fucking say?'

Well, yes, it is, without pissing myself.

'Are you going to do absolutely fuck all like you did last time?'

I allow my right arm to uncross and my right-hand creeps up to my chin. Oh, come on, have you ever seen such a caring face? I'm a lover not a fighter, please just calm the fuck down, my whole body is a picture of concern. I'm giving her all my best moves here, but inside I couldn't give a shit, she's bloody rumbled me.

'No, no, I'm not going to do that.' Me.

'Not going to do fucking what?' 'Er.

'Er, um, whatever it is that you don't want me to do.' Fucking hell, desperate times call for desperate measures, I'm going to bring out The Invincible. The carefully positioned index finger starts to tap on my chin, I could not look any more concerned. It has served me well for so long.

'Are you just going to stand there tapping one of your fucking chins or are you going to arrest the fat schizophrenic bitch?' And being an obnoxious bitch has served her well for so long. The Invincible is not only defeated, The Invincible has been slaughtered.

'You've called the police because you're a victim of crime, I've arrived within five minutes. I've just been dealing with someone who's had his head stoved in by a metal bar, and the offender has been tasered, and all you have done is be obnoxious, rude and abusive towards me.'

'I couldn't give a shit about his fucking head. I'm a professional person, I'm a financial advisor, and I'm a victim and I want the fat schizophrenic bitch arrested.'

I just felt so deflated, not only had The Invincible become The Uninvincible but I hate wasted talent. Being so obnoxious, rude and abusive to be a financial advisor is such a waste of talent, she'd make a great barrister.

29 March 2018

Mr and Mrs Dumbfuck live in Barton off the Roundabout, a quiet little suburb of Oxford, full of colourful characters.

Mr and Mrs Dumbfuck are from a long line of Dumbfucks and the genes are getting stronger and stronger, and because there is very small gene pool for Dumbfucks, the Dumbfuck gene has run riot in these dumbfuckers.

Mr Dumbfuck has phoned to say that he has stabbed his wife three times and she is dead. Armed Response Vehicles and police officers from all over the county blatted to get to the Dumbfucks. She opened the door of their studio apartment with a lovely little smile. Mr Dumbfuck pretended that he was dead on the bed. TeeTee and Heidi pinched his lobe and touched his eyelids, but the Dumbfuck squeezed them closed.

Like all my colleagues, Heidi and TeeTee are so incredibly professional, compassionate, courageous and discerning, that they remained respectful.

To cut a long story short, he came out of his feigned death when he thought that the ambulance would be called. TeeTee told the Dumbfuck that if he repeated this gross act of dumbfuckery he would be arrested.

'Why have you phoned the police to say that you have stabbed your lovely wife three times?'

'I didn't.' I think he's lying.

'We will phone the phone.'

'Go on then, I didn't do it.' He's got to be lying.

Ring ring, his phone rang with the ringtone of Alanis Morrisette song 'Ironic' as the ringtone just to add to the drama. He's lying.

Not satisfied with his night's work, Mr Dumbfuck has phoned into complain, obviously.

'So, Mr Dumbfuck, let's get this absolutely straight, you've behaved like a complete dumbfuck, by saying that you'd stabbed Mrs Dumbfuck, and now you want to be an even bigger dumbfuck by complaining that my officers didn't buy your dumbfuckery and waste more of my dumbfucking time by treating me like a dumbfuck. Well, listen, Mr Dumbfuck, I'll be dumbfucked if I'll let you treat me like a dumbfuck, so if you could do us all a massive favour and dumbfuck the fuck off, tata.'

The never-ending drivel of pointless PDRs, where no-one can express how they feel is another reason as to how it has come to this. Dunt ma''er in December me and Party 3 are off to Amsterdam. Hey ho nine months to go

APRIL

The New Operating Model and the De-skilled

Completely Disillusioned

Ten months on and it's BACOOMA Time all the time.

I mean, it was pretty bloody obvious really.

Officers have left in their droves, completely disillusioned with the difference between what they believed they were joining and what the reality of what the police service had been transformed into. The officers remaining on the frontline are completely bewildered.

I'm thinking of becoming a consultant, I'm not clever enough to become an academic.

And this is my New Operating Model, the AIRoberating Model. Apart from the extremely hardworking CID officers, and a couple of other departments, everyone would be proud to wear the uniform. Everyone would come into work, stick their big hat and radios on and get out and serve the public – do the job they joined to do. We need plenty more pointing action. It appears to me that for every officer who's taken off the beat, they've been replaced by four or five officers or civilians stuck in offices producing precisely bugger all.

All of this was predicted by my predecessors in the police service, but it has become far worse than anyone could've ever predicted. All the chickens of predictions made by my predecessors have come home to roost.

We've lost the art of policing; it was a craft, a skill. A police officer would get to know an area and speak and get to know people. They knew when someone or something was out of place and they'd find out what was going on and challenge it, and if necessary, stop and search it. We'd sneak up on people. We were sneaky.

That's what it was all about. Officers had presence, it's what the public love to see.

That's the art, the craft, the skill. That's where terms like 'copper's nose' and 'thieftaker' came from. We've lost the good old-fashioned copper who had an eye and an instinct.

Somewhere along the way we lost our way and our soul. The criminals must be laughing at us. We lost too many good old-fashioned coppers. We lost too many coppers. We don't have any officers to pass on their experience, and even if we did the officers are far too busy blasting from job to job to be proactive, that is how County Lines have flourished.

I'm grateful that part of my service was during a time when officers could use their initiative, it wasn't so painfully prescriptive, I feel the pain of the new recruits.

The art, the craft, the skill were killed off by consultants and academics who believed that a coppers nose could be replaced by taskings, hotspot areas, 'top five offenders', and any other stupid idea that would stop an officer from getting out and about and getting to know the people they serve. They thought a bobby on the beat could be replaced by meaningless engagement events. The consultants and academics thought that the copper's instinct could be replaced by risk assessments and soul-destroying processes. Everything's been replaced by soulless processes. They took away the bobby's creativity and replaced it with joyless, meaningless detection rates.

It was traumatic to see an institution lose its identity and soul.

I am indebted to my ex-Sergeant and friend Billy Adams for reminding me of an extremely important piece of legislation that had an enormous impact on policing. This will've been lost in the midst of time, but it's vital.

The Conservatives sneaked the Police Act 1996 (building on the Police and Magistrates Court Act 1994) through Parliament just as they were losing power to Tony Blair's Labour Party. We were extremely sneaky, but we could never be as sneaky as the Conservative Party. Amongst other things the Act led to the boundaries of policing areas being coterminous (oooh, get me) to those of local government for ease of communication and co-operation between the institutions. But far more importantly, it outlined the role of the Secretary of State in determining objectives and setting budgets for the police. So, people who had no idea of policing were going to tell police how to police. This is a huge reason as to how policing lost its soul.

It was like strapping a skeleton bobsled to the back of someone who's ill, it went downhill pretty rapidly after that. The Police were at the mercy of every whim and fancy of Whitehall. There were so many knee jerk reactions it turned the CCMT into the Ministry of Funny Walks. This is where the wretched performance indicators/detection rates/ target culture and risk assessments have come from.

When everything is a priority nothing is a priority. 'Priorities' is a word only an academic would use. To the officers who had to deliver the 'Priorities' it made absolutely no difference, they continued to give the best possible service at every incident, irrespective of whether it was a 'Priority' or not. A 'Priority' is only a priority to enable a manager to shake their shitty stick at an officer.

I cannot profess to be an expert, but the NHS and teaching must've been subjected to their equivalent of the Police Act 1996. I would be extremely interested if someone could tell me.

Let the police, police.

Let the teachers, teach.

Let the doctors, doctor.

These used to be plum jobs, but now you have to be a bit of a plum to do it.

The government have meddled to the point of making them useless. Thanks for that fella, but I think we can take it from here.

I've never known the police to do a national telly campaign to try and entice new recruits. But they are now. Nobody wants to join, and few want to stay, I'd love to ask Boris why he thinks that is. Because it's not because of house prices, and it's not even because of The Culture, it's because of having to continually deal with other people's shit. It's relentless. Who'd want that as a job? Not me.

Imagine the legends that are going to join. Maybe the legends who want to be social workers will, and deal with the vulllllllnnnnneraaaable, who'll just piss off the officers who want to fight crime.

Old Bull

Do, do,

Do a review,

That's all that I ever do,

Is review and review and review.

May, may,

May I just say,

That this is day after day,

After day after day after day.

This is

Not, what I should do,

Review and review and

Review and review and review.

I just

Wish I could do

Something other than review, and review, and review,

Down at the Old Bull and Shit.

Because there are so many incidents being passed from the response team to the IHub, I spend my entire day reviewing whether the 'golden hour' (completing house to house enquiries, seizing CCTV footage, obtaining essential statements, tasking CSI attendance and, if possible, arresting the suspect) enquiries have been completed, and the incident/job is IHub-ready.

Jake Nutt's nuts have swollen.

All these bloody reviews are all his bloody idea, and it's an absolute classic. I cannot articulate how fucked off I am.

This is known as Nosnibor's Law because it's all the wrong way around. It appeals to my narcissistic nature. I'm not, honestly, I'm not.

This law states that the people who instigate change aren't affected by it. And the people who are affected by change can't instigate it. Actually, it's even worse than that. Not only is change instigated by people who aren't affected by it, it's instigated by people who've never even done the job and haven't got a clue what they're chatting about.

Little wonder the whole organisation is such a clusterfuck.

If it was down to me, all the major changes for the police service should be instigated by people who are affected by it, who know what they're doing and care tremendously about the organisation, their colleagues and the community they serve. This will be known as Robinson's Law. Yep, yep, all right, I may be a little narcissistic.

Jake Nutt won't have to do reviews and handovers. Yet he's instigated me having to do them all day, every day, day in, day out and he's instigated that I have to do them because it makes his life easier, but it makes my life incredibly difficult. Here's a novel idea: how about, just for once, doing something – almost anything – to make the response officers' lives a bit easier?

There's no need for people like The Academic or The Consultant – they're laughing all the way to the bank – they bring about the New Operating Model, and an awful shift pattern, risk assessments and detection rates (more about them in a bit) and many other initiatives and procedures that frustrate an officer from getting out on patrol, which makes police work incredibly inefficient and ineffective. If I was to be cynical, I would think that this is all in an effort to make us so ineffective and so inefficient that the public would be grateful for an alternative, any alternative that would involve seeing a bobby on the beat. And that would mean privatisation.

In the Happy Valley consultants were paid £12 million last year. Twelve million pounds – the equivalent of the salary of 400 police officers. It's outrageous. Why can't they trust the people who do the job to instigate the change that's needed? What's the point of having a hierarchy?

You can have my advice for a pint of Guinness.

'Sarge, sarge, sarge, Al, Al, Alan, sarge, sarge, sergeant, sergeant, Alan, Alan, Al, Al, sarge, Al, sergeant, Alan, Alan, Alan, sergeant, al, sergeant.'

I was beginning to get the impression that one of my lovely officers wanted a word with me.

'How can I help?' I was good like that.

'You'll never guess what, sarge, Alan, Al, sergeant?'

'No, no, I don't think I will, I think you'll have to give me a bit of a hint.'

'You remember that high risk dommy yesterday, I was there for over two hours?'

'Yeah, it was a bad un.'

'The DAU (Domestic Abuse Unit) have only sent me an e-mail telling me to complete the form with the kids dates of birth and schools.'

'Oh, for fuck's sake.'

It would've been quicker for the DAU to've contacted them themselves and obtained the info.

The DAU are usually extremely good, most officers in there appreciate how difficult it is on the frontline, but a couple just don't get it.

But this is the mentality on a lot of the departments that should support the officer.

It's ingrained. Bounce it back to the officer. The scrutineers are the worst. Continually bouncing things back. Waste of fuckin' time, just file the fuckin' thing. Please.

We're far too busy scoring petty points over our colleagues at the expense of providing a meaningful service.

I'd love to see a spearheady sorta thing going on. Everybody moves the investigation on. Progresses it, instead of batting it back. If anyone bats anything back, they should get a bat right on the back of their head.

And now that I'm on a roll. Instead of being hellbent on retribution for a petty crime, show a bit of kindness, love and compassion, give them some support, help 'em out, show them that you care, but that wouldn't show up on any piechart.

And if it dunt show up on a piechart, it dunt get done.

That's the sort of advice I'd give if I was a consultant, and it wouldn't cost £12 million.

I'm anyone's for a couple of pints of Guinness.

Homeless community

Gazza the Gazelle is a homeless lad in Oxford, and he's a right pain in the arse.

For one reason or another, I get a daily update from him, his girlfriend, from his other girlfriend, from the other girlfriend's other boyfriend, or anyone else foolish enough to stick their sticky beak into his nonsense.

In fact, he was the one who'd had his head stoved in a couple of days ago when the obnoxious bitch defeated The Invincible – it still hurts. I'll get over it, records are made to be broken.

For some unfathomable reason Gazza the Gazelle is highly desirable among the homeless community. Men want to fuck him up and women just want to fuck him. So much so, that he's the central player in a bizarre love dodecagon. If he carries on the way he is going he will be fucked and fucked up simultaneously.

His care worker has just informed the police that Gazza the Gazelle has told him that a bloke whose girlfriend has been shagging the Gazelle wants to shoot him. So many women, so little time.

Now his crazy shit is going to drive me crazy.

What am I supposed to do about that? If the Gazelle gets shot it will be all my fault. Calm down, think clearly, there are four things to consider when the police receive information that there is a threat to kill.

1. Is there a very real intent to kill? I should blimmin' well cocoa. The suspect has got a previous conviction for shooting a bloke some years back for doing exactly the same thing.

2. Has the suspect got the capability? I should blimmin' well cocoa. The gun that he used was never found.

3. What is the proximity between suspect and victim, is it likely to happen imminently? I should blimmin' well cocoa. They're probably within 100 yards of each other. And, and my fourth point overrides the previous three considerations.

4. Do I give a fuck? No. No, I don't. I need a cup of cocoa or better still, a cup of Yorkshire tea and a Bourbon. This gazelle shit has been going on for years and it will be going on for years after I retire.

So, I had a lovely cup of tea and dunked me Bourbons and the world seems a much better place, and obviously nothing happens to Gazelle, it was only the care worker passing their responsibility to me.

Ooh, sailor

And we're out and about, mixing it up with the crazy cats of Oxford.

'Hey, mate, you've gotta bit of tissue on the back of your shoe.'

The poor sod lifts his heel and looks back at it.

'Oooooh, sailor.'

'You bastards.'

As Ash and I drive away high fiving.

Oh, hang on, what's going on here? Some mad lady with crazy hair is waving frantically at us. Sweet Jesus, I only go out of the office to get away from the incessant calls from the Laura in the Contact Management Platform asking ridiculous questions. For some unknown reason they're all called Laura, even the blokes. I think it might be one of the qualifications you need to work there. I think I might've been a little bit out of order when I told her to fuck off (well, I didn't exactly tell her to fuck off, but I might as well have done, when she asked me how often the tampon machine in St Aldates gets replenished. But there are an awful lorra, lorra Lauras asking a lorra lorra questions, causing me a lorra lorra stress).

The mad lady with the crazy hair told us that someone was going to kill herself in a very specific and peculiar way, and any experienced officers worth their salt, would immediately know who the suicidal person was, and how to prevent it from happening. I'm going to call the suicidal person SP.

Whenever I find myself in the middle of a particularly sticky problem, I quietly think to myself, what would The Academic do?

He's loved and revered across Happy Valley for his pragmatic approach.

The Easter revellers are doing everything they can to help, well, when I say they're doing everything they can to help, what I actually mean is that they've all got their smartphones out and are busying themselves recording it.

So, what would The Academic do?

Bore poor ol' SP shitless with bollocks about operational fairness. Oh my God, if I was SP, I'd take my chances on the other side. What am I talking about? If I were me, I'd take my chances on the other side. Fuck this for a game of soldiers, even the heroes recording the spectacle would want to take their chances. There would be a massive queue of people lining up. We'd need more police for crowd control, but we haven't got any police officers because it's all fucked up.

He'd be asking for negotiators, Armed Response teams, someone from the media team, road closures, support from other areas, etc, etc.

Yes Sir, you could do all that, or you could get an experienced officer who's got knowledge of SP and who knows what they're doing, and who knows the little secret knack of gaining rapport with SP and resolve the situation within seconds.

That's the value of having experienced officers on the frontline. People who get out and get to know the people they're serving. But we've got a Government and Senior Management who are hellbent on getting rid of experienced officers. There's no substitute for experience, but when you've only got one person on the response team with more than five years' service (and it's getting worse as the years go by) it's a very scarce and valuable commodity.

What a topsy-turvy ol' world we live in, when someone can record and upload a video on social media and it can be viewed by millions within seconds with all the people involved easily identified, but I've got to be extremely careful writing about it in a book which will be read by a couple of hundred people, if I'm lucky.

Too bloody late

They arrive at the Early Turn briefing at five past seven.

'Sorry we're a little late, er, we're from the Service Improvement Unit.'

Late, late? About twenty-five years too bloody late, mate.

'We're here to see how we can help you improve our service to our service users.'

Fuckin' service users, dofuckinwot? Where are we going with this?

Ah great. I have waited twenty-five years for this moment.

'We have five officers trying to police at least 170,000 people in Oxford, can ... anyone ... see ... why ... on a few occasions … our... service ... is not ... quite...'

'So, we will be in St Aldates for the next couple of weeks to hear ideas from you as to how we can improve our service.'

I jotted down a few notes and off I jolly well fucked.

And my rant begins. I reel off issues with recruitment, discipline, consultants and academics, the Ferkin' Merkin', just to start off with. Move up a level and we've got: Resource Management, the PDR and High Potential Development scheme (HPDS) – that bloody scheme that The Consultant instigated. Which means officers move to the rank of incompetence far too quickly. And cruise into the PCC, officers leaving, officers with stress, duty changes and not allowed to book leave. And round it off with the belief that everything gets dumped on the response teams; other departments are there to support us, but nothing could be further from their minds. And reeeeelaaaaax, deep breaths.

And then the realisation that the man from the Service Improvement Unit is not here to listen to any of my bollocks. He's here to ensure that what we're doing is recorded properly. He starts questioning me about the recording of burglaries, assaults, modern slavery and domestics.

It's very apparent that we're not singing from the same hymn sheet, we've not got blue sky thinking, we're not going to put it on the back burner, we're not going to run it up the flag post and see who salutes it. We're not going to be doing any of those things.

The police service is limping from crisis to crisis but all the CCMT are doing is ensuring that their arses are well and truly covered, from their elevated position up the greasy pole, and it's all being recorded properly. Just like the legends recording SP's antics.

Gory details

Ah no.

This whole chapter was going to be dominated by an incredibly witty diatribe about the latest instalment of the on-going drama about the Didn'tKnowItWasNewYear'sEve Department, I mean, the Didn'tKnowItWasEaster Department. In the latest episode the useless Resource Management Department has been re-christened: It Would Appear They Didn'tKnowItWasTheRoyalWedding Department. Also known as the Meghan Markle Debacle. In this episode, police officers were going to have to time travel to enable them to be in two places at one time. However, I've made the decision to delete it and spare you the gory details, think yourselves very lucky. But I will take this opportunity to say that this is how you get to see so many police officers at protests and demonstrations and yet no police officer attends your crime. The officers are subjected to duty changes at extremely short notice, sometimes giving up their rest days, which need to be reallocated, which obviously has the effect of there being no officers on area (at their normal station). There needs to be a definition in Regulations of what an exigency of duty is, I think I may've mentioned that a couple of times already. Officers can only be in one place at one time, and they can only spend their time once. And that is the reason why you never see a police officer.

It was at this time that I was subjected to loads of duty changes to supervise Op Nightsafe (because the neighbourhood sergeants didn't want to join in with this policing malarkey).

I had a serious sense of humour failure and wrote an e-mail to Civilian Thoughtless in the Resource Management Department. I told him that I was leaving the service at Christmas and they could fuck off (well, I didn't exactly tell him to fuck off, but I may as well've done) and do his worst.

I should've taken the opportunity to remind him that Christmas Day falls on 25 December every year and Boxing Day is the day after, and the big one, that catches them out every year, New Year's Eve is on 31 December. Always the same, never changes.

That reminds me, if you ever bump into Mrs R ask her to say, 'fuck off'. It's a thing of absolute beauty, she holds onto the 'o' so whoever is on the receiving end of it, is left in no doubt that they are not worthy of any emotion, it's like she's bored with the whole damn thing, fuck ooff. I'm going to use it at every opportunity, what are they going to do to me? Put me on a five-week rotating shift system on a response team at Cowley? Or 'stick me on'. 'Stick you on' is an expression peculiar to the police service, all through my illustrious career I never had a clue what it meant. Stick me on what? The wall? I've got no idea.

'Al, if you don't complete the domestic form, I'll stick you on.'

'Crack on, mate. I've got no idea what you're chatting about.'

I must remember that this job is growing me.

1977

I've got two days of training. The first day is teaching me how to be an Evidential Review Officer (ERO) – yep, yep, I know what you're thinking, but Al, I thought that you were a police officer. Yep, yep, so did I but hey ho, you know. And the second is the rather nattily titled 'From Report to Court'.

Now, when I was applying to become a police officer, I thought it would be plenty of pointing action, a bit of biff and scud on a Friday and Saturday night, chasing down a few robbers, catching the odd burglar, and maybe even a murderer. I was a man of the world; I'd played football for Witney Cygnets and been on the 1977 tour of Holland. I could handle myself.

Somehow, being a police officer has descended into reviewing inconsequential shitty incidents, batting off endless phone calls from Laura and telling her to fuck ooff (well, I didn't exactly tell her to fuck ooff, but I may as well've done), telling Civilian Thoughtless, in the Didn'tKnowItWasTheRoyalWedding Department to fuck ooff (well I didn't exactly tell him to fuck ooff but I may as well've done); and avoiding Nutt, Wyng and PieChartMan. Together with living with the trauma of seeing a six-foot three officer dry hump some poor sod on The Blabber bridge; when you see me, I'll tell you all about it.

But things have just taken a turn for the worse.

The lecturer kicks it off with, 'So, you want to be an evidential review officer.'

And I thought, no, no I don't, if I wanted to be an evidential review officer, I would've applied for the job called evidential review officer but I didn't want to be an evidential review officer, I wanted to be a police officer, so I made the rather wise decision, bearing all this in mind and taking all things into consideration, to become a police officer, not an evidential review officer, and my family and friends were very proud of me. So no, no I don't want to be an evidential review officer. I've got nothing against them, they're all lovely people, and they do a marvellous job, but I don't want to be one. A civilian should be an Evidential Review Officer and a police officer should be a police officer, it'd all work extremely well that way. You'd be a very rare beast if you could be a great evidential review officer and a just below average police officer, they require two completely different skillsets.

So no, no, I don't want to be an evidential review officer at all, thanks ever so much for asking. I'd desperately love to be a police officer and go out and do all the wonderful things that a police officer does, if it's all the same to you, thank you.'

I couldn't think of anything worse. I would rather have a root canal filling or listen to a lecture by The Academic … well, no, I draw the line at that, I would far rather be an ERO. Come on, Robinson, let's get things in proportion.

'The first thing that you must ensure, is that the file is EPIC. Evidential, in the Public Interest, and Court-ready.'

Wow, and this has to be done by a police officer, right?

Just tell me where I need to sign.

'And you'll have to go through a three to six month 'buddy' period, to become an accredited ERO.'

I wish you the very best of luck with that one, my friend; that won't be happening, not on your nelly. And this has to be done by an almost physically fit police officer, right?

Just tell me where I need to sign.

'So, what you have to do is identify offences and lines of enquiry, apply the Full Code Test, and make No Further Action (NFA), and Out of Court Disposal Decisions...'

I'm terribly sorry, my good man, you've totally lost me; and this has to be done by an almost physically fit, kind of mentally well police officer, right?

Just tell me where I need to sign.

'Which leads nicely on to the golden ARC of evidence: Admissible, Reliable, Credible...;

You're not even trying to find me; and this has to be done by an almost physically fit, kind of mentally well, fully operational police officer, right? Just tell me where I need to sign.

'And you need to give your rationale...'

Anything, just fucking anything; and this has to be done by a physically fit, kind of mentally well, fully operational police officer, with twenty-five years' experience, right?

Just tell me where I need to sign.

'And then you have to complete the National Case File Quality Assessment...'

Just. Fucking. Tell. Me. Where. I. Fucking. Need. To. Fucking. Sign.

Crying off

The Boss wants a word with me in his office.

The Boss is my inspector. A really great ol' boy, a kind, caring and decent man, it cannot be overstated what a great ol' boy he is. He shouldn't be an inspector after only four years in the job, but it doesn't stop him being a great person. He's on some kind of Accelerated Promotion Scheme. Ironically, The Boss will go on to be a great leader, which somewhat undermines my argument. But, the truth trumps everything.

He informs me that Laura from the Contact Management Platform and Civilian Thoughtless from Resource Management have contacted him because they think that I've told them to fuck ooff. Well, I didn't actually tell them to fuck ooff, but I may as well've done and should've done. He also considered that I hadn't taken the PDR seriously, and I'd taken so little interest in it that I couldn't even be bothered to delete the last couple of lines that I'd obviously left in after copying and pasting it from last year's review.

I asked him, 'How on earth should I know when the tampon machine is going to be replenished? And why on earth should I have to suffer doing Nightsafe all the time because of a bloody awful Operating Model and other sergeants crying off doing it all the time? These are organisational failings and not mine. But I take your point about the PDR.'

He said, 'Apart from that I'm really pleased with your work.'

I said, 'It's all in a day's work.'

We both walked away respecting the other's point of view, and that's the funny thing about it.

This job definitely, definitely grows you.

Finger

Can you help me out here please, there's something not quite right here, something not quite right at all, I just can't quite put my finger on it.

In an article in the *Daily Mirror* dated 22 April 2018 with the heading *Cop Out* (clever play on words – subtle, like it), it says that police officers are quitting their jobs at one of the highest rates since records began. It stated that voluntary resignations by officers have risen by fifty per cent since the Conservatives came to power in 2010. And the Police Federation have warned of plunging morale and damage to officers' mental health with sixty-two per cent of its members saying its workload is too high.

And an article in the *Oxford Mail* in which it reports that the Vale of White Horse Council Leader, Matthew Barber, has been appointed as full time Deputy Police and Crime Commissioner.

There's something not quite right about all this, can you see anything wrong with it?

Growing as I type.

Losing experienced officers, making police officers do jobs that should be done by civilians, and The Police Act 1996 are other reasons why it has come to this. Dunt ma''er in December me and Party 3 are off to Amsterdam. Hey ho eight months to go.

MAY

Cobbled Together

I'm sure you're all relieved to know it's No Swearing May.

Oh, for fuck's sake, those fuckers in the fuckin' Didn'tKnowIt WasMayDay Department have only gone and forgotten that it's fucking May Day. Well, that didn't last long, I'm sorry, but for fuck's sake.

May Day is a big day in Oxford. It involves 12,000 revellers seizing the opportunity to get as drunk as possible, so surely, they'll give us loads of officers to deal with it, right?

Nah.

So, they've cobbled together twelve officers, at very short notice, from all around the Happy Valley. To do that, they've robbed Peter to pay Paul, taking officers away from their usual place of work, leaving them short, and have made them police the May Day celebrations in Oxford. I thought that I'd have eight officers on patrol, but they've robbed me of four to police the celebration, leaving me with just four officers to cover all the other shenanigans. To rob officers from the area to put on an operation is a piece o'piss, anyone could do it, even I could do that, you could train a chimp to do it.

In fairness, the vast majority of people were a lot of fun but there was a bit of fisticuffs outside McDonalds on Cornmarket, a couple of drug-dealing gangstas got themselves all unnecessary because they didn't get a gherkin or summut. It'd all calmed down by the time we got there. But they couldn't resist the opportunity to get out their mobile phones and stick them right in my face.

The thing is, when you stick your mobile phone in a police officer's face you really must adopt the most wankish smirk on your most supercilious, gormless face. You know the one, that vomit-inducing expression that all newsreaders slip into when they're telling us about

106

the Royal Wedding. (I have no idea why there was so much fuss when Naga Munchetty, commented about Trump's racism, newsreaders are always biased in favour of the Royal Family.) Anyway, there it is, a rose gold, iPhone 8, right on the end of my nose. I'm not one for gender stereotypes, 'live and let live, love and let love', that's my motto, as you know, always has been, always will be, you can use it if you want. But, really, a gangsta with a rose gold iPhone, I mean, come on, really?

'Sir, Sir, what's your grandmother doing for a phone tonight?'

Cor, bloody hell, the rose gold phone, gone, wankish smirk, gone but that supercilious, gormless face, that'll be there forever.

I'm a police officer, and being a police officer makes me a very rare and very wonderful thing and I'm walking towards what can only be described as a wanker. The wanker, having had many generations and many millions of years to evolve, has developed an instinct of taking photos of rare and wonderful things. So, the wanker's many generations and many millions of years of evolution has evolved a subconscious, because as Darwin says "it is not the strongest of the species that survives, nor the most intelligent that survives. It is the one most adaptable to change."

And adapt this xkclunt has.

His subconscious has kicked in, and he is thinking.

'I' – His right hand goes into his hoody pocket.

'T'– Right hand locates his rose gold iPhone 8.

'S' – Right hand pulls out his rose gold iPhone 8.

'A' – Straight in my fucking face.

'Pol' – Selects the video function.

'Ice' – Press record.

'Off' – Adopt a wankish smirk.

'Ic' – On his supercilious, gormless fucking face.

'Er' – 'Fuck, he's made a comment about my rose gold phone and made me look like a complete cunt.' Back in the pocket, as quick as a flash. Hoping no fucker had noticed.

'Upload that to YouTube, you wanker.'

TCP

The years roll by, as quickly as you blink, enjoy yourself, enjoy yourself its later than you think a blink of an eye. Twenty-five have rolled by.

When I joined the service, I had a couple of months of training and a couple of weeks with my shift and after that I was summoned to see Chief Inspector Protheroe, who gloried in the nickname of 'Crazy Horse' because of some madcap antics in his younger days.

To his absolute credit he chose to sit right next to me instead of across at his desk, and after a few pleasantries like 'why did I join the job?' and 'what did I do before joining?', neither of which he was remotely interested in hearing, it was straight down to business.

'Come on, Al, lighten up. I was young once, I can understand you're a bit nervous, you must know what my nickname is.'

'I'd rather not say, Sir.'

'Al, don't worry, I know. I know what they call me, come on, what's my nickname?' He nudged his elbow into my arm.

'Sir, I'd rather not say.'

'Come on, Al, I won't tell them that you told me what they call me.' And he elbowed my arm again, harder.

'Sir, I just can't.'

'Al, it's all right, they call it me to my face, I know what they call me.' His voice broke into a little chuckle, and he gave me another much harder nudge with his elbow.

'Mouthwash, Sir.'

'What?'

'TCP, Sir.'

'What?'

'That Cunt Protheroe, Sir.' My voice croaked into a little chuckle as I elbowed his arm.

Six drug dealers

I'm sure that you'll all be pleased to know that Xavier's doing his silly shit again.

It would appear that there's a feud between the drug dealers in Oxford and the stress-increasing twat has got himself all unnecessary about it. Of course, he's not worried about 'it', what he's worried about is missing out on a golden opportunity of dick-swinging and putting the response teams under more pressure.

The silly twat only wants us to patrol the homes of six drug dealers and see that they're all hunky-dory. Absolutely bonkers. As I tell the five officers during our briefing, I could read all their minds, they were all thinking 'what in the bibbity bobbity holy fuckballs is this shit?' But they were all too polite to say. Just imagine if the good tax-paying folk of Oxford got to know about that? Six drug dealers have all the attention of the only deployable police resources in the city. What on earth are we looking for anyway? The silly old fool just hasn't got a clue, he just loves to wield his power, particularly when it's senseless and we haven't enough resources to deploy to incidents that need attending.

So, in a desperate bid to get himself a great PDR entry, he's forcing the incredibly limited number of response officers (five officers covering Oxford for the last week) to do his dirty work for him. Not only that, he's also insisting that he's updated with who's been tasked to do his dirty work for him and wanting to know why it's not been done. Um, yeah, tricky one that, could it possibly be that we are ever so slightly busy, while you're all toasty in your bed?

For goodness' sake, man, pull yourself together, and put that unfucking little thing away for a couple of minutes and give us all a break, or better still tuck it up your arse, where it can't do any harm.

All this achieves is animosity between two very hard-working departments: CID and the response officers. It shows his lack of understanding of just how incredibly busy response officers are, and it's embarrassing that he's in such a position without this understanding and lack of respect for his colleagues. Just to underline his ignorance he's made the statement, 'All response officers do is wait for the plane to fall out of the sky.' Oops, there it is. Give me bloody strength.

I wish this job would just stop growing me, now.

Mean feat

At last, at long, long last, we've got someone on our side.

He's noticed that there are far too few police officers, working far too hard, for far too long hours, with no breaks – not even to go to the toilet. Irony of ironies, that person is Raul, a drug dealer who is currently on poo-watch. He's been caught drug dealing and we believe that he may have a load more up his arse. A bit of the ol' crack up the crack. So, he's being watched every minute of the day and night, waiting for him to take a dump. He's up to two weeks, no mean feat, when I've got to go, I've got to go. Big respect.

'The way they treat you, man, is shit, even I get food when I want, and I can definitely go to toilet when I want, and I want to go, it's just that I can't. I'm fucked, if I shit, I'm fucked and if I don't, I'm fucked. I owe a lot of money to a lot of people. I'm really sorry to put you through all this, man, I really am.'

He genuinely couldn't give a shit.

That's all right, Raul, any time. Whenever you're passing, and don't want to take a dump, just pop in. But your humanity is greatly appreciated.

Along the line

And while I have to put up with Xavier's silly shit and Raul's lack of shit, the everyday shit of Oxford just continues to come in.

Adam used to be with Beth and Jason with Jade. But somewhere along the line they've swapped over. Adam is now with Jason and Beth is with Jade. No, they're not, I'm playing with you, just teasing. Adam is with Jade and Beth is with Jason. For some unknown reason, Adam is off on a mad one, he has threatened to kill Jason and his parents and then kill himself, if he could just see his way clear to killing himself first, that'd be just great.

Call of Duty

And right now, Chelsea has got herself in a right ol' pickle. Because, right now, she's been in an online relationship with Everton who lives 200 miles away. Right now, they 'met' while they were playing Call of Duty online and went into a chat room and right now, he gave her a call saying it's her duty to get her tits out for him. Right now, they've never met, and right now she's not got a clue what he looks like or who he is or where he is but right now, she wants him arrested. But right now, she wants to give a statement but the police can't go to her house because right now her mother has mental health issues and she can't be bothered to go to a police station right now because she's already missed four appointments to give a statement right now. Right now, Chelsea is concerned because although the photos only show her breasts everyone will know it's her because he got her to write Chelsea's Tits on them. And right now, he's sending them to people in Oxford on Facebook and right now on WhatsApp. So, Chelsea wants to give a statement to a police officer right now because he has to be arrested right now. And right now, Chelsea is feeling depressed so she should have a police officer right now. And right now, Chelsea is chasing for police attendance.

Well, right now, Chelsea, let's just say that me and Raul have something in common right now, because right now I just couldn't give a shit, right now.

Tigger into Eeyore

In the first week of May I was dragged, kicking and screaming, into the IHub on the middle floor at St Aldates. This was a joyless place. But hey ho, eight months to go. This is where I have to work, and I'll make the most of it. And I've still got the Party 3 trip to Amsterdam to look forward to.

Officers don't join the job to just go through the process of trying to record and then file an incident without doing much investigation, they want to feel like they're providing some sort of service to the victim and the community. That's the reason they join. Since the infamous Chief Inspector Poto'PinkPaint briefing concerning the introduction of the New Operating Model, the Contact Management Platform had just about materialised but they hadn't even found the kitchen, let alone the flippin' sink, to turn off the bloody gushing tap, so officers were drowning in a flood of over forty crimes that they hadn't had a chance to investigate (before the Operating Model we wouldn't allow officers to have more than ten). The misery permeated from the walls, hardly anyone wanted to be there. I saw officers who ordinarily would be fizzing and bouncing, turned into very dull beings. The Operating Merkin had turned Tigger into Eeyore. It did it to me.

Who's working in the

I to the H to the U to the B?

I don't care,

Anybody but me.

What do they do in the

I to the H to the U to the B?

No fucking police work,

as far as I can see.

So why do we have the

I to the H to the U to the B?

I think it's all for

Increased inefficiency.

This is it, this is what we've done all the training for, all the hard yards, to be stuck behind a desk in the IHub. I haven't got a clue what I'm supposed to be doing, nor why, but one thing is for absolute sure: it won't be anything to do with policing.

Pay as you Ride bikes

I really have to take this opportunity to say that working in the Control Room is enormously stressful. Some of the experienced operators were incredibly good and gave support and advice. One has an incredibly cool accent and the other has an incredibly cool surname, who was a great officer and went on to be a great operator. I think inexperienced operators would do well to follow their example. Unfortunately, a lot of the supportive and kind officers (such as Di J and others I'd like to name but can't) left during the Primetime Initiative – another foolish idea conjured up by consultants which destroyed the morale within the control room.

I've still got 'Screech' (one of the Control Room operators – who always makes an already stressful situation ten times more stressful) in the Control Room squawking on that she has three unresourced 'immediates' and four unresourced 'urgents' and I'm still asking her in my chirpy little tone if she has gone through the escalation process.

'Have you tried Force Roamers, IHub, neighbouring police areas, and Neighbourhood officers?'

'Oh, no, I haven't,' she squawks.

This lovely little charade gets played out ten or twelve times a day.

And Screech comes back with, 'I've tried the roamers, IHub, other areas, and Neighbourhood, there isn't anyone.'

It's BACOOMA Time, it's BACOOMA Time.

'Yeah, hang on, I'll just look under a few desks and in a couple of cupboards, to see if there are any hiding away.'

'Haaaahaha.' She doesn't screech or squawk, she actually laughs.

'Oh, hang on, I've just found five officers and a sergeant hiding away in an office just next to the City Centre Sergeants Office. I opened the door and five of them pelted under their desks, must've been a loose computer wire or summut. I had a sneaky peek under the desk to see what they were doing, they all had their eyes closed and I think they used the logic, 'if I can't see him, he won't be able to see me'. According to the sign on the door they're the Problem-Solving Team. I haven't got a clue what they do, and neither do they, but hey, they've just solved a massive problem. I now know where to park all those Pay as you Ride bikes littering Oxford'.

Blinking into the sunlight

And back to the Hub.

'Duh duddla duh duh.'

'Alternative Ulster, Stiff Little Fingers.'

Aaah bloody great, this is what goes on in the Hub, it's Guess the Intro. I'm going to fit right in here.

'Ding ding ding dinga dinga ding'

'The Clash, 'Should I Stay, or Should I Go'. Written in 1981 but didn't get to number one until ten years later.'

'Bloody 'ell, Al, you're good at this.'

I bloody am.

Dddddddrrrrrrrrrrrrrrriiiiiiiiiiiiiiiiiiiiiiinnnnnnnnnnnnnggggggggggggggg.

'Britney Spears, 'Baby Kiss Me One More Time'.'

'No, Al, that's the fire alarm. Come on, you silly old twat, quit yer wallygaggling...'

'Well, should I stay or should I...'

'Just fucking move.' Good ol' Danny G, bloody great bloke, always made me laugh, and always looked after me.

Obviously, I was the first at the assembly point. I don't fuck about. Just ask Mathew.

And out they all came, blinking into the sunlight, some hadn't been out for years.

'Oh hi, Steve, I thought that you'd died years ago. In fact, I'm sure you did, I remember going to your funeral, I gave the eulogy and everything, you remember me, Al Robinson? I was a response sergeant at Cowley, but I don't really know what I'm doing now. How's it all going?' He was incredibly pale and pasty, he looked like he'd just been dug up.

And still they kept coming out, the poor wee timorous beasties, wiping the slaver from their mouths, having a good old stretch, yawning and shaking their heads. Tens of them, some with dust and cobwebs and spiders on them, they'd hidden themselves away so well. It was all a bit of a shock to them. I tried to reassure them by telling them not to worry, they weren't in uniform and wouldn't be recognised as police officers, so they wouldn't be expected to do any police work but they were absolutely petrified and tried to scurry back into the station. I introduced myself to a few of them.

'Oh hi, I'm Al Robinson. I was a response sergeant up at Cowley but now I'm not really sure what I do, how's it all going? And you are?' And go in for the two-handed handshake, it's the only way.

'I'm Abi, I work in IOM.'

'Oh hi, Abi, nice to meet you, what is IOM? Are you a police officer?'

'Intensive Offender Management, and yeah, yeah, yeah, I've been in for ten years.'

'So why don't you wear a uniform and respond when someone wants to report a domestic at the front counter?'

'I'm in IOM, we don't deal with domestics.'

'When did you form the intention not to do any police work Abi?'

Abi lets out a cheeky little grin. I didn't have the heart to tell her that I wasn't bloody joking.

'Oh hi, I'm Al Robinson. I used to be the response sergeant up at Cowley but now...' I think you know the rest, but always the double handed handshake. It's the only way.

'I'm Scott, I work in the SMU.'

I ask him the same questions as Abi.

'Source Management Unit, I've been in the job eight years.'

'And when did you form the intention not to do any police work? And why don't you wear a uniform and why don't you deal with someone in their hour of need and they need our help with their domestic incident?' And then I was transfixed by a spider appearing from his right ear. And one in his mouth.

'I joined the police service not to do any police work, and I work In the SMU. We don't wear the uniform because the people who are giving us information do not like to talk to officers in uniform, and we don't deal with domestics.'

Ah nice one, Scott, I like the cut of your jib, nice bit of honesty, like it.

'Oh hi ...' I'll spare you.

'I'm Fred. I work in AIT.' It turns out Fred works in the Area Intelligence Team; he's been a police officer for twelve years and they don't wear a uniform in AIT and they don't deal with domestics and he formed the intention not to do any police work about ten years ago.

And just before the poor petrified pasty timorous wee beasties were ushered back into the safety of their offices or cupboards or hidey holes, I introduced myself to Nelly.

'Oh hi, Nelly, where do you work?'

'Oh, I work for the Domestic Abuse Unit.'

'Oh wow, Nelly from the Domestic Abuse Unit, great, that must be really interesting, are you a police officer?'

'Yeah, I've been in it for five years, I love it.'

'That's great, I love talking to people who are happy in their work. Do you mind me asking why don't you wear a uniform and radio? And why don't you help someone reporting a domestic at the front counter?'

'Al, I work for the Domestic Abuse Unit, we don't wear uniforms nor radios and we don't attend domestics.'

Not on your Nel....

And back into the station we go.

'Dudda duh duh, duh dudda duh.'

'What a Waste. Ian Dury. Not the Blockheads.'

Yep, what an almighty waste indeed.

In the good ol' days these office jobs were the reserve and preserve of the good ol' girls and boys who'd done the hard yards and earned the right to be in the office, to help and support their colleagues, and they did a magnificent job of it.

Growing as I type.

And ignored

In the second week of May I entered into an e-mail spat with Xavier.

During a night shift where someone had been on a mad one, firing at officers, two of my officers had to do a sixteen hour tour of duty, during which there had been an incident where someone had entered a student's room and Becca and Oz, two of my finest officers had attended, but due to everything else going on they had to redeploy.

Once again, I'm going to spare you the gory details, but Xavier got himself all unnecessary asking for the brilliant Becca and Oz to reattend.

Ahh, great stuff, great stuff that is, thanks for all your humanity. Message received, understood and ignored. He has Op Basil, with four or five officers who specialise in investigating burglary who obviously should investigate this incident; the poor bloke just simply doesn't get it. I said "This……. to me……. was completely and utterly……. and wholly and entirely………. what the………. New Operating Model was all about." Fuck my ol' tin 'at, I'm turning into 'im. He's so used to dumping on the response officers, he just doesn't get it.

I just wanted to tell him to fuck off and quit this growing lark.

Cauliflower

Ah no.

Ash is upsetting people again. This time it's the Operational Supervisor (Oscar 2), a civilian working in the Control Room, with the operational experience of notafuckingthing. In what sort of organisation do you allow a civilian with no operational experience tell an officer with nine years' service how to do their job?

Ash has only gone and asked her for her rationale as to why she didn't task an Officer to attempt to arrest someone who stole a bike two weeks earlier and is now riding around on it, in exactly the same clothes. Her reply fell just shy of, 'We're the police, we don't deal with crime.' She just didn't get it, well, how could she? She's never been a police officer. All she's concerned about is getting her top of the range cauliflower arse back on her top of the range wheelie chair.

In fact, that is her operational experience, knowing how to operate that bloody chair, adjustable seat height, adjustable arm rest, adjustable head rest, adjustable seat angle, this little beauty has to be fully operational, ready to go at a moment's notice.

So instead of sorting things out with Ash like a civilised human being would, speaking with him directly, she's chosen to complain about him to our inspector (this is extremely common), and this has culminated in her saying words to the effect that Ash should go and see how busy they are up there. Busy doing what? Adjusting their flipping chairs, and the biggest risk that they have to contend with is their top of the range cauliflower arse getting bigger and stuck in their top of the range fully operational chair.

Operational Supervisor, my uncauliflowered arse.

33 officers

The *Oxford Mail* dedicated the front page to a robbery in a store somewhere in Oxford. In the report they highlighted that it had taken almost a day for us to attend the store (we should've been there within twenty minutes, as Screech would screech, 'I have one unresourced immediate') but this is what happens during BACOOMA Time, it's appalling service. No doubt about it. If only they knew that the investigation won't be conducted by CID. Instead it's fallen to someone with less than two years' service, so scant are our resources because of the rate at which great people are calling it a day. Thirty-three officers in the Happy Valley left last month. (This was roughly the rate throughout the year.) Due to retirements, sacking and just generally being pissed off with it all.

I took buckets of sand to Headquarters yesterday and placed them next to the fire extinguishers. Above the extinguishers is the sign 'In case of emergency'. I put a sign above the buckets of sand: 'In case of reality.' I thought it'd be rather nice for members of the Chief Constables Management Team to have somewhere close by to stick their heads.

Frock and bollocks

Ash is furious with me. He's absolutely beside himself with anger. I've apologised but he isn't even talking to me.

It was an honest and genuine mistake, I didn't mean it, it just came out. Everyone's allowed a mistake every now and then surely, it's part of being human.

We were driving down Cornmarket and Nigella was walking straight towards the police car. Before I had a chance to engage my brain I said with a raised voice, 'Here he she is.' Ash gave me full on shit eye. He was so furious he had tears in his eyes. I tried to recover the situation by saying, 'Hershey bar, I like Hershey bars.' I was digging myself deeper and deeper. Ash was having none of it, he went puce with rage.

It's just that it's not something you see every day, a six-foot four man (who identifies as a woman) with a beard that Bin Laden would've been proud of, wearing a nice floral frock, accentuating a massive pair of bollocks flopping about. I'm getting old, I can't keep up. I am sorry, I am so very, very sorry. I mean, it was all frock and bollocks, I made a simple mistake. I wouldn't have been the first and I certainly won't be the last.

You know my motto, 'Live and let live, love and let love.' Always has been, always will be, you can use it if you want.

In a desperate bid to make it up to Ash I've offered to wear a floral dress and change my name to Alana, for a day.

Loose as a goose

Back on to a Nightsafe weekend, I've never lost the thrill of being called a wanker or having 'pigshit' shouted at me as I go past in the car. Well, being a police officer, I am a very rare and very wonderful thing.

Outside Plush nightclub they were having problems with a lad who just wouldn't go away. Seeing the problem, I asked Davey V to take his right side while I took his left to usher him away. As we got closer Davey V realised what I had already seen as the problem – that the lad didn't have a right arm. Davey V cursed me. Fortunately, the one-armed bloke was a great lad who had a sense of humour and informed us that he'd had a popper and acknowledged he'd been a bit of a tit.

Davey V asked him if he was as loose as a goose and he said that he was. I've had a very sheltered life (despite going on the Witney Cygnets 1977 tour of Holland) and didn't have a clue what they were going on about. A little bit later I sought clarification and Davey V enlightened me. Oh my God, I didn't know such a thing existed. I'm getting old. I must give it a go some time.

And then there was Princess Precious down on Middle Fisher Row threatening to take her own life. The only problem was that she needed to get maximum attention before she did it. She'd been kind enough to wait for us to arrive, waited for us to see her, and then flew into maximum Princess Precious mode and made a dash for the railings by the river. Davey V sauntered over and dragged her off.

'Why do you want to kill yourself now?' he enquired, already knowing the answer.

I think it's the drink, yep, it's definitely the drink, I'd put money on it being the drink.

'You don't know what a shit life I've had.' And then a load of old bollocks came spewing from her gob; you know the kind of thing – that same old bollocks that people keep locked away in the dark deep recesses of their mind but that make a very special guest appearance when they're drunk.

People cruised past accusing us of being racist.

'Davey V has just saved her li... Ah, it doesn't matter, you have a lovely evening,' I wished them.

'You've not had my life, you've all had privileged lives, you're all privileged, you must be to have become police officers.'

And on and on and on Princess Precious went, being abusive and obnoxious. Our mental health nurse arrived.

'So why do you want to kill yourself now?' she enquired, already knowing the answer.

I think it's the drink, yep, it's definitely the drink, I'd put money on it being the drink. It was the drink.

Princess Precious was sectioned under 136 of the Mental Health Act and taken to Littlemore Hospital where she was diagnosed with a very severe case of being a drama queen. After a good night's sleep and a couple of Alka-Seltzer she returned to normal, but this severe condition could return at any time of her life, or more accurately, at any time of her life when she has a drink.

And just down the road outside Atik, the King of all Drama Kings was turning in a performance. He really was the genuine article; a combination of drink and drugs had turned him into a complete animal.

When we got him into custody, he feigned a convulsion so convincing he would have won *Britain's Got Talent*. What a twit.

People feign convulsions, an epileptic fit or being pregnant, and lie to us an awful lot, it's very difficult to know when they're telling the truth.

The Big Day, 19 May 2018

At long, long last the big day has arrived. After all the excitement, all the planning, the visiting of the venue, the magic of trying on the dress, the choosing of the flowers, sending out the invitations, at last it was their day, a day that will live long in their memory and in those of all those guests lucky enough to have received an invitation and could actually attend. The problem was that my wonderful colleagues Holly and Butch had picked the same day that saw a little Royal Wedding going on at Windsor. So off most of their colleagues went to police the royal nuptials.

Even X Wyng had to go to Windsor, that's how desperate things had become.

'I went to get a battery ... yesterday ... and they didn't ... have any ... they didn't think of that.'

Oh dear, how dare they. Obviously, 'they' didn't think that someone in a leadership role – a leader of people – and a proper stress-inducing twat at that, would be so fucking useless that after having only six weeks to sort his shit out, would be so utterly inept that he wouldn't have a battery for his radio. Which begs the question, how long has he been screaming, 'I don't care too much about the community and I care even less about my colleagues?'

'Many of the ... back room staff ... haven't got uniform that fits them.'

When I started writing all this nonsense, I was worried that I wouldn't have enough material, but the silly little prick hands it to me on a plate, I couldn't make this stuff up.

'I'm just a ... constable today. Just ... making up ... the numbers.'

And even Jake Nutt was there, worried that Meghan might just somehow overshadow him. Using a helluva lot of lube, a copious amount of talc, and an industrial strength shoehorn, he'd miraculously squeezed himself into his uniform. It was snug. His eyes were watering, but he was back in the game. He needn't have worried about Meghan, there was no bigger head turner than him on that day.

But there is a serious point to all this. The Markle Debacle cost the Happy Valley very close to £3.5m (I think they got some money back, but nowhere near the full amount, all this during a time of extreme austerity). I would venture to suggest that due to the robbing Peter to pay Paul culture within the Didn'tKnowItWasTheRoyalWedding Department, and completely screwing over their colleagues in an effort not to pay overtime, I would imagine they saved close to £1m because very little overtime was paid to the response officers who had to attend. They had to endure duty changes, work extremely long hours during the rehearsal and the actual event with very little sleep, while the colleagues left back on area were left very short-staffed.

The relationship between The Didn'tKnowItWasTheRoyal Wedding Department and the frontline officers is strained, with the Didn'tKnowItWasTheRoyalWedding Department looked upon as a department who constantly and consistently screw their colleagues just in an effort to save money, because they can. What they do to their colleagues is disgraceful and the resentment grows. It would appear that the Code of Ethics, especially the respect element, does not apply to them, they put money before the welfare of their colleagues (money and ethics are incompatible) I dread to think of the number of days that have been lost due to sickness because of the relentless pressure placed on officers from this department. They could've easily asked for officers to volunteer to work at the Royal Wedding when it was announced and worked from there, but they left it to the last minute. They may not have broken police regulations, but they certainly broke the spirit of it. I don't know for certain, but I would imagine this is where we would find an Ulterior Motive or Hidden Agenda (an UM or a HA). Could this all be an effort to receive an outstanding in (pause) efficiency from Her Majesty's Inspectorate of Constabulary and Fire and Rescue Service? Are we seriously saying we're being had over by our colleagues, just in an effort to get an award no-one gives a shit about?

Meanwhile, back at the Markle Debacle, the television commentator coos, 'And, at long last, we get to see Meghan, looking absolutely resplendent in her ivory boat neck dress by Givench… Whooooooooooooa, hold the front page, what are we getting treated to here? I think it's someone on their way to a fetish club… Ah no, I remember, Happy Valley Police warned us about this, this is Jake Nutt in his uniform that he last wore six years ago.'

It wasn't so much head turning as decent folk having to double take, and not your normal double take; they caught a glimpse of him strutting his stuff along the Long Walk, had one look and on the double take they were hopping ninety degrees in the air and crashing into an innocent bystander who hadn't seen the spectacle and they, in turn, were doing the exact same thing. The silly sod should've carried a Government health warning. Elderly married couples were being knocked flying and having to be helped back to their feet.

'Did you just see what I just saw, darling?' one old man was heard to say.

'I did, I did, darling,' replied his husband.

'I want it, I desperately want it. I deserve it, I must have it, get it for me, darling.'

'Him or the outfit, darling?'

'Him, oh I'm just teasing. The outfit, darling.'

'Oooooh you're such a tease, David, darling.'

'I know, I know, Elton, darling.'

Mrs R was there, and she loved it. The good people of Windsor were wonderful towards her and all the officers, bringing out cakes and tea.

So, ladies and gentlemen, please be upstanding and raise your glasses to the happy couple, to Holly and Butch.

Too stoned

The Markle Debacle had left us extremely short of officers back on 'area'. The superintendent being the great old boy that he is, crewed up with me.

Emma and Louis caught three drug dealers on Carfax, you may well wonder how two officers could catch three offenders; they were dealing cannabis and I think that they had sampled a little bit too much of their wares and were too stoned to realise what was going on.

The sheer love, compassion and kindness with which the Super dealt with the lads, and everybody else he came into contact with, was amazing. To me, this is where policing has to go – love'll win the day. We've got to really care, we've got to be compassionate and respectful, to everyone we come into contact with and be proud of what we do. It's the only way. We've had death by pie charts and statistics; it couldn't possibly work. We're human beings dealing with human beings, let's just treat each other with respect. The chief constable has got it, I don't understand where this message gets lost.

Mushrooms

'You're a cunt, ent yer? You're a cunt, ent yer? You're a cunt, ent yer? You're a cunt, ent yer? You're a cunt, ent yer?'

After three or four minutes of this dipshittery, Beard, the most mild-mannered, patient and tolerant officer to have ever donned the uniform commented, 'I might very well be a cunt but at least I'm not stark bollock naked, smothered in my own shit. '

And just when you thought things couldn't get much worse, the naked swearer's mother and father arrived.

Ahhh, there he is, my second born, created in a moment of sheer bliss with his doting mother about seventeen years ago.

'In my own shit, am I? In my own shit, am I? In my own shit, am I? In my own shit, am I? In my own shit, am I?'

'Yes, you've eaten shitloads of magic mushrooms and now you're in the middle of a field just outside Oxford, stark bollock naked, smothered in your own shit, and everyone is looking at you.'

'I don't understand it, he's never done anything like this before,' the mother said.

'Well, he's certainly making up for lost time,' Beard said.

So, if poppers make you as loose as a goose, magic mushrooms have made this poor lad 'as slack as a whore on crack.'

And just when you thought things couldn't get much worse, a female officer arrived. And he's now become one for the ladies.

'She's fit, int she? She's fit, int she? She's fit, int she? She's fit, int she? She's fit, int she?'

And just when you thought things couldn't get much worse, he starts bashing his shit-ridden bishop.

'Want to be raped up the arse, do yuh? Want to be raped up the arse, do yuh? Want to be raped up the arse, do yuh? Want to be raped up the arse, do yuh? Want to be raped up the arse, do yuh?'

'Well, seeing as you have asked so politely. No, no, I don't. You're not really my type, a bit on the young side, and er, this shit thing. And may I just take this opportunity to say that the no clothes thing is a bit of a nice touch but next time wear a lovely bit of aftershave and bring some flowers, maybe a bottle of wine or even Prosecco, and take me to a nice restaurant, nothing too expensive. One last little tip – take it or leave it, it's up to you how you live your life – it may be quite a good idea to steer clear of the mushrooms.'

Hokey Cokey

It's BACOOMA Time. It's always BACOOMA Time.

'BPS92, I've got fifteen unresourced immediates and twenty unresourced urgents.' Screech is off again.

Ahh, good for you, give yourself a nice comfy chair to sit in. You've given me a problem that you know full well that I can't resolve, and the Problem-Solving Teams have made it abundantly clear that they have their job for the week.

I walked down the corridor on the middle floor of St Aldates.

Tippity, tippity, tappity, tip, tap, tip.

Where's that bloody noise coming from? I stuck my head around the IHub 'earlies' (early shifts) door.

Tappity, tappity, tippity, tip, tappity, tip, tap, tip. The noise was louder, but no one was there.

I stepped a foot inside and at least thirteen officers appeared like meerkats, stuck their heads above their computer screens, and stopped tippity tapping on their keyboards. I went to go out and they all disappeared, and the tip tapping started again.

I put my right foot in, meerkats appeared, tip tapping stopped. Right foot out, meerkats disappeared, tip tapping started. Right foot in, they appeared, tip tap stopped. Right foot out, they disappeared, tip tap, tip tap. I did the Hokey Cokey. I got it; the meerkats had felt threatened because I was encroaching on their environment.

I went into the IHub 'lates' office, another six meerkats appeared. Into a sneaky little office which was once the Warrants Office and another six. They're everywhere, producing an infinite amount of statistics, mostly for statistics' sake, with just an odd incident to investigate every now and then (and that's just a fluke). Just absolutely pointless.

It's said that if you gave an infinite number of monkeys an infinite number of typewriters and give them an infinite amount of time, they could produce the complete works of Shakespeare.

Just imagine what an infinite number of meerkats could produce: a thesis on how to completely demoralise public sector workers and destroy the glue that holds society together, or maybe even the Conservative Party manifesto; much the same thing really.

Not to put too fine a point on it, far too much of what a police officer does is completely superfluous to what they are seeking to achieve. Essential to dos, have been eclipsed by the nice to dos. There is an urgent need for someone to have a sudden and unexpected outbreak of commonsense to strip it back to where it needs to be.

Reverse cowgirl

'I need the police here now, please, he's got a gun, he's strangled me, and he's threatened to kill me, please just get someone here now.'

Davey V, Paddy, myself, the inspector, together with officers from the Armed Response Unit, get there in double-quick time and swift the bloke away. The victim was enormously grateful and enormously off her tits on cocaine and drink.'

'Thank you so much, you saved my life, thanks for coming so quickly, thank you.'

'Just doing our job, ma'am. Just doing our job.'

Davey V returned an hour later, after taking the bloke to Hotel Babylon.

'Could you provide a statement, please?' he enquired with his sunny disposition.

'No, I ain't goin' to give you a fuckin' statement, I ain't no fuckin' snitch. I know you lot you'll fuckin' stitch him up.'

Oh.

What's gone on here then?

What we have here is the classic reverse cowgirl thing. Seriously, look it up on The Google, it's quite a common position that women find themselves in. Most people become more and more obnoxious the more drink and drugs they have, but this bloody woman's normal state is to be obnoxious, so the drink and drugs turned her into a civilised human being. And now that the drink and drugs have worn off, she's back to her good old obnoxious self. It's the reverse of the norm.

Davey V has the whole situation in hand. 'Ah, thank you very much, the next time he's about to kill you, call your local crack dealer and see what he can do. Good night.'

Too many police officers not wanting to be police officers is another reason how it has come to this. Dunt ma''er in December me and Party 3 are off to Amsterdam. Hey ho seven months to go.

JUNE

Detection rates and the catastrophic consequences

Whizz around

Bored?

Lonely?

Feeling a teeny-weeny bit anxious at the thought of having to do a teeny-weeny bit of police work?

Call a meeting. Any meeting. Preferably a Strat Meeting, because they're great, because we can just sit around and talk endless bollocks and not make a decision.

Anyway, someone, somewhere, somehow please just call a fucking meeting.

Meetings: modern policing's solution to all of your problems.

In all seriousness, my understanding of a Strat(egy) Meeting is that all our partners, such as social care, school liaison officers, probation officers, etc, discuss a particular person's problems and attempt to work on a strategy to resolve their problems.

In fairness, there's a lot of value in a Strat Meeting, they give it a bit of a good old whizz around the good old NDM but neglect the most important part that someone, somewhere, somehow has to summon up the moral fibre to make a decision. And it doesn't particularly matter what decision is arrived at, because despite people from social care, probation, the schools etc, it will always be the police's responsibility. Just look at Child Sexual Exploitation and/or Child Drug dealing Exploitation. It was and always will be the police's fault. The responsibility lies a lot closer to home.

Right now, they want me to go to a Strat Meeting about Komodo, a young lad who's discovered the joy of drug dealing. Fuck that for a game of soldiers. Ash and Triff are too busy, so the multi-agency people are asking me to attend. No way. Absolutely no way. There's a whole bloody department, Op Kingleberry (or whatever they call themselves), for all this multi-agency bollocks, they should go. I've got the city and the IHub to run, I ain't going and that's it and all about it; now, if you don't mind, I've got a lot of work to do.

Do these boys and girls down at St Aldates know how to meeting? I should cocoa.

'I love a meeting with a lovely atmosphere.'

Well, I don't, they're a waste of my time, and I'll do everything I possibly can to avoid one.

'We're going to meeting like its 1999.'

'Oh yeah, baby.' Ah, good for you, go on fill yer boots, bring your own latte, I'll bring the cake and doughnuts. 'Ah yeah, good idea, I'll just nip across to Cafe Loco.'

Brilliant, just bloody brilliant, that's another half an hour down the toilet.

'You gotta fight for your right to meeeeeting.'

Oh no, you ain't. All you've gotta do is come up with some hare-brained idea that will absolve yourself of all responsibility and avoid making a decision, and the meerkats come from every corner of St Aldates. Any bloody excuse and they'll all turn up, at least twenty of them, talk endless bollocks until the cows come home, and then slink back into their offices.

'There ain't no meeting like a St Aldates meeting.'

Ain't that the truth.

And all this goes on while Ash is tear-arsing around from job to job.

Sharp

So here we go, this is my day today. It was Thursday 7 June 2018. It's a bit different to early February 2018.

0645hrs sharp – Pre-brief the briefing.

0700hrs sharp – Briefing. I've touched on this before, this is where we go through the briefing site, which summarises the places where crime is occurring (tasking), people who are on curfews, people who are wanted and arrestable, and the ID Sought. And information that assists officers with their safety, that kinda thing.

0800hrs sharp – Debrief the briefing and at the same time debrief the prebrief – we can't afford to waste any time.

0810hrs sharp – Pre-prepare the pre-plan for the Daily Morning Meeting (DMM). I think I may just've touched on the DMM, but just as a reminder and with a tiny bit more detail, the idea of the DMM is that the senior officer is apprised of all the recent incidents and mispers and assured that they are being progressed effectively. But what actually happens is about fifteen to twenty people from various departments (apart from the Domestic Abuse Unit) sit down and watch the IHub or response sergeant get their nuts roasted and where he or she is repeatedly asked why what was supposed to happen, hasn't happened. It's usually chaired by a chief inspector or superintendent and is attended by officers or civilians from CID, Op Stronghold (the drugs initiative), Op Basil (the burglary initiative), Community and Race Relations Office, Area Intelligence Team (AIT), Source Management Unit (SMU), Problem Solving Team (PST), Neighbourhood Teams (NHT) and Intensive Offender Management (IOM), and anyone else from an outside agency who would just like somewhere to pop in and have a nice latte from Café Loco and have the entertainment of me having my nuts slow roasted. All very humiliating for me. So humiliating in fact, that a sergeant collapsed when he was turning on the video-link. But they persist in doing it. Despite about fifteen to twenty people being there, only three or four people ever speak: The Chair, IHub sergeant (which is, unfortunately me), the Op Basil sergeant and someone else who chips in with something completely irrelevant which leaves everyone else completely bewildered.

0830hrs sharp – Daily Morning Meeting. I pre-need to be pre-prepared to be pre-made out to be some kind of pre-incompetent twat (I need to be so ahead of the game that I need to think what someone is going to say before they even pre-think it – I have to be right at the pre-inception of any pre-idea) because I didn't know the ins and outs of some innocuous domestic incident that happened while I was fast asleep (and, by now, Bally will have got me back). The whole point of the DMM is usually successfully achieved, the senior officer is satisfied that all the responsibility for all the decision-making has been successfully passed to me, and between everyone in attendance, I have been made to look like a complete and utter incompetent twat.

0930hrs sharp – Debrief the Daily Morning Meeting and have a good old laugh at the fact that I didn't know the ins and outs of some innocuous domestic incident that happened while I was fast asleep, and try to explain that we do, in fact, have a Domestic Abuse Unit, who, if they could be bothered to attend the DMM, would be able to explain the ins and outs of some innocuous domestic incident that happened while I was fast asleep; something that I've been saying for the last five years, oh well, early days.

1000hrs sharp – Pre-prepare the pre-plan for the health check meeting, to be chaired by the one and only Jake Nutt. The whole idea of a health check meeting is to ensure that officers do not have too many incidents to progress and investigate, and, why, if incidents are approaching or over 90 days old, why this has happened and if there is anything that could be used for shared learning. And if officers need additional support. They also randomly pick out jobs and see if it has been reviewed by a sergeant and it's being progressed expeditiously by the officer in charge (OIC).

We talk about detection rates.

Before I go into my rant about detection rates, I'd like to introduce you to a little thing called Sir Robert Peel's Nine Principles of Policing, they've been lingering around for almost 200 years, not unlike most of my jokes, but these are the very cornerstone that made British policing the envy of the world.

Principle 1 The basic mission for which the police exist is to prevent crime and disorder.

Principle 2 The ability of the police to perform their duties is dependent upon public approval of police actions

Principle 3 The police must secure the willing cooperation of the public in voluntary observance of the law to be able to secure and maintain the respect of the public.

Principle 4 The degree of cooperation of the public that can be secured diminishes proportionately to the necessity of the use of physical force.

Principle 5 Police seek and preserve public favour not by catering to the public opinion but by constantly demonstrating absolute impartial service to the law.

Principle 6 Police use of physical force to the extent necessary to secure observance of the law or to restore order only when the exercise of persuasion, advice and warning is found to be insufficient.

Principle 7 Police, at all times, should maintain a relationship with the public that gives reality to the historic tradition THAT THE POLICE ARE THE PUBLIC AND THE PUBLIC ARE THE POLICE; the police being only members of the public who are paid to give full-time attention to duties which are incumbent on every citizen In the interests of community welfare and existence.

Principle 8 Police should always direct their action strictly towards their functions and never appear to usurp the powers of the judiciary.

Principle 9 The test of police efficiency is the absence of crime and disorder, not the evidence of police action in dealing with it.

Absolutely incredible stuff, that's what I thought I'd be doing. And that is why, as I've said, we were the envy of the world.

May the rant begin.

Shady business

I'm really sorry to do this to you, but I really have to go off on a mad one about detection rates. Detection rates (also called positive outcomes or positive disposals, they're all the same thing, but whatever they're called I'm positive they serve no useful purpose and cause an enormous amount of harm – I'll be referring to them as detection rates, because I'm old skool).

It's one of the evil twins or the gruesome twosome within the police service: risk assessments are the Spawn of Satan and detection rates are the Devil's Work.

When a police officer is dealing with an incident the very last thing they should be thinking about is the blimmin', blinkin', bloody, flippin', flamin, detection rate, but somehow the blimmin', blinkin, bloody, flippin', flamin', detection rate obliterates the officer's decision making process.

The Devil's Work is a gauge used by politicians and senior officers to determine how well the police service, police departments and individual officers are performing. By using detection rates, politicians and senior officers are being lazy and show a lack of intellect and sensitivity.

A crime is said to be detected when a suspect has been charged, cautioned (the suspect has admitted to committing the offence and has not been charged or cautioned in the past), received some kind of restorative disposal (the suspect has admitted the offence and the victim is happy for the suspect not to go to Court or get a criminal record) or received something like a Fixed Penalty Notice for disorder (so someone involved in some drunken nonsense on Nightsafe could receive a fine) or a warning for being in possession of cannabis. These are looked upon as being detected.

When a crime has been committed and allocated to an officer and the officer doesn't achieve any of the above things, it's frowned upon by the organisation. It's believed that the officer has not investigated the incident thoroughly enough.

When the officer is judged in this way (to the point that they are a bad officer if they have a low detection rate and a great officer if they have a high detection rate) what occurs is officers will go after the easy detection – the 16-year-old kid bimbling along the Cowley Road with a blimble of cannabis, the detained shoplifter, the kids having a bit of a fight, or the lad who's a little bit drunk and disorderly. It's all a doddle and each 'solved crime' boosts an officer's detection rate so the obvious happens – everybody is criminalised.

The profound consequences that the detection rate culture has had on people, the Police Officer, the Police Service and society cannot be understated. It is far more dramatic than the use of stop and search. And while people are so busy bickering about stop and search, the detection rate culture has snuck by on the blindside, dare I say, completely undetected.

There are many different dynamics that take place when two people meet. Two worlds collide. Perhaps, unknowingly a power play occurs, where one person cedes control to the other. Obviously, there is an enormous power play when one of these people is a police officer. Instead of having a normal adult to adult relationship, all too often and all too quickly this relationship descends into a parent to child relationship. It's stressful for both parties, things are easily misconstrued and misinterpreted, things get out of proportion and out of control incredibly quickly. This huge problem is hugely exacerbated when you chuck the detection rate dynamic into the equation. Instead of the Police Officer conducting themselves like a normal civilised person with compassion, empathy, honesty and love they are reduced to someone lacking the power of thought. Instead of thinking what is best for the person they are dealing with, what is best for the community and society, or what is best for themselves and the police service, they are forced to think of the blimmin', blinkin',bloody, flamin', flippin' detection rate and what is best for a politician. It massively alters the dynamic in every interaction and the consequences for the relationship between the police service and the community (and the person) are immeasurable.

The horrible truth is, that people aren't half as good at reading other people as they think they are, and when you chuck different cultures and mental health issues into the mix, they are far worse. This coupled with the pressure for an Officer to get a detection leads to catastrophic consequences.

The identity of a police officer has been irreversibly damaged. I didn't join the Police Service to play any part in this utter garbage. The pressure of getting a detection doesn't show up on the National Decision-making Model (NDM) in fact it directly contradicts the Code of Ethics, and wherever there is a contradiction the ramifications are severe. It had a very severe effect on my mental health. The police service must move to become a more compassionate, empathetic and loving institution, where an officer is encouraged to use these qualities, there is a need for a calmer (karma) police. Hell yeah, let's get as Zen as fuck.

When officers are subjected to the pressure of getting a detection, mistakes are made. The detection rate culture has been forged. Society's confidence in the police has been seriously eroded and it will take years and a helluva lot of hard work to win it back. I couldn't believe I was working for such silly, easily manipulated people.

The detection rate culture was sold to us by arguing that a 'universal standard' should be applied to all incidents. What on earth does that mean? Even I could work out that there could never be a 'universal standard'. No two incidents could ever be the same. In much the same way the tiny fragments of coloured glass in a kaleidoscope could never fall the same way twice – no two incidents could ever be dealt with the same.

When I worked in Witney, I was regularly going toe to toe with the Inspector about this Goddamn awful practice.

It really hit home when I was forced to arrest a 50-year-old man. It'd been recorded that a thirteen or fourteen-year-old boy was reporting that he'd been assaulted by the 50 year-old man. It was on the report and I'd no option but to arrest or face scrutiny from the superintendent for ruining his precious detection rate. I visited the boy and his family, who explained that the boy had chucked a bag containing dog shit over the man's fence and it narrowly missed the man's three-year-old daughter. The man went out to confront the boy and ended up pushing him in the chest. This was a tiny misdemeanour – not a crime, and I should've been allowed to use my judgement, but this is the sort of decision-making that takes place when everyone has lost all sense. The boy's family wanted their son to apologise and for them to shake hands (makes absolute sense) but due to the superintendent's precious bloody detection rate this couldn't happen. I arrested the man. And he was lovely. He said, 'D'you know what, Al,

I've never done anything great in my life but the one thing that I was proud of, was that I'd never been arrested.'

It would have been better if he'd been an arse. But he wasn't. He was lovely. I felt awful. And I never wanted to have that feeling again. We had a great chat, during the 30-odd mile journey from Witney to Banbury (because that's where suspects have to go from Witney). I felt awful. The lovely man was photographed, had his fingerprints and DNA taken, all very humiliating. I felt awful. I never wanted to feel like this again. He was interviewed, admitted that he'd pushed the lad, ended up with a caution. I felt awful. Took him home. I felt awful. Finished my shift. Went home, felt awful and wept.

I was so angry I went mad at the inspector who told me that I wouldn't get promoted if I didn't promote the Devil's Work. A short time later the Inspector booted me out of Witney to Oxford to 'see what they make of you'.

It was the best thing to happen to me (as far as working for the police is concerned), because at Oxford everybody was too busy to analyse every little incident, the police officers could still, just about, be trusted and use their own judgement – they can't now. And the wonderful Officers on Party 3 looked after me, as did the incredible Inspector Ned Q.

Of course, the effect of the Devil's Work is that officers would be reluctant to take on the more complex investigations like fraud. If an officer was asked to investigate a £40,000 fraud at a school, it would very soon be plonked in the Too-Difficult Box. Nobody has the time to spend on a prolonged investigation just to get one detection, whereas you get exactly the same 'reward' for dealing with a drunk and disorderly which could take ten minutes to write out the Fixed Penalty Notice.

In this age where senior managers and politicians believe that people have such an appalling attention span that everything has to be in an easily digestible 15-second soundbite, the Devil's Work allows them to stand up and say, 'Over the past two years, our detection rate for the theft of wheelie bins has stayed at an incredible 18 per cent.'

Yawn. 'Wow, really, how fascinating, really do tell me more. When I'm having trouble falling asleep.'

When I joined the police service it was rammed home to me that arresting someone was the very last resort of a police officer. I've desperately been trying to find the quote by a famous Judge saying that it should be the last resort of a police officer, but The Google has let me down. It really should be the last resort of a police officer, to deprive someone of their liberty is an enormous step, and shouldn't be undertaken frivolously, other avenues should be explored first. But now people are just arrested willy nilly at almost every incident.

Thank you so much for staying with me on that, I wouldn't have done it to you unless it was vitally important. And I do appreciate that you guys have got an attention span that exceeds fifteen seconds.

Okay, back to the health check meeting. Jake Nutt gets to show what he'd've done with all the wisdom that hindsight brings and having all the time in the world to review it without a hundred and one other things going on. It's all right for him, he's had all the wisdom of hindsight without a hundred and one other things going on, hundreds of times. You ask anyone.

1030hrs sharp – Health check meeting.

1230hrs sharp – Debrief the health check meeting.

1300hrs sharp – Debrief the debrief of the health check meeting.

1330hrs, well, if we can squeeze it in – lunch.

1430hrs sharp – Pre-prepare a pre-plan for the Party/Team 3 meeting. Now, the Party 3 meeting is where only the elite officers of Party 3, that's the Boss, Triff, Ash, Ali and me, sit and discuss everything, the good and the bad, and just things in general that are happening within our marvellous little team. We would look at each officer and see if we're supporting their career development, how they're performing and any discipline issues, discuss the latest bit of dipshittery, and plan for the future, most notably who's going in and who's coming out of the IHub.

1500hrs sharp – Team 3 meeting.

1600hrs sharp – Debrief the Party 3 meeting.

1630hrs sharp – The pièce de résistance: the chief constable's roadshow is hitting St Aldates. This is where the great ol' boy tells us what is happening in the upper echelons of the Happy Valley and it gives the officers an opportunity to ask him any questions. I won't be going.

It's a hard life in today's police service.

I thought it'd all be about catching criminals, but it's all to do with meetings, and living with the trauma of seeing a six foot three police officer dry hump some poor sod on the Blabber Bridge. Yep, yep, yep, honestly, I promise you, I'll tell you all about it when I see you, I promise.

In all fairness, it was going swimmingly until the health check meeting and Jake said, 'It's all PC Stanstead's fault, not that we're here to point fingers, there is no blame game here. Goodness knows I make more than enough mistakes and it doesn't help if all we do is identify individual officers, it's just demoralising for that officer but, in this particular incident, PC1234 Stanstead is to blame, I mean, he has had all the training. I personally have spent at least an hour with him going through file prep, I've done it hundreds of times, you ask anybody, so he really should've known that you do not just copy and paste the MG3 (which is a précis of evidence given to the Crown Prosecution Service (CPS) solicitor onto the MG5, which is a précis of evidence given to the Crown Prosecution Service (CPS) solicitor). I hate to say it, and we're not here to make examples of anyone but this is a basic schoolboy error and PC1234 Stanstead must be put on an action plan to ensure that this does not ever happen again.'

'Yep, we need to pull out all the stops on this one!' I exclaimed.

Jake Nutt mouth dropped open and his eyes bulged with astonishment because he thought I was remotely interested in, and was agreeing with, something he had said, that ain't ever going to happen. Ever.

'Oh, sorry about that, sorry, I was on the radio, there's a fourteen-year-old kid in Littlemore who's threatened to kill himself and is heading for Sandford Lock. Sorry, as you were saying, Jake. Sorry.'

Jake didn't have a clue what was going on because he didn't have his radio on – never does, basic schoolboy error.

'That's quite alright, Al. Yeah so, if, er, PC1234 Stanstead – not to name any names – could receive some additional tr...'

'Have we got a helicopter in the area to assist or has that gone due to the cutbacks?' I say into the radio. 'Sorry about that, as you were saying.'

'Training. Maybe sit up with the Evidential Review Officers for a wee...'

'And have we still got a dog unit, or have they also gone due to the cutbacks?' I say into the radio. 'Sorry about that, as you were saying.'

'Week. And maybe he could be put on an action plan for a year, where he has to do everyone's files for a year, so he will learn his lesson and it will be a fucking warning to every other fucker not to copy and fucking paste the fucking MG3 onto the fucking MG5. But we're not here to scapegoat, we're here to supp...'

'And of course, yeah, some police officers, yeah, I forgot, if we still have a couple of police officers kicking about somewhere, maybe if Hampshire could spare a couple, while we still have some daylight,' I say into the radio.

'Ort.'

And all this was happening while Ash should've been tear-arsing around. But he was just sat there, with me.

Mrs Evidential Review Officer, the Evidential Review Officer, pipes up about the importance of the MG5, a précis of evidence.

'This is such an important document, this is the only form that the prosecutor has to read to the Judge and he or she doesn't get to read it until the day of the hearing.'

'They should sort out their time management then, shouldn't they?' I chirpily chirped.

Jake Nutt was amazed. He could've said, 'D'you know what, Al, you are absolutely correct, what a fantastic insight, why haven't we picked up on this before? Yes, Mrs Evidential Review Officer, why do incredibly intelligent, well-educated solicitors wait until the morning of the Court case to read through the case papers? Al, that is just brilliant, you've been wasted for all these years, if it was down to me, I would promote you on the spot, I'm in the company of a genius.'

But didhefuckaslike.

He and Mrs Evidential Review Officer got terribly bent outta shape. They were both attacking me with all the usual bollocks of the CPS being under resourced and being inexperienced. Like we're not.

How dare I? How bloody dare I? Have the temerity to criticise anyone other than the poor old frontline officer who has to produce a file within twenty-four hours and submit it to the Crown Prosecution Service two weeks prior to the hearing. It cannot possibly be anyone else's fault.

Jake Nutt launched in to, 'What you don't know, Al, is...'

It all went a bit blurry from there but somewhere in amongst it all I told him not to speak to me like that and him saying, 'You are right, Al.'

'I know I'm blimmin' well right, Jake, I don't need you to tell me. This shit has been going on for twenty-five years, beating up police officers due to the incompetence of others.

We had a bit of a hot debrief on that one.

But we had no time to linger on past glories, time and crime stands still for no-one.

Straight into the Team 3 Meeting, where only the elite (I think I've said that already, haven't I? yep, the elite) can attend: me (obviously), Triff and Ash, chaired by The Boss who, because he's newly promoted, is being assessed by Mrs Work-Based-Assessment-Assessor (WBAA).

Yep, I know what you're thinking, that's a very unusual name. Like Mrs Evidential Review Officer, name and nature, it's like in the good old days when people were named after their profession, you know, Mr Cooper, Mrs Carpenter, Miss Blacksmith, Mr and Mrs Pig Impregnator, that sort of thing.

'Now because the wonderful Davey V is leaving, the wonderful Louis has left, and the amazing Heidi is going across to the City Centre Unit we need to decide whether the wonderful Beard can be temporarily promoted to sergeant,' the boss ventured.

'My goodness, just look at that, if only the chief constable could see the list of names in the IHub and on Response, it would be the perfect illustration as to why this Operating Model just could not work' I said.

If Beard could become an acting sergeant – which he should – seven out of the eight officers left on the response team would have less than two years' service. And we'd have only one taser trained officer.

There was a lively discussion as to whether Beard should be allowed to leave the shift for a spell as acting sergeant. Somewhere along the line one of us mentioned the PDR and we all agreed what an astonishing waste of time the whole process is. Except Mrs WBAA who short circuited.

'You can't say that, the PDR is an essential...'

At which point it all got a bit fuzzy; I think I may have gone off on a bit of a mad one.

'*And you can shut yer fuckin' clangin' man 'ole cover an' all, I can say what I fuckin' want, you fuckin' thirty thousand pound a year drain of tax payers money, money that would be better spent on getting more coppers, coming in 'ere with yer fuckin' 'Olier Than Thou fuckin' a' 'itude just fuck off you are the absolute epitome of what is fuckin' wrong with this fuckin' service just fuck off what the fuck d'you know about fuckin' police work anyway you 'aven't got a fuckin' clue you 'aven't done a fuckin' minute of it and you have the fuckin' cheek to tell us what we're doin' is wrong just fuck off what other organisation would tolerate you, just fuck off go on you 'eard me, just fuck off what the fuck are you still doin' 'ere, I thought you'd've fucked off by now*"

Well, only part of me hoped that I only thought it and I didn't actually say it out loud. I'm sure I didn't say it out loud. I didn't, I know I didn't. I only thought it, I know I did.

So, anyway, where was I? Oh yes, so the wonderful Beard could not progress his career because of the incompetence of others.

And then Ash was up, out and tear-arsing around.

Side 'Eadwards

The next day.

'You were angry yesterday,' said my inspector who has been a police officer for four years and is a thoroughly great bloke.

Oh my God, I didn't, did I? As I gave him the biggest ever side 'eadwards (haha, my editor has put '???', you know the one, when you look at someone through the cornerest corner of your eye, your head doesn't move, just your eyes, so you're looking from the side of your head) the world has ever seen, although in my heart of hearts I really couldn't give a shit, I had only said what I believed to be correct. Everyone should be allowed to say what they believe, maybe not quite so vehemently, but everyone should be allowed to be honest enough to say what they believe.

'When, Sir?' Great move, Robinson, light and fluffy, that's the order of the day, let's not play my hand too soon, I could've easily said, 'To which of the many times yesterday are you referring, Sir?' Or, 'What, when I went completely batshit crazy on that fuckin' waste of fuckin' space Mrs Work-Based Assessment Assessor?' But light and fluffy is the order of the day, a nice open question, get him to play his hand. This could go one of two ways, either I'm going to lose my job or I'm not.

'When you were talking about the CPS getting their act together to read the Summary of Evidence, before the day of the trial,' he stated.

'Oh that, I thought it was something serious for a moment. No, no, no, no, no, I didn't get angry yesterday. Well, not then, anyway. You see, all that happened there was that I asked a very simple question and Jake Nutt and Mrs Evidential Review Officer were lacking the requisite knowledge as to how to answer such a logical question such as "Why are the highly intelligent, well-educated men and

143

women of the CPS waiting to the day of the trial to look at the files?" Something that has been going on for at least twenty-five years, and because Jake Nutt and Mrs Evidential Review Officer didn't have a Scooby Doo as to the answer, they got all nasty to me and I would've appreciated your support. Like I would appreciate your support with the Control Room who haven't got a clue what they're doing, where you have got civilians in there with less than two years' service calling themselves operational supervisors and telling us how to do our jobs and getting extremely rude when they're proved to be wrong, and a Neighbourhood Team not taking on any police work, and a certain useless tosser in the DidKnowItWasPrincessEugenie'sWeddingBut StillManagedToFuckItUpDepartment, who continues to not give a fuck about anyone but himself. And don't even get me started on Jake fucking Nutt, who, now that we've got this far, has sent a putrid e-mail that has demoralised two of our officers, one of whom has only been an officer for two weeks and that dick-swinging little xkclunt X Wyng who will come into work tomorrow morning after another fucking weekend off after we've found eight mispers, arrested someone who nearly committed murder and the myriad of other things we've accomplished over the weekend, all in an effort to keep their collective little cocks off the block and what a lovely little cock it is too, swinging away on the middle floor. And please don't say that they're short of staff, because we had eighteen Officers and two sergeants for the whole of Oxfordshire. Just imagine if I wrote a book saying that, that we're completely policeless; eighteen officers and two sergeants and all those fuckers can do is moan because an MG5 hasn't been completed properly. Or the curfew checks haven't been done or the rolling arrests haven't been done. So, no, Sir, I didn't get angry yesterday. It's all in a day's work.'

We both walked away respecting the other's point of view, and that's the funny thing about it.

Traps

And while all that was going on, Ash has been investigating a major incident.

It would appear that there has been a bad batch of grapes doing the rounds in the beautiful city of the dreaming spires and a lot of male officers – well, it could be females as well – have used the ludicrously small traps on the ground floor which has caused a backup which in turn has caused them to overflow.

The working hypothesis was that some bloody clown, for reasons best known to themselves, had jammed a whole toilet roll into the U bend. Ash has conducted a full investigation though, leaving no stone unturned, to this horrendous incident and discovered it's all down to the cheap toilet paper.

Ash is very particular about what does and does not go close to his bum, and whatever does, must be in tip top condition and this cheap shit is cutting it to shreds, and he's not happy.

But he's managed to get to the bottom of it, if you could find some place from your huge, big red pulsating heart, to forgive me such a pun.

The paper is so cheap that it reminded me of the horrific tracing paper that I had to use at primary school, which has left me both emotionally and anally scarred. When I have to use a public toilet, which is way, way, way too often, I have to check to see if that nasty stuff isn't there. It had *Now wash your hands* in red ink printed on it but it would have been far more appropriate for it to have *Hahahahahahahahahaohmygodppfffpfpfpfhaha.*'

Not fit to wipe my arse.

Even with that, it's still doing a far better job than us, at least it is putting up some kind of fight before it goes down the shitter.

Gangrene

There's a homeless lad in Oxford whose party trick is to take off his massive boots in a shop doorway (preferably Waterstones) and undress and dress his bandages on his feet … that are suffering from gangrene.

And do they smell, like fucking hell.

I vommed on the spot.

For days afterwards everything I ate tasted of the stuff.

'Would you be kind enough to do that tucked away somewhere? I really don't think the good people of Oxford, and the beautiful people who have travelled from all over the world to this magnificent city, and particularly, the wonderful people who'd love to buy a book from Waterstones but find themselves confronted by the most goddamn awful fucking smell from your boots and having great difficulty in circumnavigating the fucking things, would appreciate it if you could tuck yourself away somewhere, please.'

'Certainly, officer, but please treat me as a human being.'

'Look, I'm extremely sorry, in a desperate bid to be incredibly witty I have made an arsehole of myself, I'm truly sorry.'

'That's all right, mate, that's all I ask. I know that I've been an arsehole in the past, but all I ask is for people to treat me as a human being.'

'You're absolutely right, and I'm sorry, that seems like fair deal to me; but please, just tuck yourself away.'

'How about in the churchyard?' he enquired.

'I was going to say, "fill yer boots" but I can see you already have.'

He laughed.

'They say "before you judge anyone you should walk a mile in their shoes," that way you can say what you feel, and you've still got their shoes. But on this occasion, I think I'll give it a miss.'

Oh my God, did he laugh.

As we walked across to the churchyard, I asked him how life was treating him.

'Officer, I'm looking forward to Christmas, it's the only time that I can get any work.'

'Oh wow, what do you do?'

'Don't you recognise me? I was a very famous actor but now I'm reduced to doing just pantomime these days. In fairness it does pay very well, I get to play the lead role.'

'Oh wow, I had absolutely no idea, what do you play?'

'Puss in Boots.'

Touché, my friend, touché.

And all this was happening while Ash was tear-arsing around.

There, there, my dear

'There's a person the wrong side of the barrier on the Barns Road bridge, going over the Ring Road, any unit to make,' the Control Room operator says.

'BAS43 (me) we'll need road closures on the Rose Hill roundabout and the BMW roundabout and a couple of units to block the bridge and someone to build a rapport with them, and that will be all my units deployed, and oh yes, I nearly forgot, has anyone got any 'there, there, my dear' cream because I'm fresh out of mine.'

Well, when I say 'fresh out' I think I ran out of the stuff at exactly the same time as the officers at St Aldates stopped wearing their police radios. Years of people not taking responsibility for their own lives and dumping it on me, and the silly shit from my colleagues had taken its toll.

'Hi there, how's it all going?' I said. I thought it was quite a nice little ice breaker, it works with most people.

'Just fuck off, fuck off, fuck off, you just make it worse.' Ah, but not him. I always try to surround myself with nice things and lovely people and this one was an absolute fucking delight.

'Now, there's no need for that, you remember me, we spoke just over a year ago when you were going to jump off the railway bridge and I was as good as my word then, wasn't I?'

'Well, I'm not going to speak to you now, I don't even know you, why do you care what I do? I'm going to do it tonight. You're not going to stop me like last time. You don't care, I can tell by your face.'

Was it really obvious or was he incredibly perceptive?

Probably really obvious.

"Fuck off, you cunt." Said John.

I think that went particularly well.

"Ah, fuck you then, fuckin' do it."

"You're a cunt."

That's been a recurring theme throughout my career.

Becca arrived and applied shed loads of 'there, there, my dear' cream.

Then the negotiators arrived.

'Okay, Al, what have we got? What's his name? Shoot.'

'No, it's not shoot, it's John, definitely John, John is his name.'

'Background? Shoot.'

'Well, John is a white male, late twenties, recently split up from his girlfriend who was arrested last night for a domestic incident. John has numerous children who have been taken into care, here to serve.' And chucked up the goofiest of all goofy salutes as I stomped my right foot down.

'It's all about rapport, Al, rapport, rapport, rapport, treat him like a friend, rapport, it's all about getting off on the right foot, attention to detail. Al, they pick up on the slightest little thing. Al, watch, listen and learn from the master. Al, your opening line is vital, you never get a second chance to make a first impression, remember that. Al, what's his name again?'

'John, it's John, Sir.'

He struts over.

'So, James, what's the problem?'

Uurffff.

Fascination

Just look at this for a sad state of affairs; since the introduction of the Ferkin' Merkin', there are only eighteen officers and two sergeants covering Oxfordshire. Somebody may argue that there are Roads Policing, Firearms, and Dog Section (the Force Roamers) but they could be miles away. In reality, there are six response officers for Oxford, six for Cherwell and West (North Oxfordshire) and six for South and Vale (South Oxfordshire). Such a sad state of affairs.

I hope it doesn't come as too much of a shock, but mistakes happen, things get overlooked, stuff that happened fourteen months ago ain't happening.

Nothing too serious, just a sex pest up in one of the 'burbs, who'd been sex pesting a nineteen-year-old girl and then held a machete to his girlfriend's throat and had tried to smother her with a pillow the night before, hadn't been arrested.

Davey V sorted it out. The sex pest was arrested. And because we were being so kind to him in custody, he gave us the absolute treat of stripping stark bollock naked in the search room and then just sat there like a spoilt sex pest refusing to put his clothes on, so we just had to stand there being called 'blood clots' by the sex pest.

Now. Men's genitalia hold absolutely no fascination for me whatsoever but somehow, and I'm still not quite sure how he did it, he tucked his cock and balls up his arse. I was mildly curious as to how this had happened, my brain had great difficulty assimilating what had just happened. I couldn't say to Davey V, 'Did you just see what I what I just saw?' One minute they were there and the next minute they'd gone. Tucking them up his arse was the only logical explanation.

If I could have been sure that what I thought had happened had just happened, I was going to ask the sex pest to give lessons to Nigella and Xavier (you remember her, all frock and bollocks and you remember him, all xkclunt).

Female caller

One of the most essential roles within the police service is the handling of the initial contact with the person wanting our help. This is where the Contact Management Platform should've turned the wanky tap off but didn't.

You need people with massive kahunas to work in there, people who know how to whizz their way around the good ol' National

Decision-making Model (NDM), people who really love it, think of it as a drug, a retired ex-sergeant with about twenty-five years' experience, one who could drop a few bollocks (because that's all part of being human), knows the Association of Chief Police officers, ten or maybe eleven Risk Principles (more about this in July), someone big, and devilishly handsome and, who, on occasions quite likes to have his arse tickled. I'd have to change my name to Bugarov though.

This is the future of policing. This is how it'd be.

'Ah, good afternoon, Happy Valley Police, The Man with The Massive Kahunas, Bugarov speaking but you can call me by my first name, Iwishyoudalljuz, how may I help?'

'Yeah, well, yeah, hundred per cent, d'you know what I mean?' It was a persistent and consistent female caller who I'd recognised instantly.

'Ah hi, Kylie, how's it all going? I thought I was going to have to report you as missing as we'd not heard from you today. The Operational Supervisor in the Control Room consider people to be missing for far less.'

'Yeah, well, yeah, hundred per cent yeah, she keeps on calling me a slag on Facebook and Instagram, yeah. D'you get me, yeah?'

'Yep, I think I'm with you so far, yes, it's not as difficult as trying to understand a speech by The Academic. Please carry on, I have a massive piece of A3 paper, and a massive red pen poised, ready, willing and waiting to make a precise and accurate record of what you're about to tell me.'

'Yeah, well good, yeah, hundred per cent yeah, Tiffany, my sister, yeah, is going round telling everyone that I'm a slag yeah, and that's defecation, that is, she's saying stuff like I've slept with her boyfriend, which I have but that doesn't make me a slag. I have only done it four times, but she shouldn't say that I'm a slag on Facebook.'

'Your story has truly moved me in so many deep and meaningful ways, as you can only imagine, Kylie, I don't think my life will ever be the same again. I've made a note of it on my massive piece of paper, and what I'd like to do, Kylie, is send it to you in the post, if that's okay with you, Kylie, and then what I'd like you to do, Kylie, is scrumple it up, really nice and tight, and roll it into a cylinder shape, and then Kylie, what I would like you to do is insert it up your anus. Make sure you do not hurt yourself, Kylie but just suffer enough discomfort so you remember never to trouble me with your horseshit of a life ever again, is that all right, Kylie?'

'But you're the police, it's your job to sort my life out.'

'Yes, Kylie, you're absolutely correct. Let me just put you through to my brother, his name is Ithortmybruvjuztoldutu Bugarov, and if you don't get anywhere with him you could always try our mother, Aahfafuksakewyduntyagethefukinmessagetojuz Bugarov. Have a very long and happy life, Kylie.'

It'd be my dream job. Batting the crap into the long grass. It would reduce the demand on the police massively and allow us to see the wood for the trees.

This is equally true of good-hearted people who are kind enough to say that they don't want a police officer, they just need their crime recorded. This could be for something like a bicycle theft, where the aggrieved is realistic enough to know that there isn't a lot the police can do but would like it recorded, so as, if it was found we would know who to return it to.

There's absolutely no point in allocating it to an officer, where the job will languish on their unfiled jobs list, stinking out the computer screen, just to waste the officer's time to say that the case will be filed. It's absolutely pointless and just thwarts the officer's attempts to get to where they should be, which is to be out on the beat trying to prevent the bike theft in the first place.

Good decision-making at the very earliest opportunity is the key to making the police service more effective and efficient.

The person with the massive kahunas will have to have a good working knowledge of the workings of the Happy Valley and where the best solution lies. Instead of putting all the onus on the response sergeant, this can go directly to the sergeant best placed to allocate an officer.

If it's a domestic incident, the sergeant on the Domestic Abuse Unit would have to allocate someone to deal with the incident, and it'd be no good them saying they didn't have any resources, because that's exactly what the response sergeant has had to deal with for years. It's a domestic incident, so the Domestic Abuse Unit will have to take care of the situation, makes perfect sense. One touch policing, 'anybody can deploy a person – that is easy, but to deploy the right person to the right degree and at the right time and for the right purpose and in the right way – that is not within everybody's power and is not easy.' What a doddle, Aristotle.

If it's a burglary that had happened some time ago and the offenders have long gone, then Op Basil the Oxford burglary initiative will have to attend and deal. If it's a longer-term neighbourly dispute, then the neighbourhood team will have to sort it out. I'm sure you get the idea, spread the pain a bit.

The best department to deal wlth the job will deal with the job. One touch policing. It's so blimmin' obvious, it would stop all the nonsense of a response officer attending, and then relaying the information to an officer from the department who should've deployed in the first place, who, invariably, are kind enough to tell the hard-pressed response officer what a shit job they've done, and it would prevent something vital getting lost in translation.

Get off your arse and do the job that you're paid to do. At the moment, the majority of jobs that come in go through the Contact Management Platform, who haven't got a Scooby Doo how to make a decision, so the job gets passed to the Control Room supervisor who hasn't got the Scoobiest of all Doos how to make a decision (and it must be the cushiest job in the whole force) so they just bundle it onto the response sergeant who is one of the very few people in the whole organisation who has the remotest idea of how to make a decision so they make the decision.

And from there it just gets a little bit silly. The response sergeant tells the most appropriate sergeant that their department is going to have to attend, it was completely and utterly and wholly and entirely the point of the New Operating Model, an almighty bun fight ensues and is lost by the response sergeant because every other department says that they do not have enough resources and miraculously their lack of resources is more important than the response sergeant's lack of resources, so it all gets passed back to the response sergeant, who's just wasted an awful lot of time, effort and emotion to end up exactly where they started.

And that's the reason that Good Ol' Bugarov is so vital within the Contact Management Platform, he or she'll make the decision as to which department is best placed to deal with an incident, and if any sergeant disagrees with Mr Bugarov's decision, they too can be referred to his brother and mother. It would save thousands of hours of bickering between sergeants.

It would also save thousands of hours of bickering if the officer who attends and/or deals with the job makes the decision as to whether a crime has taken place or not. I would need to write a whole new book regaling you with horror stories of something being recorded as a crime that's not; for example, a child being returned late by the father to his mother, recorded as coercive control or harassment or I think, it has even got up to a kidnapping but it will always be a domestic incident, and many hours of wasted police time. We cannot see the wood for the trees because our incredibly scant resources are bogged down with this crap.

Making contact

Strangely enough, the only reason that I knew that the Contact Management Platform was even in existence was by finding out who's leaving the service, and people in Contact Management are leaving in their droves.

Approximately thirty officers are leaving, and thirty civilian staff are resigning every month from the Happy Valley, some of whom are leaving from Contact Management.

'Al, it's all about managing contact, managing expectations, turning that tap off, managing contact is where it's at,' one of the Senior Management Team members was explaining it to me.

Dear God, he's said it, and done it using that wanky hand gesture.

'You're absolutely right, Sir, managing contact is where it's at, people are managing to leave so fast their arses aren't even managing contact with their fucking fully operational chair.'

In eager anticipation of the wonderful chief constable, and he is truly wonderful, to the extent that it makes me wonder where it all goes wrong, was coming to town again at the end of June. Blank boards were put up on the walls for officers to ask him questions and make observations.

Here are just a few examples of the questions and observations that were written on the boards:

I have absolutely no idea of what I am supposed to be doing, I have no defined job role, and there is no clear leadership. (I think the superintendent was writing on behalf of us all when he wrote that.)

I love ... you ... do you want ... to ... see my willy? (Oh Xavier, have a day off.)

Can you remind me what the caution is, please? (Good old CID showing they still have a sense of humour.)

I know about that

I thought it would be a bit of a hoot to crew the wonderful Chief Constable, with the equally wonderful Davey V, who was leaving in three days' time.

I was in the Sergeants Office having a good ol' chuckle with someone about the size of Nigella's gonads.

'It must be the most enormous sack to've ever graced God's earth,' I was trying to explain, as Davey V came bursting in doing that strange cutting his neck with his finger's thing trying to get me to stop, closely followed by the Chief Constable. '...filled with all those toys and he's got to deliver them all in just one night, I've no idea how Father Christmas does it. Ah hello, Sir, Al Robinson, really nice to meet you.' As I leapt to my feet to shake his hand. Double-handed.

'Hi, Robert, nice to meet you too,' he replied with a warm smile.

He must've just completed his advanced negotiator's course.

Davey V took the Chief Constable out and about and just so happened to mention that we only had six officers working in the city because we had to supply officers to the South and Vale.

'I know about that. '

And … and … nothing … nothing at all. Well, that's that sorted then.

It's all in the delivery; it has to be said with enough conviction to sound concerned, but crucially, just about concerned enough to do absolutely fuck all about it.

It's a life-changer.

Mrs R says, 'I haven't got a cup of tea.'

'I know about that.'

'You've had four days off, and you haven't done a stroke of housework.'

'I know about that.'

It's brilliant, just brilliant, it's my 'go-to' response in any situation, I love it. Sometimes I chuck in an 'all' for some added drama.

'We have an unresourced murder, a high risk misper, and an uncompliant shoplifter and no officers to send,' Screech squawks.

'BAS43 (my call-sign), I know all about that.'

Go on, give it a go, it's so liberating. That's why he's a Chief Constable. Pure genius. I know about that.

In all seriousness, it's a bloody good job that officers in the lower ranks don't think that way, they do 'know about that' and they do something about it.

Esprit de corps

Everything, and I mean everything, gets reduced to a painful process, lacking personality, creativity, soul and emotion.

My friend Davey V handed me his uniform and his warrant card. I ticked a few boxes and signed the ghastly form.

Davey V and the team had shared incredible moments, always with a great sense of humour, a little bit of wit and even less wisdom but we got through it all. There can be few jobs that have such amazing camaraderie and banter, the *esprit de corps*; no matter what life chucks at us, we will always get through it. I bloody love it. Whatever the organisation and the public chuck at us, it'll always pull us closer together. I absolutely bloody love it. It makes me incredibly happy, the team spirit, the pulling together when times are tough, it's absolutely magnificent, and I'll miss it and the people terribly. I lived for it. It's the best job in the world when everybody pulls together.

And this is why I get so upset, angered, and bewildered by the likes of Xavier, Jake, and PieChartMan, the Resource Management Department, Control Room inspectors and Operational Supervisors and just a few others, well, everyone else, really, they simply don't get it.

They're too busy being self-centred, self-absorbed, self-serving, self-aggrandising selfish xkclunts to get it. They'd gladly sell their soul and their granny to get to where they want to be. There's far too many of them. There's so many of them that there's a permanent BOGOF (Buy One Get One Free) offer on grannies.

And that's one of the reasons we only had seven additional officers on New Year's Eve.

The most useful purpose they serve is to pull the people who actually want to serve the public closer together.

Fortunately, the vast majority of people within the Happy Valley get it. If we love and look after our colleagues, we can go out and deliver a service to the public. My colleagues are my sisters and brothers, I absolutely adore them, I'd like to think that I'd do anything to help them. I banter about the Domestic Abuse Unit, CID and Child Abuse Investigation Unit (CAIU) but my God, they make the biggest decisions within the service, and I absolutely appreciate and respect what they do, they truly make the big decisions. What I've said about them in my book is pure banter, I love and respect them very much.

Davey V has to leave to follow his dream of being a firefighter. He may come back, he may not, he should, he was absolutely brilliant.

'Does anyone want a ruler, for all your straight edge needs,' typical Davey V enquires.

He told his last joke. 'How does a Brummy psychoanalyst like his eggs? Freud.'

He gave everyone a massive hug and asked me what I'd miss most about him and I told him to fuck off and gave him a massive hug, and then he was gone, and then he came back for his bag, and then he was gone, and then he came back for his keys, and then he was gone.

Big love, appreciation and respect to everyone within the Happy Valley who comes in to work to make their colleagues' life easier and make the big decisions.

Detection rates, the loss of a team spirit and the lack of courage to tell people to take responsibility for their own lives are more reasons how it has come to this. Dunt ma"er in December me and Party 3 are off to Amsterdam. Hey ho six months

JULY

Wheelie bins

Can you believe it, we're halfway through the year already?

And what better way to celebrate than getting your hands on some horse tranquiliser or some other noxious substance and finding some way of pumping it into your body?

Which, quite surprisingly, disagreed with the lad (probably had a couple of grapes as well) which caused him to strip stark bollock naked and go horseshit crazy in the middle of the Cowley Road Carnival – only to have his fun spoilt by PC Beard who seemed to specialise in spoiling the fun of lads who just wanted to be stark bollock naked. Don't knock it until you've tried it, that's what I always say.

And Ash and I only went and caught Ye Olde Wheelie Bin Thief of Ye Olde Cowley Road red-handed. If I keep on the way I'm going, I'll catch up with Jake Nutt in no time.

Yep, the poor lad was only nicking them all and putting them into a shop at the bottom of Cowley Road.

Ash slapped the old handcuffs on him and said the magical words before I could say 'Al Robinson'. Well, he's been taught by the best. It would appear that Michael Jackson had told him to, "Heal the world, make it a better place." And what better way to carry out Michael's wishes than to nick all the wheelie bins you can get your white-gloved little hand on and hide them in a shop? (Some people say that Michael also said that he would like to stick his finger up Jordan's bum, but we won't be doing that will we?)

Paddy, one of my many brilliant officers on Party 3 (who isn't going to Amsterdam – he thinks he'd have more fun letting off fireworks in Moscow, but the rest of us are thoroughly looking forward to it), enjoyed his short but enjoyable time with Ye Olde Wheelie Bin Thief of Ye Olde Cowley Road. The moment the bloke arrived in his cell, he stood on the pan to have a piss and then with the sudden realisation that he had discovered water, acted on his overwhelming urge to wash his face and hair with it.

Michael would've been so proud. I can't remember him encouraging us to wash our hair and face with our own piss, but I guess it's not out of the realms of possibility.

We encountered a major problem when we were trying to find the victims of this heinous crime.

'Where's yer bin, mate?'

'I've been working on the oil rigs.'

'No, where's yer wheelie bin, mate?'

'Well, I've really been in prison, but don't tell my mum.'

Stomach pumped

During every shift at least one person threatens to take their own life.

'I'm not going to tell you where I am, no fucking way, d'you think I'm stupid? All I'm going to tell you is that you will find a body in South Park.'

'So, you're in South Park?'

'I didn't fucking say that. I ain't ever going to tell you where I am, don't you get it? I wanna fucking die. I've taken shitloads of paracetamol and you ain't ever going to find me, all you'll find is a body on the swings in South Park.'

'So, you're on the swings in South Park.'

'Nah, I'm not saying that, what I'm fucking telling you is that you'll never find me, I've got five minutes to live, tell everyone that I'm very sorry but I have to do this. You'll never find me alive on the swings in South Park, where I am going to die in four minutes, so you'd better fucking hurry up if you want to find me dead. So please fucking hurry up, please.'

'Ah, there you are, on the swings in South Park, how's it all going? Shall we have a wee trip to the JR and get your wee stomach pumped?'

'I haven't taken anything really, sorry.'

'Ah, that's great stuff, great stuff that is, now if you'd just like to pop into the wee police car for a wee trip to the big JR2 so as you can have your wee stomach pumped just in case, that'd be just great.'

He was only fucking about.

Hit me

I had just walked into the Sergeants Office in Cowley after a fairly unsuccessful tour of the station trying to find some poor innocent person to irritate.

Tomtetomtetomtetom.

And all of a sudden it hit me.

'Cor fu...Jesus bloody Christ, Ash, have you .... er...'

Ash looks bewildered.

'Oh, what do they call it?'

Ash looks even more bewildered.

'Oh God, it's on the tip of my tongue.'

Ash begins to laugh.

'Come on, Ash, help me out here, there's a funny name for it, it always makes me laugh when they say it.'

Ash is properly laughing.

'Ash, come on, there's a technical term for it, it always makes me laugh when they say it. I've heard you say it, come on, what do they call it? It's annoying me now.'

Ash is slapping the desk.

'I've got it, I've got it, it's just come to me. "Shit yerself", yes, that's it. Ash, have you shit yerself?'

Groin

At the end of last month Mrs R and I had the good fortune to go to my colleague Dan's leaving do, at All Bar One.

Having parked up on St Giles, we walked across to St John's and Balliol, close to the Martyrs' Memorial. As we walked, we saw the neatly made sleeping bag of a homeless person with the handwritten sign saying:

Just nipped off, for a cheeky little groin shot,

So please put a penny in the poor man's pot,

If you haven't got a penny

A ha'penny will do,

If you haven't got a ha'penny,

Then God bless you.

I hope it doesn't come as a massive shock to you to know that I suffer from a fair dose of *l'esprit d'escalier* as Triff would have us say. It's French, but Triff told me about it.

A mere two weeks later I was quick witted enough to think:

Oh, undoubtedly, you're so honest and funny,

It's worth a quid of anybody's money,

If you haven't got a vein in your groin

In between your toes will do,

If you haven't got one in between your toes,

Then maybe it's about time you reviewed your life choices, bruv. I mean, I don't mean to be mean, and I know that you've had a tough life, but all this self-medicating is doing you more harm than good; please take it easy on yourself, forgive those who've hurt you, and learn to trust people; you've punished yourself far too hard for far too long. I'm very sorry, I really do not mean to lecture, but please take good care of yourself.

Granted, the last line may need a little bit of work on it, but I'm getting there.

Clifton Hampden

The sheer humiliation of it all.

A lad had drowned near Clifton Hampden, his body was under the water. I had to supervise the recovery of the body and liaise with his girlfriend and friends who were understandably distraught on the riverbank.

Due to the cutbacks, I had to watch our pathetic attempts to recover the body for eight hours. Yep, eight hours. Austerity had meant the loss of Sergeant Rupert Jones, a great bloke and police officer, who left the service when they decided to scrap the underwater search team.

It was absolutely disgraceful to see police officers try to recover the body without a dive team. For three hours they hovered above the body, trying to hook him out. At 2100hrs they had to admit defeat and ask for a private company of divers to recover the body, the lad had been under water for over twenty-four hours. The family and friends were traumatised, but my goodness, they were incredibly dignified. I am immensely grateful to them, and wish them my deepest sympathies.

All members of the police service

I'd forgotten to take the phone off the hook.

'Good afternoon, Sergeants Office at Cowley, Police Constable, Sergeant soon to be Acting Inspector Al Robinson speaking, how may I help?'

'Yeah, hi, is that the police? Yeah, hi, it's Flitzy from Children's Social Care, yeah, hi, yeah, you may remember me, I'm the one with the fancy neckwear and brooch.'

'Doesn't really narrow it down.'

'Convertible Beetle?'

'No, still doesn't really narrow it down, anyway, how may I help?'

'Well yeah, well yeah, well yeah, we well, yeah, well, I … yeah, have had a massive problem with Komodo yeah, for a couple of years yeah, he's sixteen years old yeah, and yeah, he's now drug dealing for older boys, yeah, and we don't know where he is, yeah, and we, well yeah, I am very worried because he is very vulnerable, yeah, did I mention that, yeah, vulnerable, did you catch that, vulnerable, yeah, because he is very vulnerable, yeah. I have not been able to speak to him for a couple of months, yeah, and now I want you to find him, yeah, and issue Child Abduction Warning Notices (CAWN) to the older boys, yeah. I understand that you didn't want to come to the strat meeting, yeah, because you said there was a whole department to deal with that, yeah, who refused to go, yeah, and we've had strat meeting upon strat meeting about him, yeah, and, in fact yeah, that's all we seem to do about him, yeah.'

(I feel it's only fair to mention, that when someone describes somebody as 'vulnerable', although they really emphasise the word 'vullllllllnnnnneraaaable' what I actually hear is 'easily led soft lad'. Most of the time there were absolutely no issues that made a person 'vullllllllnnnnneraaaable'. 'Vullllllllnnnnneraaaable' is absolutely the wrong word to use, they should be saying 'easily led soft lad' because an 'easily led soft lad is what he is. If an 'easily led soft lad' is what he is, surely, they should be calling him an 'easily led soft lad' because he's an 'easily led soft lad' and not 'vullllllllnnnnneraaaable', and it's not fair on someone who really is 'vullllllllnnnnneraaaable' to hear an 'easily led soft lad' be called 'vullllllllnnnnneraaaable' because an 'easily led soft lad', is what he is, definitely, no doubt about that).

All I could think of saying is,

'I know about that.'

'Don't you do that fucking "I know about that" shit on me, it might work on your fucking wife, yeah, but it doesn't fucking well work on me. You fucking find Komodo, otherwise you'll have another fucking death on your hands, and it'll be all your fucking fault. And don't fucking return him to his fucking useless fucking father. I want a proper Public Protection Order (PPO, which means that we act in the best interests of the child and Social Care, on some occasions, find temporary accommodation for the child), on the little cunt, now fucking stay awake.'

We didn't want to let the incident involving Komodo drag on and on. So, the City Centre Sergeant Guy found him, invoked the PPO and told Children's Social Care who told us to return him to his father. Again.

And Komodo runs away again, and is vulnerable again, and drug deals again, and they report him missing again, and they want a strat meeting again, and they ask a police officer to attend again, and I can't be arsed again, so I don't attend again, because there is a whole department who should attend again, and they say that they aren't quite ready for a strat meeting again, so they rearrange another one for Thursday again, when they can have a proper strat meeting again, he's our priority again, we waste thousands of pounds of taxpayers' money again, finding the little chump again, on Thursday again, they haven't had a chance to have a strat meeting again, so he's returned to his father again, he assaults a police officer again, and he is arrested again, thanks a fuckin' bunch again.

And this is how it works again, all the other agencies (who are also suffering from the cuts again) think they've got us 'over a barrel' again, because they think the role of the police is to "improve the life for all citizens" again, but I know that's just one of our roles again, because I believe that our most important role is to maintain law and order again, and protect members of the public and their property again, and prevent and reduce the fear of crime again. With a tiny bit of working in partnership with our communities and partners, again; but not too much of that shit, again.

Over the years I've been on the wrong end of awful condescending comments for saying that we spend far too much time safeguarding and far too little time getting stuck into crime. We're not trained to deal with mental health problems. I've been called narrow minded, they've abused me by calling me thick and shallow, some have even called me an old dinosaur, all of which are true, but they also know that I'm right. It's only a difference of opinion, nothing to get all eggy about. But I was never given outlet, no-one would ever listen.

Obviously, all the name calling, insults and abuse were served up with liberal dollops of guilt trips "If you don't do anything, and he dies, I'll make sure your name is brought up."

"Oh. Really. Good for you. Thanks." Now where's me Bourbons.

Funnily enough all these spiteful comments came from the "be kind" brigade. And strangely enough, they're all pretty much, pretty shitty officers, who couldn't hack frontline police work, you know the type, the ones who skulk out of Nightsafe, or working nights, or weekends, or at all. They want to be social workers on police officer's wages. I wish they'd all just do the decent thing and go and be social workers and leave the rest of us to do proper police work. And funnily enough, these are also the kind of people who wonder why the mental health problems and the suicide rates for men are so high.

Fortunately for all concerned, I'd never dream of lowering myself to their standards; I could never be condescending or abusive or name call. Not my style, fucking bunch of cunts.

The Ten ACPO (Association of Chief Police Officers) Risk Principles

I'm out on patrol again, mixing it up with the crazy cats of Oxford.

"BAS43 (my callsign – I never quite got around to embracing this BPS92 nonsense) please view incident number, such and such", the control room operator would politely request.

"I'm the response sergeant, my job is to respond, you've got an inspector and an operational supervisor in there who should review incidents." This little scenario is played at two or three times each shift.

Principle 1: The willingness to make decisions in conditions of uncertainty (i.e. risk taking) is a core professional requirement of all members of the police service.

Principle 2: Maintaining or achieving the safety, security and wellbeing of individuals and communities is a primary consideration in risk decision making.

Principle 3: Risk taking involves judgment and balance. Decision makers are required to consider the value and likelihood of the possible benefits of a particular decision against the seriousness and likelihood of the possible harms.

Principle 4: Harm can never be totally prevented. Risk decisions should, therefore, be judged by the quality of the decision making, not by the outcome.

Principle 5: Making decisions, and reviewing others' risk decision making, is difficult. This needs to take into account whether they involved dilemmas or emergencies, were part of a sequence of decisions or might appropriately be taken by other agencies.

Principle 6: The standard expected and required of members of the police service is that their decisions should be consistent with those a body of officers of similar rank, specialism or experience would have taken in the same circumstances.

Principle 7: Whether to record a decision is a risk decision in itself which should be left to professional judgement. The decision whether or not to make a record, and the extent of that record, should be made after considering the likelihood of harm occurring and its seriousness.

Principle 8: To reduce risk aversion and improve decision making, policing needs a culture that learns from successes as well as failures. Good risk taking should be identified, recognised and shared.

Principle 9: Since good risk taking depends on quality information, the police service will work with partner agencies and others to share relevant information about those who pose a risk or those who are vulnerable to the risk of harm.

Principle 10: Members of the police service who make decisions consistent with these principles should receive encouragement, approval and support of their organisation.

Ah great stuff, great stuff that is.

And don't forget the most important principle of all:

Principle 11: At every opportunity pass all risk-taking to the response sergeant and forget the other ten fucking risk principles.

It's the only one the Control Room inspector (Oscar 1) knows, it's the only one they need to know. It's the role where people go when they don't want to make a decision, they just pass all the decision-making they should do to the response sergeant.

The Ten Risk Principles don't mention getting a detection.

Funny Kinda Tang

'Yes, yes, yes, yes, yes, yes, yes … yes, yes, yes … yes, yes, yes, yes, yes, yes … yes,' the lad just kept saying, repeatedly … for the last three minutes.

'Oh, come on, mate, what's your name?' I enquired.

'Yes, yes, yes, yes, yes … yes, yes, yes, yes, yes, … yes, yes … Yes, yes, yes, yes, yes.'

Yes, I think I know where this one is going. 'Where do you live?'

'Yes, yes, yes, yes, yes, yes, yes, yes … yes, yes, yes, yes, yes, yes, yes … yes, … yes, yes, yes, yes, yes, yes, yes, yes, yes, yes, yes, yes, yes … yes, yes, yes, yes … yes, yes…'

I thought he's either the Man from Del Monte, or an officer from the middle floor of St Aldates wanting to progress his career (I didn't recognise him) or a negotiator for the Happy Valley Police, who goes to one of the endless meetings where they sit down and negotiate with our partners as to who is best placed to take the lead with initiatives (I'm good to my word, I said that I'd explain that now).

'Have you taken anything?' I politely enquired.

'He's taken some ketamine and drunk a bottle of vodka, to celebrate finishing his exams,' said one of his friends.

'That's the spirit, and why the hell shouldn't he?' I said to the lad, 'Taken some ketamine, and drank a bottle of vodka have ya?' But I kinda knew what the answer would be.

'Yes, yes, yes, yes, yes, yes, yes, yes … yes, yes, yes, yes, yes, yes, yes … yes, … yes, yes, yes, yes, yes, yes, yes, yes, yes, yes, yes, yes, yes … yes, yes, yes, yes … yes, yes…'

We waited and waited for the ambulance. For about an hour. The ambulance didn't arrive due to cutbacks, so I had to put him in a police Vivaro.

'Yes, yes, yes, yes, yes, yes, yes, yes … yes, yes, yes, yes, yes, yes, yes … yes, … yes, yes, yes, yes, yes, yes, yes, yes, yes, yes, yes, yes, yes … yes, yes, yes, yes … yes, yes…'

Back in the day, just after, the great old big old days of Sergeant Mills, and just before the word 'vulnerable' became en vogue, the multi-agency approach was all the rage.

This was code for all the other agencies/partners to spam all their responsibility onto the police, but we negotiated hard.

They'd all be there: Social Services, county, town, and parish councillors, representatives from domestic abuse charities, and the probation service and anyone else who didn't have a meeting to go to that day, and of course our very own representatives from the police.

'Come in, help yourself to the water, it's free, haha, we won't charge you for it, ha, help yourself.'

'Ah, thank you very much.' Slurp, slurp. 'Got a bit of a tang, mmmm, the water's got a bit of a tang, mmmmm, has the water got a bit of a tang?' said the police representative. 'Dunno, mate, you're the only one drinking it.'

'Yeah, it's got a bit of a tang it has.' And did that silly thing of tut-tutting with her tongue and teeth and closed her eyes. 'Yeah, it's a got a funny kinda tang, it's definitely got a tang, mmm there's a tang definitely. '

'So, I think the police are best-placed to take the lead in finding all the missing people,' says the chair.

'Yes, yes, yes, yes, yes, yes, yes, yes … yes, yes, yes, yes, yes, yes, yes … yes … yes, yes, yes, yes, yes, yes, yes, yes, yes, yes, yes, yes, yes … yes, yes, yes, yes … yes, yes…'

Slurp. 'The water has a bit of a tang doesn't it, a tang, the water, yep, a bit of a tang.'

'Good, right, that's that one sorted then, and I think the police are best placed to deal with all the anti-social behaviour, and everything else the council don't want to deal with, help yourself to some water.'

'Yes, yes, yes, yes … yes, yes, yes, yes, yes … yes, yes, yes.' Slurp, with a funny look at the glass.

'Okay, this is all going a lot better than I thought it would and looking after all the domestic abuse incidents. '

'Yes, yes, yes … yes … yes, yes…'

'Okay, let's strike while the iron's hot, and all the vulnerable people…'

'Yes, yes, yes, yes, yes…'

'And taking mentally ill people to hospital because there aren't enough ambulances… I'm just going to sit back and enjoy this one…'

'Yes, yes, yes, yes, yes, yes … yes, yes, yes, yes, yes … yes, yes, yes, yes, yes, yes. Yes, yes, yes, yes, yes, yes … yes, yes, yes … yes, yes, yes.'

'Shuuut uuup, and anything else no-one wants to deal wit…'

'Yes, yes, yes, yes, yes, yes, yes, yes, yes … yes, yes, yes, yes…'

'Well, that just about concludes…"

'Yes, yes, yes, yes, yes, yes, yes … yes, yes, wh … wh … what happened'

'Phew, just in the nick of time, er nothing, we'll send you the minutes.'

'Great, thank you.'

'No, thank you.'

Gaslight

'Al, you're unhappy in the IHub, so I've decided that you're going back to Cowley … with immediate effect,' said the The Boss, who's a great ol' boy, did I mention that he really is a great ol'boy, and I'm enormously grateful to him.

Alleluyah, Alleluyah, Alleluyah, Alleluyah, Alleluyah, Alleluuuuuuuuuuyaaaaaaaaah.

'Oh really? That's a shame, that's a real shame that is.'

But I think my face may have given it away. And the cartwheel. And the running around the middle floor with the front of my shirt thrown over my face, running up to everyone with my arms above my head and yelling 'yeaaaaaaaah' right in their face. And returning to my seat. And sitting down nice and serenely. Because I am.

'You don't mean that do you, Al?'

Perceptive. I thought I'd been subtle.

The strategy had worked. I had been awkward and obtuse, refusing to go to the Komodo's strat meeting, amongst many other things.

'But, but, but, why?' I ask.

'You have been awkward and obtuse, refusing to go Komodo's strat meeting, amongst many other things, Al.'

'Oh, but I'm going back to Cowley, right?'

'Yes, Al. People are worried about you though, Al, why are you so unhappy? '

'They've got to scrap the New Operating Model, and this floor has too many dick-swingers.'

'But you can't go around telling people that. '

'It's just a little thing but I am really quite proud of it, it's called honesty. The model just isn't working, and senior officers have got to acknowledge the truth, boss.'

'They do know it, Al but they can't admit it, because it will seriously sink, they have to prop it up.'

'Oh wow, I'd rather be honest.'

'I think you should see your GP, Al.'

'Because of being honest? Will it require surgery, or do I just have to go up through the ranks?'

'No, Al, I think you're suffering from stress.'

'Don't you dare fleshlight me.'

'I think you mean gaslight.'

'Yeah, well, both, actually.'

'You're suffering from stress, you keep snapping at everyone.'

'I snap at people because I'm angry, there's a world of difference between being stressed and being angry. Look, this is what my face looks like when I'm angry ... and this is what it is like when I'm stressed... Angry ... stressed ... angry ... see? Completely different.' This doesn't work particularly well written down.

We both walked away respecting the other's point of view and that's the funny thing about it.

About nine months ago I had to take some time off, I'd had a very minor Transient Global Amnesia (TGA), my blood pressure was sky high, I was stressed and suffered from anxiety. I was in a bad way. My condition was exacerbated by being off work. Because when I wasn't in work, I suffered more stress by knowing that the people in work had to do my work and suffer more duty changes to cover my shift. And constantly receiving phone calls from the very people who had made me poorly. This makes it incredibly difficult for a police officer to recuperate, I should imagine it's just the same for all public servants.

Anyway, me, awkward and obtuse, I rather like it.

I'd rather like it on my gravestone.

And I want it placed across all three lanes of the eastbound carriageway, just outside Barton off the Roundabout, during rush-hour, at a rather jaunty angle.

Here lies the body of Alan Gordon Robinson

Known to his mates as Robert

Born 21st December 1963 – Died far too soon.

Fuck was he awkward and obtuse.

And now that I've got everyone's attention, can I just mention the police service is broken, yep, that's about all really.

Take good care of yourselves.

Al

It's what you do during that tiny – that counts.

Help me out

Please be kind enough to help me out for a couple of minutes, what's the female equivalent to a dick-swinger?

I have to say that within the police I've never met the female equivalent. Almost without exception female officers are incredible, they all just get on with it, get stuck in, and get through it. But I would like you to tell me what the female equivalent to a dick-swinger is. Thanks, please give it some thought.

Radio

After skilfully managing to avoid the Daily Morning Meeting for many months, I'm back and we're proudly sporting the old 5, 4, 3, 2, 1 formation, yep, out of the fifteen in there, there were:

Five, who had no radio, who are police officers, who had no intention of doing any police work, and never ever had, and never ever will, and just thought that attending the morning meeting would be a bit of a laugh and quite an entertaining way to spend half an hour of their life. Watching me being asked questions that I didn't have the remotest idea of what the question was, let alone what the answer could possibly be, they could see me diligently making notes on a scrap piece of paper (which would be diligently chucked into the nearest bin the moment the painful charade had ended) and making myself look a tiny bit interested in something that I had no reason to be interested in, and I personally think that I turned in a sterling performance and I, for one, very much hope that everyone very much enjoyed it.

Four, who had no radio, no intention of doing any police work, and who, in all fairness, were not police officers anyway.

Three, who at least looked smart, and sat there without a radio, who, about a year ago, had some inclination to do some police work but now the novelty had worn off.

Two, who gave it a bit of a go, no radio, but had found something black to wear, and some inclination to do some police work.

One, who remotely resembled a police officer, er, that'd be me then, (God help us all) with a radio and wearing a uniform.

The one question I get asked every single time I'm forced to attend this pantomime is 'how many officers have you got today, Al?' Usually its five or six, and the PieChartMan says, 'Oh we're below minimum, get our officers back from South and Vale, Al.'

'I would Sir, but they've had to go over there because they're below minimum and even with our officers they're still below minimum.'

'Well get our officers back from Cherwell and West, Al.'

'I would Sir, but they've had to go over there because they're below minimum and even with our officers they're still below minimum.'

'Have you highlighted this to someone, Al? So, they can do something about it.'

'I just have, Sir, can you do something about it now, please, Sir.'

This little charade gets played out at almost every morning meeting.

Flag

A mere six months after being awarded the incredibly prestigious outstanding in (pause) efficiency from the incredibly prestigious Her Majesty's Inspectorate of Constabulary and Fire and Rescue Service (HMICFRS), the senior officers are still banging on about it. In fairness, it's all they can bang on about, because they refuse to accept the bleedin' obvious, that the Ferkin Merkin' just ain't ferkin' workin'.

The HMICFRS, like all these QUANGOS or self-empowered committees or whatever they are, is led by a Special Kinda Guy. I wonder if he'll have the bollocks to wear the old brass fire officer's helmet and weld it to his brass neck to make him look like the bell end he really is, and wear it with the police uniform to a National Police Memorial Day Service to show what a Special Kinda Guy he really is?

The Special Kinda Guy is the bloke who wrote a report recommending that the Government welched on their pension contracts with the serving police officers. This caused tremendous hardship to nearly all my colleagues, of all ranks. When we joined, the deal was, we worked hard for 25 to 30 years, putting up with all the crap that society and the organisation could throw at us, but at the end of it we'd get our pension. That was the deal. His report caused an entire workforce to be completely demoralised, it was a complete breach of trust that could never be won back. It was absolutely devastating.

My dad cracked it within seconds, he used the word, within seconds. 'But that's unBritish, Al.'

Yep he said the word. How very unBritish to welch on a contract. I still can't believe he's got away with it, he's a special kinda wanker. And just to rub salt into the wound, they've gone and appointed him Head of Her Majesty's Inspectorate of Constabulary and Fire and Rescue Service. There should be some kind of crowdfunding to take this wanker to court – it just cannot be right for him to write a report that recommends welching on a contract. If he can get away with doing this, then there is no point in signing any contract. (Update – it has gone to Court and the police have won the case! I hope all the officers who suffered hugely as a result of his welching, claim a huge amount of compensation.)

And this special kinda guy has the brass neck to sit in judgement of me; if it's all the same to you, I'll take my moral compass from someone else, almost anyone else other than you.

In fairness, every cloud and all that, at least it's got rid of the notion that an officer gets tied to a soulless job, where they have to sell their soul and hold on like grim death so as they can get their pension after 25 to 35 years. At least they will say 'fuck this for a game of police officers, I'm off to have a far more fulfilling life, where my skills will be recognised, and I'll feel valued'. Yep, that's what'll happen.

Anyway, the Special Kinda Guy has awarded us 'outstanding in (pause) efficiency' and the senior officers can't get enough of it. So, the Special Kinda Guy now gets to preside over what is efficient and what is not, and considering we are a product of his making he's hardly going to say we are a pile of shit is he?

It's like an architect admiring a building that she's designed that looks like a turd with a flag stuck in it.

'Just look at that, isn't it the most attractive thing ever built?'

'I'm terribly sorry, sis, any way you look at it, it looks like a turd with a flag stuck in it. Now if you'd be kind enough to fuck off and take your steaming pile of turd with a flag stuck in it, with you, I would be enormously grateful.'

When you've got such a person at the very top of the organisation, and we've taken responsibility for all the things that other public servants should be responsible for, these are big reasons why it has come to this. Dunt ma"er in December me and Party 3 are off to Amsterdam. Hey ho, five months to go.

AUGUST

PECKED

The blue line gets ever thinner

From political games that they've played

The light dims and gutters

Disgruntled mutters

As the hue of the blue even fades.

At a stroke of a pen,

Five years is ten

And lump sums are slashed to a third

The knighthoods they gain

From the blood that they drain

Are nothing short of absurd.

Every failing a drama,

In the media blood count

Pecked by the vulture

Of contrived blame culture

As we're ever more held to account.

The shining lie of streamlining

Of doing more with less

Can we ever even the score

Or clutch at the hope of success?

But every nine o'clock wash up

The precision of hindsight a joy

Adds drag to your step and caution indeed

To each tactic you employ.

Timid souls with ambition inclined

To leave the filth and the fray behind

Offer their input, never sought

About how we hadn't done what we ought.

From ivory towers, always complaining

They piss on our backs

And tell us it's raining.

And while the timid prevail and praise the Emperors new suit...

Just keep your powder dry my friend,

Don't give them ammo to shoot

Tim Parker

Naughty

It was about the beginning of August; I had a word with Xavier's boss. I explained to him that the comment about waiting for the plane to fall out of the sky hadn't gone down well with response officers, together with his overall tone towards me. To try and make the conversation more memorable I told him that Xavier was 'naughty'. I just wanted him to know that being kind and compassionate isn't for everyone but if he ever gets tired of behaving like the horse's arse, there's always the option to stop.

In the Daily Morning Meeting (DMM) on the first Sunday of August we were proudly sporting the 0, 0, 0, 1, 2 formation, that's just the way the mop flops, and it all works swimmingly.

We had no-one who had no radio, who are police officers, who had no intention of doing any police work, and never ever had, and never ever will, and just thought that attending the morning meeting would be a bit of a laugh and quite an entertaining way to spend half an hour of their life.

We had no-one, who had no radio, no intention of doing any police work, and who, in all fairness, weren't police officers anyway.

We had no-one, who at least looked smart, and sat there without a radio, who, about a year ago, had some inclination to do some police work but now the novelty had worn off.

But we did have one person, Ash, who was at least prepared to give it a bit of a go, no radio, but had found something black to wear, and some inclination to do some police work.

And two, me and The Boss who remotely resembled police officers, with a radio and looking resplendent in our uniform.

I really enjoyed going to work on Sunday morning. The Senior Management Team (SMT), apart from our Superintendent, are halfway through the time they don't deem it necessary to grace us with their presence.

And it all works a lot better, despite it being the busiest time of the week.

Well, you know what it's like. Just like New Year's Eve or any time a career-limiting decision has to be made, the Senior Management Team (SMT) are nowhere to be seen. When the going gets tough, the SMT get going – home. As long as the endless bureaucracy is taken care of and they get awarded outstanding in (pause) efficiency, they're laughing kitbags all the way to NAAFI breaks

Off the back burner

Eight days later, on Monday morning, and we're back to the good the good old 5, 4, 3, 2, 1, and all the silly shit resumes. This time over a video link between St Aldates and Cowley. I wisely chose to have my nuts roasted in the comfort of Cowley Police Station, two miles away from the carpet botherers who I try so desperately to avoid. It also buys me a bit of time. 'I'm terribly sorry, the sound went a bit there, can you repeat that, please?'

When they try to give me some kind of meaningless bollocking for the rolling arrests not being done, it completely deflates them by the time they've had to repeat themselves three or four times. Or I just sit perfectly still, to make them think the link has frozen. That's my usual tactic but this time I decided to try something a bit different. One of the five piped up, 'The taskings haven't been updated for five days.'

If you remember, the taskings are areas that have been identified by somebody who doesn't work weekends or evenings or nights (or at all) as places that the six officers who do work weekends and evenings, and nights, are to visit during quiet times. Pfff, they don't 'alf come out with them don't they, ha, 'quiet times' pfff, just like that, off the top of their heads, absolute comedy gold.

Anyway, dunt ma''er, as I was saying, he said, 'The taskings haven't been updated for five days' and glared into the camera at me. And, so did the other thirteen.

I just stared into the camera for about thirty seconds and made them wonder whether the screen has frozen, before speaking.

'Oh, er, um, yes, well, obviously you've every right to make that observation, and errr, it could just be, errr, and, errr bear with me on this one and you do have every right to ask the question, and please bear in mind that I was on rest days for four of those five days, and this is just a little theory that, errr, I've been working on, and nothing to be too concerned about but I think, and I'm, errr, not too sure, but it just could be that we, errr, haven't got enough officers, just throwing it out there, let's get that one off the back burner, have a bit of blue sky thinking, run it up the flagpole and see who salutes it.'

'Um, interesting, really.'

'Um, yes, I'm glad that you find it interesting but to my officers it's a tad stressful and just a bit insulting to sit and listen to this. I've had six officers, two of whom were off, seven hours, seven bloody hours late because they found a cannabis factory, while the others had to deal with a high-risk misper; a father had attacked a son with an axe around the corner from Cowley Police Station and was arrested; someone was threatened with a knife and ran into the petrol station at Headington; and there was a big incident in The Clarendon Centre. I really wish you would give me the courtesy of acknowledging that, and who knows, in time, no rush, you may even appreciate it, and show the tiniest bit of gratitude but you have every right to ask the question. It's called *esprit de corps*, as the French would have us say, team spirit to you and me. You may wish to join in some time, instead of buggering off for the weekend,' I pointlessly try to explain.

179

Another one of the five piped up, 'And the rolling arrests haven't been done, JoHi has not been arrested and Xavier will not be happy.' The rolling arrests are arrestable people who are suspected to be offenders, identified by somebody who doesn't work weekends or evenings or nights, (or at all) as people that the six officers who do work weekends and evenings, and nights, are to attempt to arrest during the quiet times. Pfff, they don't alf' come out with them don't they, ha, 'quiet times' pfff, just like that, absolute comedy gold.

Oh, for fuck's sake, have you listened to a single word that I just said?

'May I refer the honourable gentleman to my previous answer?' I gracefully replied.

It grows you.

Collapsing deck chair

For some inexplicable reason I've found myself in St Aldates. I tried to avoid it at all cost, but somehow, I've found myself in there and I'm trying to explain to Steve – great old boy and civilian investigator – the size of Nigella's balls.

'Honestly, Steve, you've never seen anything like 'em. Apart from the Great Wall of China they must be the only thing that an astronaut can see from outta space, I tell you, those flippin' balls are enormous... '

As Chris, great ol' boy and police officer comes rushing in holding his index finger vertically to his mouth and flicking his head back, I see The Boss emerging from behind him.

'...So, I got into one and Mrs R got into the other, and some ol' boy zipped 'em up and pushed us off and we tumbled right the way down the hill, it was bloody brilliant. Ah hello, boss, how's it all going?'

'Oh hi, Al,' says The Boss. 'Al, in a bit, can you just nip down the corridor, we need to discuss the cultivation job and the seven hours, yep, seven hours overtime for Oz and Paddy. Oh, and er, Al, just so it's no surprise, Mrs Work-Based Assessment Assessor (WBAA) is in da house.'

Ah no, everybody best be on their best behaviour, Mrs WBAA is in da house.

'Nipping as we speak, boss.' And he walks back down the corridor.

Fuck fuckity fuck fuck, that's the fucking last thing I wanted, I must've been a right bad bastard in a previous life, I knew I shouldn't've gone to St Aldates. I really haven't got time for this shit, let's just get this hideous ordeal over and done with. It's no big deal really, all the boss has to do is say what a great job he's doing and all I've got to do is agree with him.

I say to Chris and Steve, 'Lads, I've just got to put my acting skills to good use. He can get every box ticked apart from "leadership and management point 2.6 – take action to maintain morale through difficult times." No-one has ever got that off me, and no-one ever will, it just ain't happening. Please answer the phone, wish me luck.'

They chuckled. 'Good luck, Al.'

I was off and in. 'Ah, Boss, how's it all going? Ah, and Mrs WBAA this is an unexpected pleasure, only it's not unexpected, and it's not a pleasure.'

'Hi, Al, yeah, Mrs WBAA is in da house to do some assessing on me, not you, so you can relax, make out she isn't here, just relax.'

'Yes, Al, I don't exist,' she chipped in.

I say, 'I really wish you didn't. More than anything else in the world right now I really wish you didn't. Oh, I'm sorry, I don't mean you as a person, I have no doubt that you're a really nice person, as a person I am really glad that you do exist, but your job role really must cease to exist. Did you hear anything Boss?'

'Right, Al, that incident where James Bond nearly killed his mum,' says the boss.

Boom, we're straight in, there are some boxes that need to be ticked under the heading of 'supervise the response to critical incidents', and I'm not going to get in anyone's way.

'Oh yeah, yeah I dropped a bit of a bollock …'

'Ah, now, Al, please do not swear in front of Mrs WBAA.'

He's only gone and got a tick under the 'provide leadership and management 'heading 2.5 – 'win the trust and support of colleagues and other key stakeholders (who dey?) through exemplary performance and behaviour'. It's a biggie but not as big as the 2.6, it's a masterstroke and the boss is happy, and if the boss is happy, I'm happy. This is great, I'm loving this.

Mrs WBAA's hand is all aquiver as she ticks the box and she lets out a groan, it's like the boss is controlling her most intimate bits.

'But, but, but she just said that she doesn't exist, does she exist? Or doesn't she? I'm confused, I need clarity.'

'Al, I exist,' she exclaimed.

'Did you hear something, boss?'

'Al, she did exist, then she didn't but then she did and now doesn't.'

'Will she again?'

'Yes, I think she will.'

'Oh, that's a pity.'

The boss continues, 'Anyway, back to this James Bond incident. It's a critical incident because owing to the police response, the public may have felt let down, you didn't respond quickly enough. I, obviously, ensured the golden hour enquiries were completed, and I made absolutely sure the offender was arrested, obviously. Obviously, the scene was identified, and the victim was obviously looked after. Obviously, it could've had a massive impact on the victim. Obviously, I, all by myself, without the help of anyone else, liaised with partners in the mental health services, and I – me, your boss – identified the responsibilities within the command structure. I – yes, me – continued to risk assess, and checked that actions were taken promptly, and I escalated it, and, above all else, I obviously deployed resources appropriately, and informed the Superintendent, obviously.'

Gee whizz, boss, where did all that come from? That wasn't exactly how I remembered it. But yeah, love it.

Mrs WBAA couldn't get enough of this, her hands were far too shaky to tick the multitude of boxes that deserved to be ticked, she just about managed to put a squiggle, let out an enormous groan and her body went into convulsions.

'Obviously, boss, that is obviously what you did,' I agreed.

'Anyway, Al, that's enough about me, what about you? How are you feeling at the moment?'

Oh my God, he was chancing his arm a bit, he'd bloody gone for it, he'd only gone for the elusive 2.6. Never, not on your bloody nelly, no-one will ever get a 2.6 off me, not then, not now, not never.

'Oh, I feel like I've been put on the spot a bit here. Er, I dunno, I've not really had much of a chance to think about it. Ahem, I dunno, you know, it's not something I really think about, that much. Well, yeah, just off the top of my head, er, I guess, I'm a little perturbed, shall we say, maybe even traumatised by the lack of officers on the fron—'

'Yes I am awa—'

'—tline. And, well, you know, there is the compassion fatigue, you know, how can I go out there and give compassion to people when I don't receive any compassion here? No-one cares for the frontline officers who actually have to deliver this nonsense, credit where credit's due, anyone who's not a frontline officer doesn't even pretend to care. And then there has always been that cognitive dissonance, you know, I was recruited because they identified that I had common sense and discretion, but I'm never allowed to use it, am I? Because all my decision-making is obliterated by the ghastly detection culture. I mean, everything is just reduced to a mind-numbing process, of assessment upon assessment and of course the constant pressure of being politically correct but I think overall—'

'You are hap—'

'The Senior Management Team really need to know that officers are deeply unhappy, and they feel undervalued by not only the community but also by them as well. I mean, the job is difficult enough, with all the unpleasant things we have to deal with, but there is no appreciation or gratitu—'

'Yes, thank you, Al, that's enou—'

'And then of course, there is the lack of support and the blame culture. I mean, just look at that poor Doctor Hatiza Bawa-Garba, I know it was the NHS but that is exactly what it's like; if I made a mistake because of being exhausted or human, I know full well that I will be hung out to dry and, constantly being in a state of hypervigilance, and the press constantly getting their facts—'

'Yes, that's eno—'

'Incorrect. I thank my lucky stars all this stress, constantly coming into work early, going home late, no lunch breaks, constant criticism, has not spilled over and affected my home life. I'm still the cheeky, cheerful chappie I always was, you can ask Mrs R, I am an absolute joy to have around, she'll tell you. I dunno, just off the top of my head, and making it up as I go along, I think the cuts have gone far too far, constantly wanting more with less and less. You know what I mean don't you, boss, and knowing that all the blame will be on me when it goes wrong because nobody will ever be able to say that the cuts are to blame. Oh, blimey, Sir, I wish you'd given me a bit of warning for that question, because obviously—'

'Well, Al, I think you have said en—'

'There are the constant shift changes, leave embargoes, officers constantly poorly and leaving and getting injured, and it just appears that we're not being listened to and nobody cares, they seem to think this New Operating Model is working. I mean, boss, whose idea was that? Who's going to be brave enough to admit to being responsible for this debacle? Sir, they are splitting us into tinier and tinier parts, it's like they're going to privatise us. Sir, they won't do that will they, Sir? Like the Probation Service, Sir, and look what a mess that is. It would be easy to civilianise and then just privatise us wouldn't it, Sir? Are they trying to divide and conquer us, Sir? That would be awful wouldn't it? Just imagine all this hard work and stress and anxiety just to make Sir Dickie Branflake even more money, did you know he has already made £2bn out of the NHS, that's evil isn't it, Sir? Two billion pounds at the expense of the health of the people, I don't want it to happen to the police, Sir, but it's like they are running us into the ground; it's cruel, Sir, officers working so hard to try and keep the public safe when we ourselves are broken. The organisation itself is broken. I look upon it like an alcoholic mother, I love it with all my heart but there just comes a point where you've just given it chance upon chance and all I'm doing is throwing good emotion after bad. I've just got to let it go, it's draining me, it just takes and takes without giving back, in the end for my own welfare I have just got to cut it loose, I find it really traum—'

'Yes, if we could just mov—'

'...atic. Yeah, I think that I'm traumatised and I'm really sorry, boss, I know there are a lot of boxes there to be ticked but I really haven't really got a lot to say about how I am, not a lot to say at all, I mean, what is there to say? Just look at the constantly moving goalposts, I do not know what is expected of me anymore, all these priorities, we've got more priorities than officers, boss. And then there's the constant thought that I have to cover a massive area and go on a forty-minute blue light run, to somewhere that I've never heard of to support officers I've never heard of. I dunno, I just find it shambolic and traumatic. And the poor officers, they all want to leave, two are wanting to go to the Met and one to West Mids, there is a lack of faith in the decision-making of the higher-ups and I can't see them ever winning back the trust of their officers. I really wish you'd warned me that you were going to ask me how I am, I would've had a bit more of a comprehensive answer. I'm sorry.'

'Boss, that reminds me, I'm reading this brilliant book at the moment by a psychologist who I think was or is married to a police officer. I think her name is Claire Carter, the book is called *Duty of Care*, it's absolutely brilliant, I'll give it to you when I've finished. I think this organisation just don't believe they have a duty of care for you and me and all the officers, honestly, no wonder everyone is leaving or wanting to leave, they need to wake up to what's going on. If someone sued this force for the stress that they've endured they wouldn't have a leg to stand on. I haven't got strong feelings about it one way or the other, and what I do have I keep pretty much to myself. I wish I had more to say really.'

'Well, at least you sound happy Al, and things will only get better.'

Fuck me, boss, that is a stroke of pure genius, he's only gone and done me. He's shot from his own penalty box and curled it into the top right-hand corner. Pure genius.

As Mrs WBAA screeched, 'Two point six.'

Well, I think that is what screeched, as the last word was so fucking high-pitched it was inaudible to the human ear, but sent the dogs in Rose Hill into a mating frenzy, as she slithered, slid and slipped off her seat, and buckled like a collapsing deckchair. I managed to react quickly as she dropped to her knees and was about to face plant, and luckily enough, I caught her with her nose about 3 inches from the carpet.

I picked up her pen, put a massive tick in 2.6, step over her, and said, 'It's all in a day's work.'

We both walked away respecting the fact that he'd completely done me, and I was completely fucked off, and that's the funny thing about it.

Hillman Hunter

Friday night, fight night, Nightsafe night, shite night, hate it night, Stupid Little Cunt Just Down The Hill From The Police Station (SLCJDTHFTPS) night.

After all the usual shit of people having a fight and then claiming they had been assaulted, and my officers being abused and insulted for stopping some wanker from getting a well-deserved kicking, all of my resources were allocated to taking people into custody in Abingdon.

And just when we were on our knees, the SLCJDTHFTPS inevitably was on hers, giving some Hillman Hunter a blowie in Marsh Park. So just like every Friday night for the last three weeks on the stroke of three o'clock, you could set your clock by her, the

SLCJDTHFTPS phoned up to say that she's been raped. So, because she's been flat on her back, she wants us to be on ours.

Through her junkie-, crack-, alcohol-addled brain, she has conjured up a load of bollocks that makes perfect sense to her but no-one else. Never mind, it gives her the perfect excuse to be rude and obnoxious to some poor unexpecting officer who I've had to drag across from the South and Vale. The officer, against all the odds, remains perfectly professional despite enormous provocation, which only serves to anger her even more but at least it has brought her to some level of sobriety to make even her come to the realisation that she is talking absolute bollocks.

And in light of this epiphany the only way to react is to become even more abusive, rude and obnoxious to the professional officers, who sit and take it because they have to, it's their job, and all they will get is the scrutiny from management asking them why they didn't take a report of rape, and eventually the SLCJDTHFTPS kicked them out of her flat. See ya soon, same time, same place, next week, be there or be somewhere else, absolutely anywhere else, please.

And I will be. I'm off to Turkey on me holibobs.

Ben Nevis

One day, in the very near future, you'll be going about your normal everyday business, jogging your daily 10k, like me, or just driving to work, something like that, and your attention will be drawn to a mountain about the size of Ben Nevis that wasn't there the day before. And you may think quietly to yourself, hmm, that's funny, there's a mountain about the size of Ben Nevis over there, that wasn't there yesterday, I wonder how it got there?

I wouldn't, I wouldn't bat an eyelid, I'd just take it all in my stride, I'd just think, I know what that is, that's just a pile of completed Domestic Abuse, Stalking and Honour-based Violence (DASH) forms that has been filled in by the wonderful police officers of England and Wales over the past ten years, when their time would've been better spent doing something else. I often wondered what they were going to do with them all. And now I know.' Yep, that's what I'd think.

Domestic abuse, stalking and honour-based violence is dreadful, and the police service treat every single incident incredibly seriously and work extremely hard to ensure the victim is given the very best service possible.

You can only imagine how harassed, alarmed and distressed I was to hear Flora Frichards (the person who designed the DASH form) on 24 July 2018, shimmy-shammying her flim flam (I asked you to think of the female equivalent of dick-swinging, there you go, my knees are buckling having to carry you lot the whole time) on national television and any other media outlet available.

'Cops stalker fail, death of forty-nine women linked to failure by police to act on stalking and domestic abuse.' Followed by, 'These are the most dangerous cases – they are murders in slow motion – yet women are still not being believed or taken seriously when they report it to police.'

According to the Office for National Statistics (NOS), the police service in England and Wales dealt with over 1.1 million domestic incidents in the year ending March 2017 (over a hundred an hour). Hardly the actions of a service that doesn't take domestic abuse seriously. And there were almost 100,000 court cases for domestic incidents in that year, hardly something we would do if we did not believe or take seriously any allegations, is it, Flora? And out of that, seventy-six per cent were convicted. And Flora, it would be incredibly interesting to know how many of those were victimless prosecutions. But hey ho, these are all just little details. I fully appreciate that because you are human you are fallible and you can make mistakes, no dramas. And, it is of no significance at all that over 83,000 multi-agency risk assessment conferences were held to prevent serious incidents. This is where multi-agency meetings do have value.

It must've just slipped her attention that in the three years that the forty-nine people have been killed, we have dealt with roughly three million domestic and stalking incidents. This means a failure rate of less than 0.002 per cent. And this could be due to the very policy of taking every domestic incident so damn seriously that we have no filter to enable us to bin the nonsense and focus on the serious.

In recent years there are roughly 120 domestic related murders each year. Seventy-five percent are women, so roughly ninety females and thirty males are killed.

In three years approximately 270 women will have been killed, meaning that if forty-nine can be attributed to police failures, 221 murders didn't have police contact. (Please be aware that this may be slightly inaccurate because Flora could not obtain the figures from all Constabularies – including the Met; even so, I believe that more women were killed without contact with the police than those who did. I might be wrong).

Every time we attend a domestic or stalking incident, we have to dutifully complete a five-page risk assessment devised by Flora. I believe that unless the officer considers the incident to be particularly serious, the form should not be completed. This would have the effect of a much more focussed approach to domestic incidents, instead of risk assessing every single one. It's unmanageable. The only true reason for a risk assessment to be completed is to make some poor sod accountable and responsible for everything that happens subsequently.

The officer should attend a domestic incident and give it all the time and consideration it needs. Talking to both parties separately, without judging whether one is the victim or suspect (at this stage we've no way of knowing), but speak to them as people and not as a ticky box exercise, which would make them feel valued. And then, make a judgement, and if it's a storm in a teacup write it off appropriately.

And, a huge proportion of domestic incidents involve people who, ordinarily, in everyday life are enormously capable,, but now that they've had a minor tiff, over something like the estranged husband returning the kids ten minutes late, they've descended into moronic douchebags and pass all their responsibility onto the poor ol' police officer.

I cannot profess to be an expert on domestic abuse, but it's very strange that when a police officer is involved in a domestic incident in their personal life the organisation doesn't seem to hesitate in chucking the poor ol' officer under the bus. I know of at least two incredible officers who've suffered in this way. The job spills out into the home, but there doesn't appear to be a tremendous amount of compassion towards the officer.

Crikey, do you remember me telling you about the Two Evil Twins or The Gruesome Twosome operating within the Police Service? It seems such a long time ago doesn't it? I stressed the damage that the detection culture (The Devil's Work) has done, please be kind enough to read about risk assessments (The Spawn of Satan).

The Spawn of Satan (Risk Assessments)

Who'd want to join an organisation where their judgement is being questioned all the time? Officers have good judgement, that's why they become police officers. It's debilitating and, to use another Flora word, 'disempowering' to have their judgement challenged continually. The act of completing the risk assessment suggests that there is something to assess, whereas the vast majority of the time the complaint is a load of old drivel. It makes officers reluctant to attend any incidents where a risk assessment has to be completed, which is almost every incident they attend. Honestly, we have to risk assess almost everything, we're drowning under a tsunami of risk assessments, we're completing so many that we're in danger of disappearing up our own arses(sments).

Scrap the Spawn of Satan.

The officer is supposed to risk assess the vulnerability of a victim by asking if the perpetrator has said things of a sexual nature, used a weapon, assaulted her while she was pregnant or put their hands around her neck, and even if the perpetrator has raped her, it's supposed to be an indicator as to whether more serious offences will occur in the future.

I was a pretty ordinary police officer. I would make an even worse Nostrafuckindamus so how am I supposed to know what's going to happen in the future? (Within moments of me leaving they could be humping or thumping each other – how am I supposed to know?) And even worse, I am supposed to be responsible for it, and even if I could predict it, there is very little I can do about it (it would be incredibly difficult to assign a police officer to personally protect the victim – all we can do is offer a refuge). How about referring all domestic abuse victims to Flora (or her organisation) and pass all the responsibility to her and see what she can do?

Countless times I've had sleepless nights being physically sick believing that I was going to go in to work and someone will have been murdered and it will all be my fault. With every incident we deal with, we always cater for the worst possible scenario – instead of, what in the officer's judgment, is MOST LIKELY going to happen.

And then there's something called personal responsibility. This is a very old and underused concept where somebody, please bear with me on this one, actually takes responsibility to sort out their own problems, I know, I know, it's crazy. Why would anyone want to do that when all they've got to do is pick up the phone and pass their responsibility to the police? They must be mad.

We spend millions and millions of pounds of taxpayers' money every year on policing and taking responsibility for domestic abuse incidents. (It would be incredibly interesting to know the precise figure, but it is millions upon millions). I believe that it's long overdue that we revisited the domestic abuse policy and with the help of Mr Bugarov in the Contact Management Platform, work out a policy which is realistic and workable, one which enables us to see the wood for the trees and to focus on the more dangerous cases. The policy has got completely out of hand, it's unworkable, we need to be more focussed.

We're far too blinded by some dopey chief inspector encouraging us to complete the Spawn of Satan. 'If it saves one person's life' while a crocodile tear makes an unexpected appearance. (His wife must have told him to imagine he's been passed over for promotion, after having sold his soul, and given up all his morals, just to promote a meaningless diktat coming from an anonymous unaccountable bureaucrat, that's the only time a tear would ever appear in his bloody eye. Bloody great performance, though – bloody love it). But if the aim of the game is to 'save one person's life' we'd have to wrap everyone up in one of those great big balls me and Mrs R bounced down the hill in. Life's a risk. This applies to all risk assessments, not just domestic abuse risk assessments.

A commonly used phrase used when talking about domestic abuse is 'it's like a frog jumping into a pan of boiling water, it'd jump straight out. But if it's in a pan of cold water and the pan is heated up it doesn't know what's happening and ends up getting boiled.' Can I just suggest that if that's what happening in a domestic situation and it's getting a bit hot to the point of you needing to take your jumper off, it might be just about the time to hop out. You know, take a bit of personal responsibility.

The doctors and nurses in the NHS have to make huge life and death decisions every day, they have to make decisions on whether people will have money spent on them to save their life or not; this is not easy, but someone, somewhere, somehow needs to make decisions, as to whether this is a viable policy. Other parts of our service are being left short, to the extent that we cannot properly resource a major incident because we're so bloody bogged down with this policy.

I know that I'm going to upset a lot of people, but lively discussion and debate never hurt anyone and it's more important to be right than nice.

And it's not just at domestic incidents that risk assessments have to have their arse kicked out of, it's anti-social behaviour, speaking to homeless people and ongoing neighbourly issues, these risk assessments are so important they get their very own mnemonic, get a load of this: OSARA (Objective, Scanning, Analysis, Response, Assessment).

OSARAs do funny things to PieChartMan, he can't get enough of the wretched things.

The police service is made up of people with many different skills, some are good at arresting people, some are good at gathering evidence and detecting, some are good at talking to people and getting intelligence, I'm sure you get the idea, everybody brings something to the table. Apart from PieChartMan. All he brings is piecharts. If only *he could see his way clear to leaving the charts somewhere where he can't remember where they are, like next to his radio, and just bring the pies that'd be great that would. Or better still, if he could just see his way clear to leave himself with his charts, next to his radio, and just send the pies, that'd be greater still, that would. I love a good pie. Steak and Guinness is my favourite, I had one of them at the Victoria Arms in Jericho, when Davey V's girlfriend Janet left, bloody brilliant it was, I'd thoroughly recommend it, Mrs R had a veggie one and said we'd have to go back some time. So, pies I like, piecharts I don't, in fairness there are very few non-edible things that I do like.*

But anyway, PieChartMan loves his OSARAs, it's an easy way for someone who is good at talking to people and not so good at arresting people to justify their existence, which in turn is an easy way to justify PieChartMan's existence. On many occasions it takes longer to fill out the pointless OSARA than it does to solve the problems, and while all this is being done and stuck on a piechart real police work isn't, and that is all a very sad state of affairs.

Mo Farah

In Great Britain in 2017 twenty three people died during or after being in police custody. This is the highest number for a decade.

The Independent Office for Police Conduct (IOPC) said that seventeen people had been restrained by police before they died but that did not mean the use of force was a factor in their deaths. Out of the seventeen people, eleven were restrained in custody. Nine people died in hospital after falling ill at the point of arrest.

It is so incredibly sad. Great people. They had their whole lives ahead of them, now all are subjected to a lengthy stressful investigation process where they will be treated worse than the criminals they've had to deal with.

One of those who died in hospital was in Oxford and involved my amazing colleagues.

Out of the millions of interactions that police have to deal with each year including almost 800,000 arrests, twenty-three people have died. A huge percentage of people we have to deal with have massive medical and/or mental health problems and have used copious amounts of drugs. We're not dealing with the likes of the Brownlee brothers or Mo Farah; we're dealing with the very poorest and the very poorliest in society. What I witnessed from police officers was complete kindness, respect, compassion and empathy with everyone we came into contact with.

What you'll never know is the number of lives police officers save each year.

According to the Office for National Statistics, deaths of police officers that were classified as suicide or undetermined intent has almost doubled from fifteen in 2009 to twenty-nine in 2013. Nobody leaves the police service unscathed.

I suffer terribly with dissociation, I never feel like I am properly involved in what is going on around me. Possibly due to years of being involved in traumatic incidents, instead of being engrossed in what is going on I continually had to worry about how the incident was going to be viewed by the 0830hrs hindsight brigade. I consider I got off lightly, a lot of Police Officers suffer terribly with PTSD.

A great friend and colleague committed suicide very shortly after retiring.

We are the Police

We're scarred.

We live,

We love,

We laugh,

We see things that should never be seen,

To do the things that need to be done,

By not giving up on others,

We end up giving up ourselves.

Suicide is the biggest killer of men under the age of forty-five, please talk to someone. Samaritans 116 123. Please, the world is a better place for having you on it.

Especially if you're a police officer and you're suffering, and I find it almost impossible to believe that you're not, please talk to your colleagues, it's a sign of immense strength.

Josh Etheridge and Andy Rhodes

I never thought I'd see the day where a senior officer would support his or her officers, but it has actually happened. Yep, officers had to taser an 87-year-old woman, not ideal I grant you, but if it has to be done… Despite being asked repeatedly to put a knife down, the silly old biddy refused, the officers even demonstrated what they wanted her to do, but she still refused so it was decided to taser her. Do you remember me explaining the Conflict Management Model, and how excited you got? This is what the police officers have to do, desperate times, desperate measures. It turns out she didn't speak the lingo, but next time, when someone shows you to put your knife down, probably best to do it.

So good old Josh Etheridge from the Georgia Police Department USA has supported his officers.

Ha, had ya. I bet you thought I was talking about a senior officer supporting his officers in Blighty. Not a chance. It would be career suicide. And career preservation is all they ever care about. It just would never, ever, ever, ever, never, ever, never, never, ever, happen ever.

What the hell. Hold the front page.

I take it all back, I sincerely apologise, I am so sorry. The legend that is Andy Rhodes, Chief Constable of Lancashire Police has only gone and supported his officers after they had to get a bit 'hands on' with a teenage girl when she got herself a bit unnecessary.

The legend that is Andy Rhodes not only supported his officers he went one step further.

'Perhaps those filming the incident may have better used their time helping the officers to calm the situation,' the legend said.

Ain't that the truth.

So, the ludicrous amount of risk assessments that we have to complete is another reason for how it has come to this. Dunt ma"er in December me and Party 3 are off to Amsterdam. Hey ho four months to go.

SEPTEMBER

PieChartMan and the Hotel Babylon

Drug-dealing stabbing

The inevitable happened and Komodo (the lad that we'd had countless strat meetings about) got himself involved in a drug-dealing stabbing. Really, who'd've predicted that, after all those meetings and support and wasted police hours trying to find him, all the thousands of pounds of taxpayer's money, he was involved in trying to kill someone.

Staffy

And then I've got to work a good ol' Saturday night Nightsafe.

We're treated to another episode with a lad called SuperMario, who's had exactly the same amount of support as Komodo, and is out drug dealing with his mate, beats someone up and gets arrested the next day. His mate is a complete arsehole and assaulted a detention officer when being put into a cell and hurt his hand, so he had to have two police officers to look after him at the JR2 Hospital.

A drunken lad on Park End Street says that he's going to run in front of a car if another drunken lad doesn't go out with him and goes and does it. Good work, brother, only breaks his leg.

And two cousins have a scrap on Middle Fisher Row, which continues into Worcester Street Car Park; fair play, they didn't kick off with the officers. But it means that at least seven officers are either at the hospital (with SuperMario's mate) or in custody. And it's rolling around to three o'clock and we will have to look after SLCJDTHFTPS. Miraculously she hasn't pumped her body full of drink and drugs and so has just about managed to deny herself that initial rush of pleasure she gets from wasting our time.

And there's a Staffy on a mad one on the North Way estate. It's taken it upon itself to try and maul the face off his owner and gets tasered by PC TeeTee for its trouble. To everyone's astonishment it has the desired effect of getting the bloody thing's teeth off the owner's nose and it makes good its escape, with the barbs still in it.

In the debrief PC Teetee stated, 'I shouted to Ozzy, "sit on it, Oz" and he didn't.' 'Fuck that. I wasn't going to do that,' Oz politely stated.

So, I said, 'Oh yes, and why not, Oz? You'd better have a pretty good excuse as to why you didn't sit on it, you'd better think pretty damn quicksmart and come up with just one bloody good reason as to why you didn't lower your Crown Jewels onto the teeth of a nasty bastard land shark who'd almost just bitten off his owner's nose… Hmm, just as I thought, you've got nothing to say for yourself.'

Cantankerous

Just like PCSOs (who should all become police officers, but please don't tell Boris that because that is where he'll get his additional 20000 officers from), civilian investigators, the good ol' station duty officers (SDOs), and detention officers in the custody suites, are the unsung heroes of the police service. They have to put up with the worst kind of behaviour from the people in custody, and that's just from the custody sergeant, they also have to deal with some fairly unsavoury behaviour from the prisoners.

PCSOs, civilian investigators, SDOs and detention officers are more frontline than most police officers.

A few years ago, I had the very great pleasure of looking after the custody suite as a custody sergeant. Here are a few tales from my time in Hotel Babylon.

'Ah no, what are we getting treated to 'ere?'

A bloke wearing reactolites (which never quite got around to reacting to light), thin on top with a ponytail, with a touch o' the Shipmans about him, comes through the air lock with a couple of officers.

No, no, be fair, give him a chance.

He was wearing his uniform. His spunk and piss stained grey joggers were a bit of a giveaway. And I was looking absolutely fabulous in mine.

Come on, give him a chance, innocent until proven guilty.

'Good afternoon, sergeant, this is Mr Pile, he's been arrested on suspicion of indecent exposure, we caught him masturbating outside the school.' The arresting officer explained, fair play, at least you gave him a chance.

'Okay, you understand why you've been arrested, what's your name, please?'

'Mr Fido Pile, it is spelt Fido but it is pronounced Fedo.'

'I'm sure it is, Mr Pile, I'm sure it is, no doubt about that. And why were you born?'

'Why was I born? What sort of question is that? Why is anyone born? Why were you born?

'I said, "where were you born?"'

'Oxford.'

'Okay, I am here to look after you whilst you are in custody, you have three rights, you've the right to have someone to hold your ear...'

'Someone to hold my ear, what would I want someone to hold my ear for?'

'As I was saying, you have the right to have someone told you're here, you have the right to have a sister...'

'What do you mean I have the right to have a sister, you're just making this up, you haven't got a clue what you're doing.'

'You have the right to have a solicitor, and you have the right to look at this book, the *Codes of Practice*, which tells meee, how I should look after youuuuu.' I said all sycophantic, dutifully and beautifully holding the book to my right, like I was advertising Persil, as I waft my left hand up and down in front of it.

'Yeah, well, you've looked at it for long enough now, d'you want someone told you've been a dirty Bertie or not? And d'you want a solicitor?'

'I haven't been found guilty yet, so you can't say that I've been a dirty Bertie.'

'Yep, you're absolutely correct, Mr Pile, you haven't been found guilty yet, and I unreservedly apologise. I am sorry, so sorry but you are a bit of a cunt...'

'Huh.' As he inhaled, 'You heard that he just called me a cunt? He just called me a cunt.'

All the detention officers suddenly found that the nib of their pen had something absolutely fascinating on the end of it that deserved much closer attention. The Nibbage Moment.

'Cantankerous person, if you'd just let me finish, now apologise for jumping to conclusions, I would never call anyone a cunt, it's not in my nature.'

'I thought that's what you said, I'm sorry.'

'That's fine, all I said was that you're a bit of a cantankerous person, that's all, nothing more, nothing less, nothing to get all bent out of shape about but undoubtedly you're a bit of a cunt as well.'

'Okay. You're a cunt an' all.'

'I beg your arsey pardon, 'ark at the dog calling the cat furry arse, yep, Mr Fido Pile, you're absolutely correct, I'm an absolute cunt, and I'm an absolute cunt that's got to look after you while you're in here, it is meeee who has to look after yoouu, no matter what disgusting thing you may or may not have done. How much citalopram or fluoxetine do you take?'

'How do you know I take anti-depressants?'

'Shucks, well, you know. Just a wild guess, I guess, I've been doing this job for a little while, y'know.'

After a few more questions I ask the officers to take Mr Pile to Cell 20. 'It doesn't overlook the playing field; we don't want him going off like a firecracker and coughing and spluttering into his undergrowlers.'

There's a doorbell kinda thing in each cell, and the guy in number thirteen keeps ringing the damn thing.

'That bloke in cell 13 keeps ringin' the bell,' I inform Pip.

'That's all right, Al, if they're ringing, they're not swinging,' Pip informs me.

'Ah no, what are we getting treated to here?'

'Good afternoon, sergeant, this is Mr Mushtash, we've just arrested him after an allegation of shoplifting.'

'Ah, hello, Mr Mushtash, I hope that your stay with us will be a short but pleasant one. What's your first name, please?'

'Mustafa Mushtash.'

'Ah that's a shame, I've just shaved it off, I thought it made me look very distinguished, but Mrs R didn't like it. Only kidding, only kidding, and why were you born?'

He laughed. I never deviated, always the same.

When I did my silly shit with the *Codes of Practice*, he politely requested the Qu'ran.

I handed it to him in the cell. 'Pip, Pip, that guy in thirteen, he keeps banging,' I inform Pip.

'That's all right, Al, if they're banging, they're not hanging,' Pip informs me.

'Thanks, Pip, is Mustapha all right?'

'Well, he's been facing Mecca for the last hour praying to Allah.'

I went to see if he was okay, and I could hear him saying, 'The great all-knowing Allah, please forgive me … the all forgiving Allah, please look after me … the all loving Allah, please love and forgive me … the all merciful Allah, please show mercy … the great all loving Allah, please love me … "

I think you get the general idea, but it had been going on for a terribly long time, so I opened the door.

'Mustapha, I really don't like seeing you in this state, is there anything I can do to help?'

'Allah?'

'No, sorry, I'm Alan. As you were.'

And then back to the charging desk 'Okay, Emma, you've been charged with drug dealing and child neglect, and before you go, I hope it doesn't come as any great surprise when I tell you that while you've been in here your two beautiful children have been taken into care.'

'You fuckin' what? You fuckin' cunt.'

She was absolutely apoplectic; she was frothing at the mouth. The froth ended all over my face. My face was like an astronaut's when they are subjected to a certain G force, but with loads of saliva on it. I stoically just stood there, deadpan.

'You fuckin' cunt, so you've fuckin' kept me in here while you, you, you fuckin' cunt, you took my fuckin' children away.'

'Yep, that's it.' My ears ringing and my face starting to drip.

'They're my fuckin' life, and you, you, you fuckin' cunt have taken them away, I'm going to kill myfuckin'self. I hope your fuckin' proud of yourself…'

'Well, no actually…' As much as I wanted to stand there stoically, I had the sudden urge to wipe my face, which was rather wet by now.

'You, you, you fuckin' cunt, sneaky cunt, they're my fuckin' kids, no cunt can take them from me, I'm going to kill myfuckin'self, you cuuuuunt.'

She had blistered my ears. 'One more time, Emma, but this time with emotion. 'And had the presence of mind to raise the *Codes of Practice* in front of my face.

'Fuuuuuuuuuckiiiiiiiiiiiiiiiiin' cuuuuuuuuunnnnt.'

And I tossed the *Codes of Practice* on the desk – I knew it would come in handy one day.

And she left.

'Well, I think that all went rather well.'

Band of brothers and sisters

And back to the present. On my four days off, on my boss's recommendation, I watched *Band of Brothers*.

On the morning of Friday 7 September 2018 Ash says, 'Al, this is going to upset you but you know you dropped a bollock the other week, when you were on your own and you were running Oxford and South Oxfordshire, and you were incredibly busy, and you let that old boy out of custody when you shouldn't've.'

'Er, yes, er, that does ring a very vague bell.'

'Well, the good old boys down in Stronghold, D'ange an' all are all happy with it and rallying around to keep you out of trouble, but X Wyng got to hear of it and he's now gunning for you. He's told the boss.'

Oh well. Ho hum.

'But I apologised. I couldn't be more apologetic. I sent an e-mail apologising and taking full responsibility.'

'Yeah, well. I'm sorry Al, he's gunning for ya.'

Oh well. Ho hum. Well, if I play with feathers, I'm going to get my arse tickled. And sometimes I rather like having my arse tickled.

I walked along the corridor and a putrid toxic smell, usually only found on the middle floor of St Aldates, filled my lungs. As I went into the Briefing Room, I found the source. PieChartMan was sat there, stinking the place out.

'Are you all right, Al?'

'Yep. Extremely, Sir. Thank you ever so much for asking. You?'

'I'm okay.'

We had about six officers to respond and three in the IHub. He loves the All Blacks mantra – 'Leave the jersey in a better place.' Well, you ain't, mate, you've left yours in a right shit state. Graham Henry you're not. You place far too much emphasis on statistics, not everything that matters can be counted and not everything that can be counted matters.

Of course, this was on a Friday, and I knew that we were going to be incredibly short of resources over the weekend. Even by the breathtakingly low standards of Resource Management, they had only one (instead of six) officers on response, so the IHub officers had to cover response and the Problem-Solving Team had to cover the IHub. (It would've solved a problem if they'd've put the Problem-Solving

Team on to response but hey ho. It was an absolute clusteroffuck, I mentioned it to PieChartMan but he didn't seem in the least bit interested, he appeared to be preoccupied. And over the weekend I'd find out why.

I also received an e-mail from the DidKnowItWasPrincess Eugenie'sWeddingButStillManagedToFuckItUp who, despite having seven months to sort out the resourcing for Eugenie's wedding, still managed to leave it to within a month to tell me that I had to work on a rest day to cover it. Any chance for a civilian to bully a police officer, they can't get enough of it. Especially in the DidKnow ItWasEugenie'sWeddingButCouldn'tMissTheOpportunityToBully APoliceOfficerDepartment.

Late on that Friday afternoon we received the usual hospital pass from Children's Social Care. They phoned in to say that SuperMario failed to attend an appointment and therefore they consider him to be missing. I don't. But I'll never win the bun fight with the Operational Supervisor in the Control Room so all the responsibility for SuperMario falls to me. This is where Mr Bugarov is so vital. I wanted The Boss to support me, but he didn't.

SuperMario is identical to Komodo. Somebody, somewhere, somehow, has to summon up the wisdom to cut through all the endless bollocks of all the endless bloody meetings and do what is best for these lovely kids (and I am being absolutely sincere here, they are truly lovely). Make a bloody decision, give it a good old whizz around the good old NDM and make a bloody decision. If they really have to be taken from their parents, because the parents are too busy battling their own demons, crack on and do it. Love'll win the day. If the decision is to support them in their home, crack on and do it. But stop passing all your responsibility on to me.

On Saturday 8 September 2018, the wonderful PC JayBee came along to assess and support the student officer, the equally wonderful PC CeeDoubleu. We had a very short meeting just to ensure that PC CeeDoubleu was being supported and was on course to successfully complete his probationary period. Due to the cutbacks this is an area that has been woefully neglected. During the meeting, The Boss tried to contact me. I informed him that I was in a meeting and I would get back to him. I told PC CeeDoubleu and PC JayBee that I loved them muchly and wished them all the very best for the day.

I was responsible for all the complaints and the mispers, as Ash was responsible for attending and supervising the incidents. I couldn't give a fuck about SuperMario. Well, actually, I could, I could give an almighty fuck about him actually. What I mean is, I couldn't give a fuck about where he is, he'll be all right, tucked up somewhere, not wanting to be found by us. I was enormously concerned about him and Komodo, they ain't gonna see old bones. They're going to flush their lives down the toilet. They're amazing lads. SuperMario had nothing but kindness and respect for me, but we've lost him, thanks to his own silly decision-making.

But, given the choice between flipping burgers with a boss constantly on your back or drug-dealing, I'd be seriously tempted. Absolutely nothing wrong with flipping burgers, but if you're constantly having to meet targets and being scrutinised, I know what I'd rather do. I can see the attraction.

I could see that an Inspector had conducted a review of SuperMario being missing, and I'd assigned one of the officers from the IHub, PC Cee, to look for mispers, and he knew full well what was expected of him. I was not going to chuck loads of officers to run around like headless chickens to try and find him – we didn't have any anyway.

John or James or whatever his name is, the lad that Becca had talked off the bridge a few months previously, had texted the wonderful PC PeeGee, who was kind enough to give John or James her own personal mobile phone number, (what an amazing thing to do, that's how much she cares) telling her that he was in Swindon and wanting to kill himself.

Well, Swindon is a shithole, it has that effect on most people, it has that effect on me, you're not alone there, my friend. Just leave.

No. He had to have his three-hour dosage of attention. High risk missing person, all our resources are focussed on this idiot.

Thousands and thousands of pounds of taxpayers' money down the pan.

As I said in my Introoy Thingy, I am not the Dalai Lama, but in a certain light etc… I haven't reached the point of self-actualisation, and a year previously I would've had all the compassion in the world for the guy, but I'd be being absolutely dishonest if I said that I cared.

Every city has four or five of these people who think it's acceptable to behave in this way. It'd all taken its toll. I'm certain most officers would still be compassionate, but if he did what he was threatening to do, it would be a whole world of pain for me. And I was trying to spin too many plates.

I went to try and find a three-year-old misper who was last seen on Shotover; probably overegged a game of hide and seek a bit. PC CeeDoubleu and PC JayBee with the help of other people found her – no dramas.

This was all punctuated with, 'What meeting are you in?' 'I told you four hours ago to do a review for SuperMario.' And, 'I have to have words with you.' From The Boss. That's what PieChartMan was preoccupied with. He was setting him up to do a number on me, that was why he was stinking out the place on Friday.

And bugger me, if half an hour later some old boy had the sudden overwhelming urge to hang himself in the Shotover woods. Back up I went. PC CeeDoubleu phoned him, and the lad told him where he was, job done. Three high risk mispers found in about two hours, back to the station for tea and medals. The Boss'll be chuffed to bits.

Sunday 9 September 2018

Ring ring. It's the Boss. 'Al, can you come to my office, please?'

'Coming as we speak, Boss.'

We had only just left briefing together so I'm not altogether sure why he didn't ask me then, but hey ho, here I go. I know what's coming.

'How did you sleep last night, Al?'

A wee bit unconventional but nothing I couldn't handle.

'I haven't slept at all Boss, I was sick throughout the night, and I've been sick this morning.'

'Why?'

'You said to me yesterday that you wanted to "have words with me", and I have literally been worried sick.'

We had a little bit of a bicker over his lack of support for me over the amount of Nightsafes I have to supervise. Eventually I got around to saying, 'You're trying to get around to bollocking me for dropping a bollock when I let that ol' boy go in the Met. Listen, I've apologised unreservedly for that, and I've taken all responsibility for what has happened and I'm ashamed at what I've done, and I stand by that apology, I am so incredibly sorry. But I've got enough confidence in my own ability to admit when I've made a mistake, and I've enough self-belief to make a decision and take the responsibility, and that's something that none of those people on the middle floor could ever do. And I'm proud of that.

'D'you know what, I sat and watched *Band of Brothers* over my four days off and there's a classic line in there. "Lieutenant Dike wasn't a bad leader because he made bad decisions. He was a bad leader because he made no decisions." They never make a decision, and it's far worse even than *Band of Brothers*; they not only never make decisions, they then come in after their weekend off and have the temerity to snipe at people who have.'

I didn't have the presence of mind to say it, but not only do they not make decisions, they then come in and criticise (they are far too cowardly to snipe), they delegate to someone else to do their sniping for them, and who better to delegate their sniping to than an Inspector who's only been a police officer for four years, and that's one of the many reasons why we should never have accelerated promotion, or high potential development or direct entry to God schemes. These wonderful people are far too easily manipulated by wankers.

I continued, 'Where are they now, Sunday afternoon? When the going gets tough, those fuckers fuck off. Come on, Sir, I bet you never thought that when you joined the police that all the senior officers would take every weekend off, it's deplorable and yet no-one challenges it, this is the precise reason why we're in this shambles – no-one challenges it.'

'Al, I can't change anything, it happens at such a high level...'

'Sir, you've got pips on your shoulders, why do you have such limiting beliefs? You can change everything. Please, boss, try.'

'Al, I unreservedly apologise to you, for giving you a sleepless night, I am so sorry. Somebody did that to me once and it isn't nice. I cannot apologise enough.'

'Apology accepted. It will not be mentioned again. D'you know what? That's the first time in twenty-five years that anyone has ever apologised to me.'

The boss also apologised for the lack of support and said that he would sort out Nightsafes for me. We went through the incident where I let the old boy go, which Xavier was kind enough to highlight to him so as The Boss could do his dirty work and take my legs. It was worse than I thought, not only had I let him go but I'd also noted the incorrect log number which clearly stated that he should not be released.

Oh well. Ho hum. I played with feathers and got my arse tickled, but I rather liked it.

The fabric of society ain't going to fall apart because of my mistake, the fabric of society fell apart years ago.

And then something really strange happened.

'How do you think you're performing, Al?' I scoured his face for any sign that he was having a laugh, no, nothing there. Oh my God, PieChartMan had done a proper number on him and now he was going to do a proper number on me.

'Pfoff, oh, boss, I'm sorry, I don't know; great, there you go, I'm performing great. I'm amazing. What d'you want me to say?'

I watched his face intently and intensely. I couldn't believe this was happening. His eyes went like saucers as if to say 'shit, this isn't supposed to happen, this didn't happen in *Leadership for Dummies*, (he definitely isn't a dummy, he's very smart) where do I go from here?' He hasn't got anything to play with. I could just sit there.

After an interminable silence, 'Well, Al, where do you see your weakness?'

Fuck me, did he just say that? Surely, he's taking the piss. I thought about saying, 'I'm a little bit partial to a Boss's chicken kebab.' But thought better of it.

'Pfoff, I don't know, you've got me on that one. No, no, I don't think I have any, and with sixty working days to go I'm not going to do a lot about it, even if there were, which there aren't.'

'Come on, Al, there must be something you can improve on?'

This is absurd. Up, down, side to side, all around, no, no sign he was having a laugh at my expense. My eyes darted around the room looking for cameras, this would go viral.

'Pfofffoff, no, you have got me on that one, too, sorry. I make that three-nil. I'm not very good at this game, am I? You got me, fair and square. I don't think I can come back from this, d'you mind if we don't play this game anymore? I'm not going to do a Liverpool and come back from three-nil down like they did on that glorious night on 25 May 2005 in Istanbul.'

I sat there in stunned silence waiting for the pearls of wisdom that a wonderful person who had been in the job for four years was going to impart. It was a long wait. Never mind, it gave me a chance to have a look for the camera.

'What I would like you to do is more checks on their investigations with officers, and file more of their jobs,' he stated.

Ohbejeezuz man, why didn't you just say that? Instead of chatting shit.

'Ash does all that, there's no need for me to do it,' I insisted.

There were a couple of other equally banal things that he would like to see an improvement on over the last sixty days of my service, which I won't bore you with, I'm sure you get the general idea.

'So that is what is expected of you and if you want, we will meet up every month...'

'You're all right, boss, if it's all the same to you, I'll pass on that o...' I'd rather have a burning hot needle stuck down my Japseye.

'What I mean is that we will meet up every month. Just to ensure that we get you safely to your retirement.'

Great.

Genuinely, he's a great, nice, kind, compassionate man but the Middle Floor Massive had got their teeth into him.

'And I'll be referring you to Occy Health because you said that you are sick when you come into work.'

'I get all the help and support that I need from Mrs R. I don't want or need it from anyone else. Being stressed with coming in here is a perfectly normal human reaction, it would be abnormal if I wasn't stressed coming in and having to deal with all this with four or five officers.'

He said that he'd send me an e-mail summarising our meeting.

'Yeah, great, thank you. It's all in a day's work.'

I walked away completely bewildered by what had just happened, and that was the funny thing about it.

Message received, understood, and ignored.

It grows you.

The e-mail was long, detailed and comprehensive, leaving no stone unturned, covering every possible salient point. I was incredibly impressed. It was a masterpiece; I couldn't get enough of it. I couldn't pick any fault in it whatsoever. There was absolutely nothing left out.

Except his fuck up.

Just as I was about to go home.

Ring ring.

'Al, can you pop upstairs?'

'Popping as we speak, Boss.'

'Al, have you had a chance to read through my e-mail?'

Fortunately, I had put aside the couple of hours required.

'Yes, Boss, it was extremely comprehensive, I was very impressed.'

'And of course, you think it is very um, er, erm, um, balanced account of our meeting?'

'Oh yes, boss, um, er, erm, um balanced is the precise word I would use to describe it.'

'So, you will be doing something about it and with it?'

'Yeah, well obviously I haven't had much of a chance to fully figure out its entire contents because it was quite comprehensive, and um, er, erm, um balanced, obviously. But at this very early and raw stage of processing its um, erm, er balanced contents, I think what I am going to do with it is find the very thinnest paper that can be used for photocopying, possibly even A3, and run off a copy. And then, I know a fair few hench dealers who have got some mighty fine dank nugs and combined with that photocopy, I will roll myself the longest, biggest, widest, finest, fattest doobie the world has ever seen and have a good old fashioned toke on a fat one. And I, for one, am going to thoroughly enjoy it, it's all in a day's work.'

And he sat there, completely bewildered by what had just happened, and that was the funny thing about it.

Make sure we get a detection

That night I just couldn't sleep. What on earth was that all about? I kept on having a recurring image.

The Middle Floor Massive have got me on my knees, handcuffed to the back, blindfolded. Yep, I know I'm entering into the realms of fantasy, none of them would be able to apply the handcuffs, but please go with me on this one.

'It'll be in the head, Al. It won't ruin your jersey, Al, you'll leave it in a better condition than you were given it, Al,' said one of them.

'Oh, that's good then, Sir, thank you.'

As he hands the pistol to someone else.

'Soooooomeoooooone wiiiiiill … compleeeeeete theee seven-pooooooooint … plaaaaan.'

Ah, I can't quite put a name to the voice.

As the pistol gets passed to Jake.

'Al, I've been shot, over a hundred times, you ask anybody, and it doesn't hurt. You'll be all right.' No, again the voice is familiar, but I can't quite place it.

As the gun gets passed to the boss.

Oh, Stanley Milgram where art thou, when a social experiment needs halting? Please go on The Google to find out who Stanley Milgram is, he's well worth going on The Google for. Stanley is what The Google was invented for.

I plead, 'Please tell Mrs R I love her with all my heart.'

Bang.

'What the fuck is a heart?' the Middle Floor Massive say in unison.

As I lie there with blood streaming from my head.

And then the full enormity of the horror of what had just happened hit each and every one of them. They just couldn't contain themselves. They just couldn't keep their emotions in check.

'Fucking hell, mate, what have you done? You fucking idiot… We didn't think you'd actually fucking do it… Well, not like that anyway… You see, what you should've done is gone around to the front and shot him in the temple,' said PieChartMan

'Nah, nah, nah in the ear, I've seen it hundreds of times, you ask anybody.'

'Up throoooooough the … chiiiiiiiin … and ooooooout the baaaaaaaack … of the heeeeeead.'

'Make sure we get a detection out of it please, lads. Shit job, but the jersey's in a better state. Now you really must excuse me, I have to record this on a pie chart.'

Girl splattered

Nine missing people, fuck the fucking lot of 'em, I don't even know where to start, I want to go out for a bit of a laugh. So, I do.

I'm out on patrol.

I'm out on patrol.

Eee aye adeeoo I'm out on patrol.

With Ash.

When we were travelling back from Marks and Spencers with a couple of sandwiches for the homeless people, I spotted a girl splattered on the floor close to St John's College at the beginning of St Giles. I shouted to Ash to stop the Vivaro. Honestly, I carry that bloody bloke, my knees buckle some days, he was in a world of his own.

'Come on Ash, where's your community spirit? That's the second time I've had to say that in two days, and to tell you the truth I'm getting pretty tired of it. If I have to say it again, I won't be too happy. Buck your bloody ideas up, the public are relying on us. I can't keep carrying you like this, my knees are buckling.'

The splattered woman was on her phone, obviously, to her mate. I took it off her and started talking to the person on the other end of her phone.

"Hi, good evening, Police Constable Sergeant soon to be Acting Inspector Al Robinson. Well, I won't actually be an acting Inspector. Can you believe it? It used to be that you'd get a period of acting for a year before you retired so as it'd bump up your police pension but for some unknown reason, they haven't done that for me. There was a job going on the Problem-Solving Team as an inspector. If they thought I couldn't solve problems, they're chatting shit, I'm a dab hand at sudoku and no-one even comes close to me on Candy Crush. It was all sorted. I thought I had it in the bag. But it's like I've upset them people on the middle floor, I mean, I don't mean to upset them, I just do, imagine how much damage I could do if I actually meant to do it. Anyway, I am Police Constable Sergeant never to be Acting Inspector

213

Al Robinson currently stationed at Cowley but I could easily be in Henley, Banbury, Windsor, anywhere really. Anyway, I'm with your mate, who I thought had jumped from a roof but she hasn't, she's just drunk, and having a bit of a laugh. I'm next to the Martyrs' Memorial, how may I help?'

'The Martha's Memorial?'

'Yep, that's it, the Memorial for Latimer, Cranmer and Ridley, all extremely well known Marthas. Who is this, please?'

'It's the ambulance service.'

'Oh fuck, it isn't is it? Have you been recording this?'

'All our calls are recorded.'

'Ah that's great, great stuff that is. Yeah, as I was saying, I am Jake Nutt, we don't need an ambulance. I've dealt with hundreds of people jumping off roofs, usually just after talking with me, you ask anyone, leave it with me. Good night.'

Jake Nutt has that effect on me, after speaking with him I usually have the sudden urge to jump off tall buildings.

The splattered woman had made a miraculous recovery and Ash had her sat in the Vivaro.

'I was really worried about you there, I thought you'd fallen from the roof, what with your legs all mangled an' all. I had even asked Ash to pass me the chalk so I could draw around your body. D'you know, when I was a boy, and I watched all those crime programmes, like Colombo and all that, I always thought it was crazy how people always managed to die exactly in those chalk outlines, I only found out how we do it when I joined the police. D'you know how people manage to die exactly in their chalk outline?'

'No, how?'

'Well, I'll tell you only if you promise not to tell anyone, not a single soul except your friends, and everyone else you want to tell, but what we do is, we chalk round them when they're dead and not before. Heyyy.'

Smarter than the average bear, Booboo.

'You're really good at your job, extremely good, you should get promoted,' splattered lady slurred – I kid you not, and if you don't believe me ask Paddy and Becca, they were there, she did, she actually said it.

'Yeah, well, that's a bit of a sore subject at the moment.'

Phase 2

At the end of September came the news that every frontline officer in the Happy Valley had wanted to hear for sixteen months, that the New Operating model was going to be scrapped.

It was pretty bloody obvious really.

The implementation of the horrible thing was referred to as Phase 1 and because the people who instigated the horrible thing wouldn't like to think of it as the abject failure that it undoubtedly was, they insisted that its dumping had to be referred to as Phase 2, because, obviously, Phase 2 is what it is, no doubt about that, surely no-one can disagree with that. And they insisted that moving to Phase 2 was what they were always planning to do all along, obviously.

So, please refer to it as Phase 2 at all times.

That'd be great.

Thank you.

I've absolutely no doubt that the moving to Phase 2 was entirely down to the senior officers being overwhelmed by the answers to my incredibly insightful Freedom of Information request, absolutely no doubt about it. More about that in a bit.

Wot no apology.

Wot no apology, for all the stress and trauma you've caused your officers.

No senior officer had the common decency to apologise for their horrific bollock drop. And the suffering it caused to their employees.

I was by no means the only one to suffer from stress, and although we're moving to Phase 2 I have absolutely no doubt, as sure as eggs is eggs, in the near future there will be another, even worse operating model. No doubt about it.

They've already introduced the Smarter Resolution Team, let's hope it's a vast improvement on the Dumb As Fuck Resolution Team. It just sounds to me like a place to stick someone who no longer wants to be a police officer. Let's just get the bobby back on the beat.

The glitch

Those fuckin' fuckers in the DidKnowItWasPrincessEugenie's WeddingButStillManagedToFuckItUp Department have only gone and fucked it up, again. All Party 3 Response and IHub officers are going to have to be on duty in Windsor, for Princess Eugenie's (whoever she is) wedding. They've had seven months to sort this out, and now, with less than three weeks to go they're asking officers to give up their rest days. Officers had booked weekends away with their families, bought theatre tickets and were planning on going to sporting events. Y'know, having a life outside the police. They're devastated.

The Superintendent had a little word with the good people of DidKnowItWasPrincessEugenie'sWeddingButStillManagedToFuckIt Up Department and they've issued a very sincere apology for a glitch in the system, and Party 3 no longer have to be on duty on that day.

There you go, great old boys in the DidKnowItWasPrincess Eugenie'sWeddingButStillManagedToFuckItUp Department..

That's what I've been trying to tell you.

Bless that poor little glitch, she gets the blame for everything around here, the poor little thing must be working overtime just trying to keep us all on a flat rate.

Suicide note

On Nightsafe, with Smithy, a great lad and officer who'd come across from Witney.

It's all got a bit too much for some poor chap, so he'd left a suicide note, and we traipsed all around the fields of Greater Leys looking for him.

The helicopter was up, the whole circus came to town, as we ran around like headless chickens.

His family were panicking and so were we.

His phone was cell-sited in the city centre.

He was found, on the piss, having a bit of a laugh, in a nightclub on Park End Street. Great work fella, thousands of pounds of taxpayers flushed down the toilet. Big love.

Ah now, this is a bit more like it. A lad had been mugged on Broad Street; our CCTV operator pick up on the offenders cycling down The High. We got all three of them by the kebab wagon, well, it was PC Stanstead (you remember him, the one who's shit at doing MG3s) and loads of the good old girls and boys on Party 2, and good old Smithy found the stolen phone in a hedge by the gates of one of the colleges.

That's what we joined for.

Saturday 29 September 2018

A combination of consultants and academics had conspired to implement a shift pattern where the late shift go home at 0300hrs on a Friday and Saturday night, just at the time the pubs and clubs are kicking out, a pretty easy decision to make when you're not affected by it, you don't know what you're doing, and you don't give a fuck. So, I crewed-up with my good friend and colleague Streeter.

The CCTV Operator had seen a pissed lad getting into his car on Worcester Street. As we went down St Aldates, I knew that three officers were taking a comfort break.

Anyway, to cut a very long story short, which I very seldom do, but will on this occasion, we stopped the offending car just past the ice rink. I knew the driver would drive away, but I put myself on offer by walking towards the drunk person's car ('Ooh, my hero.' I know, I know, shucks, it was nothing, no, really it was nothing). I told the officers on their comfort break to get a wiggle on and block him bumper to bumper. I was talking to the drunken bloke, thinking, the officers will be coming, and I asked him to get out of the car. I looked at the keys in the ignition and thought about grabbing them, but he would've pegged it, taking my arm with him. The inevitable happened. He was long gone. And the three officers bumbled around the corner, using callsign Bimble 1. Tomtetomtetomtetom. Fucking fuckers. I was livid.

I got into the back of the Vivaro and I was so fucking livid it was right on the tip of my tongue to say, 'How do you think you are performing? Where do you see your weaknesses? How do you think you can improve?' But I didn't want them to suffer, so, fortunately for everyone, I composed myself sufficiently to say, 'What the fuck happened to you? Where the fuck were you? I'm so fucked off. Bunch of bimbling tossers.' You know, old skool, no being put on action plans, no PDR entries, just a good old fashioned bollocking.

Because we place so much emphasis on meaningless statistics and SOME of our leaders are so awful and we can no longer give a good old fashioned bollocking, and have to give action plans – where the whole thing gets blown up out of all proportion – are further reasons how it has come to this.

Dunt ma''er in December me and Party 3 are off to Amsterdam. Hey ho three months to go.

OCTOBER

Autonomy and the Empowerments

Rebecca Humphries

Some kind soul drew my attention to a story in the news, which puts a lot of what's going on in the police, into some sort of perspective.

Allegedly, there's a show on the old goggleybox called *Strictly Come Dancing* or summut like that. I've never seen it myself but apparently, it's quite good. It involves a few people who think they're famous (I've never heard of them) having a go at dancing with someone who thinks they can pull off a couple of moves. All good stuff. This year, it would appear that the incredibly famous Seann (yep, Seann, you know him with the double n, so unbelievably cool) Walsh, yes, really, him, has been stumbling and bumbling around with the equally famous Katya Jones.

The incredibly famous international superstar who is Seann Walsh, thought it would be a bit of a hoot to take the incredibly talented Jonesy for 'just an innocent drink' on his girlfriend's birthday. A thoroughly nasty thing to do. Amazingly this 'just an innocent drink' turned into a full on, snogging the face off each other.

Rebecca Humphries who had been the superstar's girlfriend for five years wrote on The Twitter (whatever that is).

My name is Rebecca Humphries and I am not a victim. It's incredibly good of Sean (huh) and Katya to apologise in the media. I have received nothing other than the support of my family, friends and a host of strangers on the internet who all wanted to make sure I was OK.

I was alone at home when Sean (huh, what happened to the unbelievably cool double n) texted at 10pm saying the two of them were going for one innocent drink. We spoke and I told him, not for the first time, that his actions over the past three weeks had led me to believe something inappropriate was going on. He aggressively, and repeatedly, called me a psycho/nuts/mental. As he has done countless times throughout our relationship when I've questioned his inappropriate, hurtful behaviour.

But this whole business has served to remind me that I am a strong, capable person who is now free; and no victim. I have a voice and will use it by saying this to any woman out there who deep down feels worthless and trapped with a man they love.

Believe in yourself and your instincts. It's more than lying. It's controlling. Tell some very close friends who, if they're anything like my wonderful network, will swoop in and take care of the logistics and of you.

It's important also to recognise that in these situations those who hold power over you are insecure and fragile, and their needs for control comes from a place of vulnerability. I think it certainly does in Sean's case. Despite everything, I hope he gets what he wants from this. I'm not sorry I took the cat though.

Having been so accustomed to people not taking responsibility for their lives, and worse still, being told that it was all my responsibility, I felt enlightened. Absolutely remarkable.

Wit and humility. Autonomy and empowerment. They're the kiddies.

This should be on the wall of every woman's refuge.

It'll do more good against domestic violence than millions of completed DASH forms, that Flora insists we have to complete.

It should be handed out at every domestic incident.

1 October 2018

The night before going back to work after four days off, I must've slept for about thirty minutes. I had a nightmare about not having enough police officers. I was left with the dilemma of going back to sleep and not having any police officers or going into work and not having any police officers and either way, the Middle Floor Massive would be gunning for me, so I plumped for going into work. It had the effect that my heart raced to such an extent that I felt like I was going to die. Seriously, I thought my time was up. I was in one helluva state.

I needed to get a grip.

I went into work and put my kit on. At the bottom of the stairs that led up to the main part of the police station, there's something that thinks it's a door. All of a sudden, I was consumed by the bloody thing. I was overwhelmed by its lack of doorness.

'Call yourself a fuckin' door, just look at yerself, stood there all high and mighty, all full of yerself. You haven't even got a handle. You haven't even got an architrave. No self-respecting door hasn't got an architrave, where's yer fuckin' architrave? Ha, gotcha. Six by three block of wood is what you are, and it's all you ever have been and all you ever will be. Get yerself an architrave and then come back and tell me you're a door. Now if you don't mind, I've got some work to do.'

Fucking hell, I was losing the plot, maybe it was hidden behind that thing that called itself a door. I'm not going to use it; it would give it some credibility to think that it was a door if I actually go through it. Fuck that, not until it gets an architrave.

One of my officers, I think it was Paddy, managed to prise me away from the lump of wood and I made my way upstairs.

I was suffering badly from stress and anxiety, but if I took time off with stress, it would be more stressful to be sat at home thinking about the amount of stress I've caused my colleagues. I was in a very bad way, and the occy health referral The Boss tried to arrange never quite materialised. It may come as a shock to you but I have a problem with over-analysing and I'm dreadful for getting things out of proportion and having been subjected to such an appalling working environment, I had developed a grey mushy mess where a brain used to be.

It wasn't just the constant lack of officers, the constant duty changes, the leave embargoes, the nonsense from the control room, resource management, the Middle Floor Massive, the Evil Twins and all the other stuff I've mentioned, it was the fact that I (and all officers) couldn't express myself, and even if I could, no-one would listen.

There was no outlet. And when someone can't express themselves, no good grows and they pop, and when people pop, they do all sorts of weird and horrible and horrific things. Like write books.

'Anger is an energy' as the great man once sang, where on earth would this country be without him? And I was angry, upset, bewildered and frustrated.

When I did try to express myself, no-one would listen. The way I saw it, and I may be completely wrong, was that people from the lower ranks would complain, and it would go as high as an inspector but it would be career suicide for them to go any higher because the chief inspector only wants to hear that everything in the garden is coming up roses. As I say, this is how I saw it and I may be completely wrong. And I wouldn't ever want to accuse anyone of wilfully harming anyone, but, to me, this was a system failing and not the individual inspectors, the vast majority of which I loved very much.

I couldn't understand any of it, it was painful for me. I was in a state of paralysis and I couldn't do right for doing wrong. Some officers were in a worse state than me, some coped better, but I could see I was nowhere near the person that I once was, I was damaged. Family and friends saw me withdraw; I couldn't stand to be near anyone. And no-one could stand to be near me. I was consumed by how awful this great institution had become.

I couldn't stand to listen to any more corporate bullshit as to why they had to introduce the Ferkin' Merkin – it was pure bullshit. Austerity under the guise of greater efficiency. It insulted my intelligence and it made me angry, and the only way I could cope with it was to zone out, it was just white noise. I had to go to my happy place – on honeymoon on the Maldives, obviously, with Mrs R.

I never thought that I would see the organisation that I was so proud to serve in such an awful state, and this is why I'm leaving almost four years early.

Get a grip

Eventually, I managed to get up the stairs and into the Sergeants Office to hear the officers from the night shift all talking about Daisy, a woman wanting to commit suicide on the Shotover bridge. She needed to get a grip.

The Eastern Bypass had to be closed as officers tried to talk her down. She was acting out. At what point in your life do you think, I know, what I'd really love to do is go onto a bridge and give all the responsibility for my life, to some other poor sod? Anyway, the officers were talking to her, and for reasons best known to herself, she turns around and gets a grip of a fence post and dangles her legs and body off the bridge.

And yells at the female officers, 'You've got to save me, it's your job to saaaaaaaaaaaaaaaaaaaa...' as she fell. '...ve me.' As she splattered on the Eastern Bypass. She seriously needed to have got a grip.

Oopsadaisy.

Looks like you've overcooked it a tad there, my love.

She didn't get a grip; she didn't get a grip at all.

As I should've said throughout my book, police officers are the most compassionate, courageous, lovely, proud and loyal people you could ever meet, I'm not, but I wasn't very well.

The poor woman, she'll have to live with that for the rest of her life. The trauma of it all. It's absolutely tragic, how does someone ever recover from something as terrible as that? Obviously, she'll need extensive counselling and therapy. Good Ol' PC Stoical, no police officer should have to suffer seeing something like that. And Daisy will be all right within a year.

Puts it all into perspective; talking to lumps of wood that are pretending to be doors is nothing compared to that.

I was also told that they'd found someone hanging. I sought clarification: did they mean that they found someone with a noose around their neck, or someone feeling shit after a heavy night out. It turned out that they had a noose around their neck. I guess that's what they call gallows humour.

There were so many missing people I didn't know where to start, and there weren't enough officers to look anyway. So, bollocks to it.

Over the weekend, we had a woman with serious issues wanting to kill herself on Shotover. I've no idea why people choose Shotover, it's absolutely beautiful.

On Friday night she decided to unleash her own unique brand of dipshittery on an unsuspecting world. She does it every couple of weeks. Takes loads of pills, cuts herself, telephones a friend and then we have to find her. Helicopters and dogs, as many police officers as we can muster, all of whom have far better things to be doing. She's found. See ya again in a couple of weeks, my love. Thanks for that. It's been emotional.

Wahey, this is more like it.

Sixty or seventy kids in Witney are so used to never seeing a police officer that the rare appearance of the lesser spotted po-po had spooked them beyond all self-control. The overwhelming urge to lob a bottle in his direction is their understandable reaction.

I bombed the twelve miles down the A40 with every other police car overtaking me (both of them), arriving at Burwell Hall, to see about ten police officers being yelled at by about sixty or seventy sixteen-year-old kids.

I've got a couple of seconds to give a quick whizz around the good old NDM, and made the decision to move the kids on, identify and arrest the person who threw the bottle and bring the whole saga to a nice peaceful conclusion. Most of the kids were great, they're from Witney – which is where I'm from so, obviously extremely posh, like me. Some of them got themselves a bit unnecessary – 'Fuck the Feds, fuck the Feds.' At what point in your life do you think that that it's acceptable to chant that? You don't even know me. If you actually took the time and trouble to get to know me as a person, you'd be far more abusive than that.

'What the fuck d'you think you're doing?' one said, as I gently assisted him up the road.

'Fuck ooff,' I replied, in Mrs R style.

The silly little chump gives me the indignant look of a middle-aged woman who has just diligently packed away her week's shopping at Waitrose and the person on the checkout says, 'one hundred and twenty pounds and thirty pence, please.' The woman looks absolutely staggered, her eyes widen, and her jaw drops. It's all too much for her. She has just packed her shopping and now, yes now, she is bloody well being asked to pay for it. It's all come as a terrible shock to her. She's flummoxed and starts flapping around looking for a purse. It's an interaction that she's participated in hundreds, if not, thousands of times, and she still manages to be shocked when it happens. Anyway, that's the look the silly little chump gives me, and then he thinks it's funny, and then he gives me a fist bump. And I liked him. A lot.

The officers managed to identify and arrest the person who threw the bottle at the officer. It was a brilliant bit of work, caught him in a pincer movement and the rest of us all walked on, up through Burwell Drive. There was a ninny who just didn't get it, just kept on going, 'Fuck the Feds, fuck the pigs.' I liked him. At least he has the courage of his convictions. Well, he's saying what he thinks after having alcohol for the first time. It's a damn sight better than not having the courage to stand up for what you believe. If you've something to say, say it, be proud of it, open up dialogue, don't mumble into your beard, give people a fighting chance of understanding what's annoying you.

He was about ten metres away, yelling at me, 'Fuck off, pig, come on then.' If I was thirty years younger and four stones lighter, he wouldn't have stood a chance. But I was thirty years older and four stones heavier so he did stick a chance, until the brilliant PC Harry C who is thirty years younger and seven stone lighter (and stood a chance) heard what was going on (and didn't like seeing his sergeant being abused) and chased him around the Burwell shopping car park and back into my rather fat tummy. I couldn't get out of the way quick enough. What a way to go.

If he'd admitted the offence when he was interviewed, he would've received a caution, if I'd've had my way we would've hugged it out, but we had to get a detection. Last I heard was that he was going to Court.

Later that night three offenders had tried to burgle and assault a well-known drug dealer in his house on The Blabber. There is an enormous amount of criminal on criminal, drug dealer on drug dealer crime (it used to be called shit on shit, I don't like that, 'there by the grace of God' and all that). The fact remains it does account for a huge percentage of crime and explains why we don't look after true victims of crime as we should.

The three offenders were caught after driving across the fields close to The Blabber, they would've been caught a lot quicker if we had more officers and particularly if we had a stop stick, which is a device to burst the tyres of offender's vehicles.

We ended up with the bizarre situation that we had three offenders and no aggrieved, because the aggrieved only phoned because he was being attacked and needed our help.

'Thanks ever so much for your help, my good man, but if you could just leave me in peace, I've rather a lot of drugs to be dealing, because you've rather kindly got rid of my opposition. Thank you'

Great, innit?

That'll stink out someone's computer screen for months to come.

Killed in the rush

'Any unit, any unit, please, the Cobb brothers are on Thames Street.' The Cobb brothers were Op Basil's targets, having been identified as being responsible for a burglary.

Ash and I ran past the office.

'Quick, Ash, let's get there, before that dynamic lot in there, get there, I hope we don't get killed in the rush,' I yell as I run past and look into their office with five officers including Jake Nutt, playing a pretty mean game of statues, he didn't move a single muscle, not a bloody muscle (it's alright, he's done it hundreds of times, you ask anyone) as I went pelting past the sick, lame and lazy office.

The Sick are the awesome officers who've been involved in horrific incidents. One of whom is a tremendous person and officer who saw something truly, truly horrific. These incredible people should be given medical pensions. And it can't help when they have to sit there, wanting to be involved, and some arse, in this case, me, shouts some sarcy comment.

The Lame, are the wonderful officers, who, against all the odds try and keep their heads above the water, but the job keeps fucking them over, and they just keep wanting to make some kind of contribution despite suffering from injury, stress, anxiety or depression. But if they take time off work they're constantly pestered by the organisation (and, most times, the very person) who's caused the problem.

And then there's The Lazy, Princess Fluffy Bunnies, the Fluffiest of all Fluffy Bunnies, (it's always Princess even if they're a bloke) who just take the job for a ride, every organisation has them, I'm sure you know the types of people I'm writing about. But it's always, welfare, welfare, welfare, training and development. Fuck the fuckin' welfare, welfare, welfare, and fire a few fucks into the fuckin' fuckers.

And then they'll pull out their trump card, the good ol' protected characteristic, having the inability to apply handcuffs doesn't quite cut it as a disability, so a touch o' the ol' dyslexias is an absolute bloody master stroke (I take my hat off and salute you). Chuck in a bit of, you're an old black, atheist, married lesbian, and the job's a good 'un for forever and a day.

'Any unit, any unit, for an immediate commitment.'

All of my officers (all six of them) had arrested someone for loads of tool thefts, dealing with the prisoner, seizing exhibits, and house searches.

Even I was out responding to jobs.

'Anyone in the Problem-Solving Team able to help?' I politely enquire.

'We would love to, we really would, but there are no car keys in the key cabinet.'

'I put my keys in there five minutes ago,' says the wonderful Heidi C.

227

'So, did I,' pipes up (the not so wonderful) Matty W (he is really).

'Yes, well, as I say I would really love to, but I have my own stuff to do.' That's the spirit. Everyone else has got fuck all else to do.

Having been run ragged for the whole shift and my constant 'Are the Problem-Solving Team still busy?' jibes over the radio, a job comes through, and an IHub officer says, 'I am just getting some fuel and then I have my own stuff to do.'

'Well done, you've just passed your Problem-Solving Team interview, when can you start?'

This is all as a result of the Operating Model.

The next day, a Top Five burglary offender who was wanted for breaching his bail popped into St Aldates. Ash was frantically trying to get officers there to arrest him. Now you just hold on a goddamn minute, it's a goddamn police station, for God's sake. There were at least twenty officers just sat there like puddings. Without their radios on. They've forgotten the reason why they joined the job. Blissfully oblivious to the obvious. I never thought I would see it like this. Someone, somehow has divided and conquered us, there is absolutely no *esprit de corps*, there was a time when it was all we had.

On the old goggleybox, *Dispatches*, a Channel 4 programme, is informing everyone good enough to listen that the police service is 'screening out' jobs they used to attend and saying that due to the Tory austerity, we have lost 20,000 police officers. Tony Nash, an ex-Metropolitan Police Commander, has set up his own little police service for those rich enough to pay for it. I think we all know where this is going.

Jumped In

At about half past four on a Friday afternoon I was sitting in the Sergeants Office in Cowley. It was close to handover time. The team that I was covering were all at incidents and the oncoming team hadn't arrived, when Control informed me that there was an unresourced incident in a village on South and Vale's area where a house had been burgled, a gunshot had been heard and the fourteen-year-old boy inside the property had been threatened. My friend and colleague, the wonderful Tom Reeves (he was the one who cracked the sexual assault case at the beginning of my book) who'd already done his ten hours, ran into my office and said that he was happy to go but I'd have to get an inspector to authorise his overtime. (Just while I think of it, no other department is subjected to this level of scrutiny for their overtime – another example of how the Response Teams are regarded. Oops, there it is.)

The work ethic, amongst the frontline officers, is something that I couldn't possibly overstate, and I've hardly mentioned it at all. I could've filled this book with stories of the sheer determination of officers to provide some sort of service to the public. This 'can do, never give up' attitude doesn't come from any desire to satisfy the Chief Constable's Management Team (officers lost faith in them years ago) and it certainly doesn't come from any burning desire to satisfy government targets, nothing could be further from the officers' minds. Their attitude is based on a desire purely to serve the public.

I loved talking and working with Tom, so I jumped in with him and blasted over to the village. You know me well enough by now to know that I'm no hero, but Tom and I did put our lives on the line to ensure that the lovely lad was all right. Anyone who'd been in the house had fled.

Tom and I had to stay on for another four hours to ensure that the most minimal police response was given to the victims.

No Armed Response officers. No dog handlers. No scenes of crime. No helicopter. No hope.

It gave Tom the opportunity to tell me about an incident he'd recently attended. Apparently, a lady with mental health issues had recently cut off four of her toes, leaving the middle one intact as if to give a middle toe to the world. She'd sent the four toes to people who'd wronged her.

'That's her dancing days over, Al.'

'Yep, won't be able to chuck those crazy shapes like she used to, Tom.'

'Not so much that, Al, she won't be able to get into any nightclubs.'

'Why not?'

'Too many doormen are lactose intolerant.'

Dumb silence

In a certain light, I bear an uncanny resemblance to Jason Statham. And on a night out, Mrs R is getting mightily fed up with all the young ladies just throwing themselves at me. And it's beginning to wear me down a bit, to be honest.

Equally, in a certain light, I bear an uncanny resemblance to Matt Lucas. And on a night out Mrs R finds it mightily hilarious at the amount of young men throwing themselves at me, and so do I.

In fact, if you're incredibly poor at chronology, biology and maths I would easily be mistaken for Jason and Matt's lovechild.

In January 2017, Ras Judah ADUNBI, a race relations adviser to the Avon and Somerset Constabulary, was confronted by Acting Police Sergeant Claire and Police Constable Darren. They believed Ras Judah was Royston McCalla who was wanted for an arrestable offence. Two worlds collided. As I tried to explain when I was attempting to highlight the perils of the detection culture.

Fortunately, a neighbour was doing all he could to help, well, when I say doing all he could to help, what I mean is that he recorded it all and had very kindly uploaded it to YouTube.

You can see Claire and Darren pleading with Ras Judah for his name and telling him that they believe he is Royston. As the incident descended into a *Dad's Army* type farce, Ras Judah yells, 'You don't know who you are fucking talking to, now leave me alone to go about my business.' The silly old sausage wouldn't give them his name, all the farce lacked was the neighbour shouting, 'Don't tell 'em your name, Ras Judah Adunbi, race relations advisor to the Avon and Somerset Constabulary, who lives just there.'

For two and a half minutes it goes on. The officers showing a tremendous amount of love, compassion, courage, kindness, empathy and patience. And Ras Judah showing absolutely bugger all of these qualities, where was his love for another human being? Where was his humanity? And please don't say he would be on the middle floor at St Aldates, it was a Saturday morning, he doesn't work weekends and evenings.

One love.

At one point, Ras Judah calls Claire and Darren 'fucking racists'.

Now just hang on there a minute my good man. You can call me a white privilege wanker, ye olde baldy bastard, speccy twat, a fuckin' fat fuck, whatever your conscience allows you to say, all of which are true, but I would be enormously grateful if you could just refrain from imposing on me an ideology that I find putrid, repulsive and vile. And now that I am on a roll, this is equally true of homophobia, transphobia, sexism, islamophobia, disablism, ageism, or any other despicable and disgusting ideology that discriminates and marginalises people. I joined the police to fight this crazy shit and this goes for every single one of my colleagues.

Ras Judah goes through a gate and Claire and Darren have their hand forced which culminates in Claire tasering the silly old sausage, a fried sausage I'll grant you, but a silly old sausage, nonetheless.

Claire's world was turned upside down and still is.

Claire was charged with common assault and was on a gross misconduct charge within the Avon and Somerset Constabulary. She was cleared of both sixteen months and twenty months later respectively. She must've gone through and is probably living in hell.

I do not understand why Judah didn't show some humility throughout this time and offer some kind of reconciliation, to show some kind of kindness and tried to understand what an awful predicament Claire and Darren had found themselves in. It's never too late to have a hug. Build bridges.

Darren and Claire were acting under Section 24 of the Police and Criminal Evidence Act (PACE) 1984. Please use The Google. Section 24 of PACE is always worth a look at on The Google.

Claire and Darren were acting lawfully, and that is why Claire was found not guilty. To me, it's not a matter of law, it's a matter of doing the decent thing.

If you scroll down from the recording on YouTube you can read what the keyboard warriors have to say about it all. About half of them support the officers, the other half have somehow managed to tear themselves away from throwing themselves around to Porn Hub's latest offering to be an even bigger wanker towards the police.

Some of the comments say what a great old boy Ras Judah is and what a great job he's been doing within the community, but he shouldn't have been so nasty towards the officers. I would like to know what has happened in these people's lives that makes them believe that this is an acceptable way to behave towards another human being.

Anyway, the incident is in the news again because following Claire being cleared in her gross misconduct hearing, two of Avon and Somerset Constabulary's finest have spotted Ras Judah and thought that it would be fun (ah yes, fun, I remember that, somewhere in the dim and distant past, before I was a police officer) to keep going past Ras Judah and repeatedly call him Royston.

Apparently, they pulled alongside him in their car, yelling, 'Hey, Royston, Royston!' and, 'Are you Royston or are you Ras?', giggling as they did so. ADUNBI is adamant they knew who he was, they were 'having a joke'. ADUNBI considered this to be police harassment.

Oh no, it ain't. It's a bloody joke, stop taking yourself so bloody seriously.

What this country needs right now is to lighten up a bit and having been lit up I would have thought Ras Judah would've found this quite easy.

The Golden Rule of Life is, if it's funny – do it.

In these horrendous, dour, humourless politically correct days, everyone just sits there in dumb silence scared shitless that they may offend someone. A whole wonderful dynamic of life is disappearing. There comes a point in every relationship where someone has to chance their arm and say something contentious and have a bit of banter, bonds and friendships form, and then something amazing happens. People don't take themselves so seriously, they take the mickey, and they have the mickey taken out of them. It's absolutely magical. There is no better sound than the sound of laughter, if my memory serves me right.

I can honestly say that if the police had done it to me and said, 'Hey Alan, Alan Statham-Lucas, Statham-Lucas' and 'Hey, are you Statham-Lucas, or are you Robert Robinson?' I'd've found it absolutely hilarious, I'd've been in hysterics and asked them in for a cup of coffee. That's just me though, that's how life has made me. I've not had Ras Judah's life, I haven't been continually harassed by the police, unless you include the Middle Floor Massive.

I think that this is the right time to explain that there are times when I am in conversation with someone and I can look into their eyes and I can feel the whole interconnectedness of life, I have nothing but love and respect for that person, I see them as my brother, made from the same flesh and blood. I appreciate that I haven't had their life and I want so desperately to understand. I really, really hope that this makes sense. I love people. But that's not to say that we cannot still have a laugh at ourselves and each other.

Hula hoops

Oh no, it's an end of an era. Ladies and gentlemen, the wonderful Chief Constable is hanging up his slippers.

'At the end of March 2019, my term as Chief Constable concludes and I have decided that it is the right time for both me and the force that I retire.

'I will always love policing and it's been an honour to serve the public, most recently as Chief Constable of Thames Valley Police.

'TVP is an excellent force and I am privileged to lead the dedicated officers, staff and volunteers who work for us.

'In the coming months I'll remain fully committed to meeting the challenges we face and will continue to work tirelessly to make our communities safer.

'And I'm exceedingly sorry that I fucked it all up with the New Operating Model.' I may have just made up that last little bit.

The PCC said, 'It is with considerable regret that I have received notice from the Chief Constable, Francis Habgood, that he will be leaving Thames Valley Police when his contract ends on 31 March 2019.'

He waffled on and on about how the Chief Constable had been an outstanding Chief Constable, how they had a wonderful relationship and that they had been ranked one of the highest ranked police forces by the completely meaningless HMICFRS.

And then, according to my reliable source (a good copper never reveals his source, and neither do I) who was there, his eyes went like Kaa the snake in The Jungle Book, and he stared into space and he sniffed the air, he sniffed all around the ground like a cat before realising that the goddamn awful smell of cat shit had emanated from his own arse. Thankfully, according to my reliable source, he spared everyone the sight of him licking his own arse (I'm pretty sure my reliable source would've remembered if he'd done that) and then he launched in to, 'WTFuck, WTFuck, the stupid little twat really should've listened to that treacherous cretinous creature Robert Robinson, the pisstakin' thundercunt had it fuckin' sussed when he called that operfuckinatin' model a fuckin' ferkin' cuntin' merkin. The fucking thing should never have seen the light of fuckin' day. I'm not going to rest until that man Robinson is promoted to Director of People. Robinson's genius has been overlooked for far too long.'

Shucks.

Well, that's what my reliable source told me, but he might've just been winding me up. I'd be pretty bloody gutted if he was.

'Sir, it isn't being scrapped, we're moving to Phase 2, like we always planned,' he was corrected by one of his aides.

'It's being scrapped, you cunt.'

Good ol' PCC, that's what I've been trying to tell you.

For anyone reading this in five years' time, I've been asked to explain that this is a joke. Obviously, I didn't have a reliable source, obviously, and, obviously, our wonderful PCC, didn't use such dreadful language and he wouldn't involve himself in investigations, or anything like that: I mean, come on, obviously, and obviously his eyes didn't go like Kaa the snake's, I mean, come on obviously, it's a joke. And he didn't say that I should be promoted to Director of People, it's all just ludicrous, crikey, obviously, it's a joke, now can everyone just calm the fuck down.

Like Madonna

I'm quietly confident that you lovely readers have got the general gist that there is no shortage of people all too ready, willing and able to waste the all too valuable time of the all too few police officers. Every officer could write a book on it.

If you possibly can, please overlook the seriousness of the alleged offence and the obvious mental health issues of someone reporting being raped by a very famous actor, whilst being filmed by a very famous film director, on numerous occasions and, somehow, against all the odds, she has managed to cram all this in, while being dead for five years.

Bloody great stuff, that is. Imagine the number of wasted hours on that. From the attending officer, sergeant, CID, being scrutinised in the morning meeting, and the assistant crime registrar, yep, we actually employ assistant crime registrars or scrutineers, because we don't trust sergeants, to ensure that all crime is recorded and filed correctly "Have you obtained statements from Sylvester Stallone and Steven Spielberg stating where they were on that evening, and can you be absolutely sure that she wasn't dead for five years?"

"Er, quietly confident, Mr Scrutineer, quietly confident."

I used to've a right laugh with the scrutineers, they were a right funny bunch.

To conveniently close and file any incident we'd have to choose from about 21 filing codes and then copy and paste some blurb that I'd preprepared (I was so organised) to go with that filing code.

The filing codes were things like

1 – suspect has been charged, 5 – suspect died (bearing in mind how long it took for us to do anything, this was used quite often), 13 – aggrieved or key witness has died (yep), my favourite 18 – all lines of enquiry have been explored and a suspect has not been identified. I'm sure you get the general idea. NFLOE (no further lines of enquiry).

I've given this is a lot of thought , and I think we just need one more.

Code 22–just file the fuckin' thing.

This thing has stunk out the poor ol' Officer In Charge's (OIC's) computer screen fer far too long. In fact, it has stunk out the whole of the police station fer far too long; at one point we thought a long lost misper had snuck into the police station and died in one PC O's many paperwork trays.

We've fiffed and farted, fannied and fucked about with it for far too long. I've had enough of playing ping-pissin'-pong with this bloody thing. I didn't study long and hard fer four 'ours to pass my Sergeants Exam to play ping-pissin'-pong. You've scored your pissy petty little points, now, just file the fuckin' thing.

Hidden deep amongst the endless Victim Contact Contracts and Reviews and 7-point plans, I amazingly discovered that, against all the odds, the Officer In Charge (OIC) had miraculously conducted an extremely comprehensive investigation.

This case involves the extremely serious offence of kidnap, but through the extremely comprehensive investigation, the OIC has discovered that the estranged husband, had, indeed, returned his children at the correct time, but after the estranged wife had comprehensively abused him, and returned to look at the clock it was ten minutes later. All parties are extremely happy with police action, they've moved on, the estranged husband has gone on to have three beautiful children with his new wife. He's no longer remotely interested in this incident. The estranged wife has acknowledged that she was only getting at him because they were in the middle of a custody battle, and she's no longer remotely interested in this incident. I'm no longer remotely interested in this incident (in fairness, I don't think I ever was) and I think it would be fair to say the OIC is no longer remotely interested in this incident. In fact, the only fucker remotely interested in this fucking incident, is you. Please, please, please, before I lose the will to live, just fuckin' file the fuckin' thing, er, ahem, please.'

It would've saved me a lot of time, effort and emotion just to have that saved on a Word Document, ready to go at a moment's notice.

We've overcomplicated a very simple job. We just need to get an officer there, as soon as possible, don't record it as a crime until they make their decision, let them use their discretion, and go on their merry way, and let the sergeant file the job. Hours and hours of police time flushed down the toilet.

Becoming irrelevant

Oh hello, what's this?

There will be 'dire consequences for public safety and criminal justice if there is not an increase in funding to the police from the government', the Home Affairs Committee has stated. It also stated that policing is at risk of 'becoming irrelevant' to most people as crime rises and the proportion of solved crime falls.

The *Policing for the Future* report found that while the number of recorded offences had risen by a third in three years – with violent crime going crazy – charges and summons have plummeted by twenty-six per cent. Yvette Cooper, the Labour chair of the Committee, said the 18-month inquiry showed the service 'urgently needs more money'.

'Police officers across the country are performing a remarkable public service in increasingly difficult circumstances, but forces are badly overstretched,' she added.

'Crime is up, charges and arrests are down, and the police service is struggling to respond effectively to emerging and growing challenges, such as online fraud and online child abuse.'

That's what I've been trying to tell you.

And while all this is going on Chief Inspector Poto'PinkPaint (who's inexplicably been promoted to Superintendent) is revelling in their very own special 'nibbage moment'. Whilst the whole of Happy

Valley Police has been collapsing around their lugholes, they've spent time and taxpayers' money on a project to paint the juvenile cell pink. This, it is believed, will make the juvenile calmer. A lot of the older people who are habitual residents of the Hotel Babylon have informed me that a nice massage from Fifi, with a happy ending, would make them calmer, but that won't be happening will it? Now, I know that a little bit of kindness can go a long way, but, come on, you could paint the bloody thing with unicorn piss, and it wouldn't make an ounce of difference. Legend has it that the first lad in there said, 'What've you put me in here for, I ain't a poof.'

Right there

I was out and about on Nightsafe and Paddy and Matt arrested a wanted man.

And, my God, did he kick off.

We had to use straps on his legs to get him in the Vivaro. My usual fan club had gathered and I was blinded by the lights on the phones that were recording the police officers working so hard to keep Oxford safe. They always tend to gather at such events.

Some right on, lefty woman enquired, 'What's he done?'

'Who?'

'Him.'

'Oh him, oh, he's just a rapist. So, do you know when you, and people like you, get involved when we arrest people and say, "why aren't you out catching rapists and murderers", well, there's one ... right there ... him ... that one.'

I was fully expecting to become an overnight sensation on YouTube.

I hung around for autographs and selfies, but no-one was interested.

Down the corridor

We had to take a girl who had been behaving like the horse's arse into care, (under a Police Protection Order -PPO – which, if memory serves me right, is under Section 46 of the Children Act 1989, yeah, I'm fairly sure it is.)

'Oh hi, I'm AIRob…'

'Oh yes, I know you from your numerous forays on to YouTube,' said one of the nice ladies from Children's Social Care, with the lovely neckwear and brooch and the Volkswagen Beetle.

'Yes, well anyway, we haven't got time for all that, we've had to take a young girl into care, and you work for Children's Social Care, can you find her a placement, please? What with it being what you're supposed to do an' all that.'

'I would love to, I really would, but unfortunately we don't have any beds tonight, can you put her up?'

'Oh, I'd love to, I really would but I have my stepdaughter staying with us in my two-bedroom…'

'No, not you personally, I mean the police – you've done it hundreds of times before.'

'Well, isn't that just the problem, you've always got us as a safety net, and we always bail you out, so you just bundle everything on us…'

You get the general idea. So, two out of my six officers had to babysit the girl.

'Oh hi, it's AIRob, you may know me from numerous forays on YouTube.'

'Never 'eard of yer, now what d'you want?'

'Well, yes, as I was saying, I am AIRob, a police sergeant from Cowley Police Station and we have just gone 136 (which means we can detain someone under the Mental Health Act) with a lad and I was just wondering if you have a room, what with you being a mental health hospital, and it being your job an' all?'

'I would love to, I really would but we don't have any beds, can you put him up?'

'Oh, I'd love to, I really would, but I have my stepdaughter staying tonight and I only have a two-bedroom coach house.'

'Haha, no, not you personally, I'm saying the police. Can the police put him up for the night? You've done it hundreds of times in the past.'

'And isn't that just the problem? You know that we haven't got any choice other than to bail you out, and you abuse our kindness.'

There were no hospital beds in Oxfordshire, we ended up taking the poor lad all the way to Prospect Park in Reading.

Legend has it, that as the nurses took him down the corridor, he waved cheery bye to the officers and said, 'I'm only going in there if it's pink.'

I don't know about you, but this austerity malarkey is getting right on my thre'penny bits.

Racist

I was never one for having a flyer. I was strictly a 'from the bell to the bell kinda guy'. And so, on a Friday night when everyone else was going home at three o'clock in the morning, just as the clubs were kicking out, I was hard at it when an assistance shout came from my colleagues in the city centre. I pelted down onto Queen Street, got called a racist four or five times, yawned a lot, and fucked off.

I'd always find it a little bit peculiar how people who feel that their particular cause had been wronged thought it was so incredibly right to abuse a Police Officer.

I often thought the reason for their hatred towards me was because I'm gorgeous, so I'd say, 'You only hate me coz I'm gorgeous.' And you're not going to believe this, but they tried to tell me that the reason that they are abusing me was nothing to do with my gorgeousness, and it was all to do with my uniform. I knew you wouldn't believe it. Well, I was astonished, as you can imagine, I was absolutely reeling, I thought they were chatting shit. 'Are you seriously trying to tell me that you hate me because of the clothes I wear? And not because I'm gorgeous? Well that's just silly that is, almost as silly as hating someone because of the colour of their skin that is, I don't believe anyone can be that silly. You'll be telling me next, that the only reason that you're being absolutely vile towards me is because you know that because of the clothes I wear I can't do anything about it and you're an absolute coward. So, please, it would save an awful amount of time, and an awful amount of abuse, if you just came clean and say you hate me coz I'm gorgeous.'

Back in the day when I was on the Police Support Unit (PSU) – a group of officers specially trained to deal with public order incidents – I was involved in policing many protests: anti-fox hunts, anti-genetically modified foods, and anti-cat farms and anti-so many other things. We were on the receiving end of bruisingly jaw dropping horrific abuse.

The funny thing about it is, most of the time I was on the side of the protestors even though some of them didn't even have a Scooby Doo what they were protesting about. But any excuse for a wrong 'un to have a well earned rest from throwing himself around his own bed to have a good ol' pop at the good ol' police. What a bizarre topsy-turvy world they must live in, to care more about people's behaviour towards cats than their own behaviour towards another human being. I cared more about the cats than they did. But any excuse to be thoroughly vile towards a police officer. What sort of wrong 'un, picks up a twenty-kilo boulder and hurls it at my shield with all the might they can muster? Thanks for that brother. It's only coz I'm gorgeous, I fully understand.

Another time, another place I'd probably be having a pint with them, or standing side by side at the protest, but in this time and in this place, they've got a licence to call me the most abhorrent names and question my parentage. I'm someone's son, I'm someone's husband, I'm someone's brother and I'm someone's friend and I'm just doing my job. They, on the other hand, are taking great delight in being violent towards me.

These days stoical officers have to put up with the constant chant of 'shame, shame, shame on you' and just stand there thinking 'shame, shame, shame on you, you little xkclunt'.

I can only see the world through the eyes of a white, heterosexual, devilishly handsome male, who occasionally likes to have his arse tickled. But I can honestly say that I only ever heard one racist comment from a police officer and that was in the back of the Police Transit and he was soon put in his place.

Here's the scoop on racism in the police service – there isn't any.

Unfortunately, the propensity for wonderful young black lads like Kamodo and Supermario, without fathers to turn to crime is high. Home Secretaries were increasingly worried that as a young black person they were eight times more likely to be stop and searched. The scrutiny on officers was immense and the obvious happened and there was a reluctance to stop and search black lads. County Lines flourished, more black lads were stabbed and killed, like the boy at the beginning of my book. And that is how much black lives matter.

The vast majority of our time is wasted with people not taking personal responsibility. Rebecca Humphries has demonstrated how it can be done. And that's the point, and that's how it's come to this. Dunt ma"er in December me and Party 3 are off to Amsterdam. Hey ho, two months to go.

NOVEMBER

Fight crime and the pretty frilly pink pants

Freedom of Information request

I don't think it's any great secret that the New Operating Model didn't warm me scones.

In a desperate bid to prove my point I got in touch with the good people in the Public Access – Joint Information Management Unit or whatever they call themselves, and under the Freedom of Information Act (FOIA) 2000, I asked them for the comparison between the year leading up to the introduction of the ferkin' merkin' and the year after.

The CCMT were so overwhelmed by the answers to my insightful questions they had no option other than to move to Phase 2.

1. Our response times had got worse.

2. Number of working days lost due to sickness was higher.

3. Occy Health referrals amazingly had gone down, probably because the people working in Occy Health were all off with stress themselves.

    I simply don't believe it, the referrals must've gone up. Everyone who stated that they were stressed due to the working environment (like me) were offered Occy Health referrals. Completely missing the entire point that it wasn't the officer that was ill, it was the organisation that was on its last legs.

    'Well y'know Al, it is what it is.'

    'Yep, and what it is, is completely dysfunctional.'

    And, quite frankly, if it was a functional organisation, there'd be very little need for Occy Health.

4. Amazingly, I was told that resignations had gone down, can you believe that? Inexplicably, I was told that only sixty-eight

officers had resigned, compared to seventy-five the year before, it was common knowledge that about thirty officers were leaving a month. I have absolutely no idea what Joint Access are chatting about.

5. And complaints had gone down, which was unsurprising because there was more use of Local Resolution, but what had far more impact, was that, Glorz, the most prolific of all complaints getters, had resigned.

6. I asked how much overtime had been paid due to the operating model and apparently this came to £866,983 (£433,491.50 went to Ash, he loves a bit of the old overtime does our Ash).

7. The number of leave refusals was up.

8. The amount paid to consultants was down from £14,596,630,67 to a mere £12,463,186.88. Jesus bloody Christ; who were they consulting with, Jesus bloody Christ himself? All those people who sell their soul, and their granny, just to show their arse as they shimmy up the greasy pole, just at the very point that they're unbuckling their belts, they absolve themselves of all responsibility and pass it to an anonymous consultant so as no-one can be accountable. There's absolutely no point in having a hierarchy if no-one can make a decision. For the love of God, how many time and motion studies do they have to do before someone realises that for a lot of the time there's not a lot of motion. And how many staff surveys do they have to do before they realise, we're all pissed off.

9. I also asked how many people were employed by the Happy Valley, how many officers and how many were civilians. I also wanted a breakdown of how many were employed in each department. All pretty normal stuff.

Eventually they told me that the Happy Valley employ 7703, people, 4193, are police officers, 390 are Police Community Support officers and 3120, are police staff (civilians).

But the good people in the Managing Access to the Public to Information about Joints Unit, or whatever they call themselves, went all prissy on me and refused to tell me a breakdown of how many people were employed in which department under Section 22 of the Freedom of Information Act (FOIA) 2000 – Information intended for future publication – so they, the people in the Inform the Public How to Manage to Get Access to Joints Unit, or whatever they call themselves, thought they'd have a bit of a laugh at my expense and very kindly furnished me with the data for 2006 – I can see no use for them, but if you'd like a copy please don't hesitate to contact me.

They also quoted Sections 24 and 31 of the FOIA 2000 for the reasons why they couldn't tell me that there were only five or six officers policing Oxford.

People KNOWING that there are only five or six officers policing Oxford is nowhere near as bad as HAVING five or six officers policing Oxford.

It's all the wrong way around, instead of hiding the figures as to how many deployable officers the Chief Constable has, it should be a statutory requirement to publicise the figure.

Anyway, I'm not saying the How The Public can Access Joints to Manage Information Department (and I must admit I was struggling a bit by the time), or whatever they call themselves, are lying about their figures, especially over resignations and Occy Health referrals, I'm just saying they might need to have a second look.

Ring-fenced

I never thought I'd see the day that the police service was so fragmented. 'They' have been allowed to cultivate a culture far worse than a silo mentality, far worse than a bunker mentality, far worse than a siege mentality, 'they' somehow have cultivated a ring-fenced mentality.

Ring-fenced mentality *(compound noun) A state of mind especially among members of the police service that is characterised by the sudden and irreversible ability to be a police officer. Symptoms include acute selfishness, inability to take on responsibility for absolutely anything, for fear of being accountable for absolutely anything, often coupled with self-righteousness and defensiveness.* Ring-fenced mentality is second only to not wearing a radio as a method of screaming in your colleague's face 'I don't give a fuck about you'.

'They've' fostered a culture where departments and ranks are so ring-fenced and protected that they don't do any police work. This is why so few officers wear radios. And when they do, they say, 'I'm on the Problem-Solving Team, I don't do police work' or, 'I'm on such-and-such Neighbourhood Team, we haven't got a car so I'm not going to attend that. And anyway, I'm in urgent need of some Battenberg." Seriously, I never thought I'd see the day where an officer would put some crappy engagement event before a crime in progress or the welfare of their colleagues. We've been divided and conquered.

This is what happens when you breed a culture of being bollocked for what you've done and not for what you haven't. There's no incentive for anybody to do anything. Nobody wants to do anything. So, it all gets dumped on the incredibly few officers who have no choice other than to do some police work.

I just don't understand why someone would join the police service not to do police work. If an officer is ringfenced from doing police work and doesn't wear a radio, why on earth are they police officers? I mean, come on, seriously, why have they become police officers, they need to look on their sleeve – it says 'Police' not 'engagement'. Get rid of them. At what point did they form the intention to do no police work? When they put their application form in? They're no good to man nor beast. Give their job to someone who'd love to support their colleagues.

Ring-fencing destroyed policing.

The hideous word should never be used within a police station.

The solution is so incredibly simple: every officer whenever possible should wear a radio, from the humble PCSO right down to the Chief Constable. Wearing a radio shows and reinforces a culture of co-operation and co-ordination – we're all on the same team, it'll give us back our *esprit de corps*, give us back our spring in our step and make all officers happier. It's what used to help us catch the criminal, we were better organised, and we all had a common aim. We all moved as a team.

At the moment, the 'couldn't give a fuck attitude' that emanates from the Chief Constable's Management Team (CCMT) ('I know about that' when informed that there were five police officers) infects every other facet of this once wonderful organisation. Genuinely, nobody within the CCMT could give a fuck that there is no longer a bobby on the beat who integrated into the community and was respected for using their judgement to sort out problems in a fraction of the time, you ask anybody in Witney above the age of about forty about Rocky Stallard and Pam Delahay, they'd tell you. In my lifetime I've seen the collapse of communities, the police officer was at the heart of it, that's what I thought I was joining, we should never've taken the bobby of the beat, it's caused a massive disconnect between the police and the community it serves. Nobody gives a fuck that we're drowning in risk assessments, nobody gives a fuck that we've got a positive outcome culture, nobody gives a fuck that officers are ringfenced, nobody gives a fuck that most of our time is taken up with safeguarding issues, nobody gives a fuck about anything other than themfuckingselves.

Let's get back to basics and put the bobby back on the beat and forget the ticky boxes that've gone horribly wrong. How about the senior officers rolling up their sleeves (instead of their trouser leg) and getting stuck in with their officers? Reconnect with the reasons they joined the vocation, because that's what it should be.

We've long since lost the art of apologising, 'they' see it as a sign of weakness, but it is a sign of incredible strength, the public love it, we've got it horribly wrong, we've built awful decisions upon awful decisions and its long overdue to get back on track.

Andrew

Sara Thornton, who is the chair of the National Police Chiefs Council (NPCC) and more importantly was my chief constable, has had a sudden and unexpected outbreak of common sense. She's stated at the annual NPCC conference that the police do not have the time or resources to deal with cases of misogyny.

She said, 'Treating misogyny as a hate crime is a concern for some well-organised campaigning organisations. In July, chiefs debated whether we should record such allegations even when no crime is committed.'

To which most police officers would say, 'Please don't, it's a complete waste of our time which is already being wasted with some equally meaningless crap.'

She went on to tell reporters, 'I'm not saying misogyny is not an issue. What I'm saying is, recording it as a crime isn't necessarily the best way to reduce that, to have a criminal justice solution to an issue which is about the way people behave and treat each other.'

You go girl.

She used to call me Andrew.

Zie Kyle

I've never been too sure why one form of discrimination is any more important than another – I've lost count of the amount of times I've been called a bald bastard, fat fuck and silly old twat (all of which are true).

To help me out, the Happy Valley don't hold back on sending us all on training courses to cover the nine strands of diversity.

The course was conducted by people from the GRT+Q community or whatever they call themselves. Someone who is heavily involved in group identity politics, and dutifully and beautifully, explained that he or she or zie or xem (or whatever preferred gender pronoun they wanted me to use) the reason they had to be treated completely differently but exactly the same as everyone else.

"Without fear or favour" bruv or sis or whatever you are, really simple, if you're a good ol' girl or a good ol' boy or a good ol' whatever you identify as; you'll be treated as a good ol' girl or a good ol' boy or a good ol' whatever you identify as, really simple. And if you're not, you won't be."

Police officers have an uncanny knack of sussing out whether or not you're a good ol' boy and treating you appropriately. It's a wonderful, uncanny knack that police officers have.

And we'd dutifully and beautifully go through the nine strands of diversity.

Age

Disability

Gender reassignment (what a load of old (or young – remember ageism) bollocks all that is or have bollocks and don't want to have bollocks or lack of bollocks and want to have bollocks, all that is.)

Marriage and civil partnership (I've never heard of anyone being discriminated against because they're married, have you? Ever).

Pregnancy and maternity

Race

Religion or belief

Gender

Sexual orientation

And I just sat there thinking, this is absolutely brilliant, I bloody love it, I can't get enough of this. I don't ever want to be accused of discriminating against anybody because of any of those things. She's absolutely right. From now on I'm going to have a laugh with everyone equally and fairly. I don't want anyone going around saying, 'There goes AlRob, he doesn't have a laugh with me.' Not even people without toes. No, I'm not going to be accused of that, not on your nelly. I'd hate the thought of leaving anybody out. Everyone is going to be treated the same, it'll be a piece o' piss, an absolute doddle, gimme summut difficult to do.

Right on cis sis, well, I think she was a cis sis, only I didn't like to ask, I wouldn't want to offend zie or her, whatever she is.

#wouldn'twanttooffendherorziewhateversheis

Shit, sorry.

#wouldn'twanttooffendherorziewhateversheorzieis

This is going to take a lot of getting used to, but I'm sure it'll be a lot of fun. And then she asked, 'Is banter ever acceptable?'

And I just sat there thinking, 'Hell yes, yes, yes, bloody hell yes, it's what I live for, wake up, have a cuppa Yorkshire tea, have a bit of banter, love it, can't get enough of the stuff. It's my *raison d'être*. Banter's the only reason I go to work, it's certainly not for the Evil Twins. If you stopped me having a bit of banter, my life wouldn't be worth living; it'd be like asking Xavier not to dick-swing, or PieChartMan to stop doing his flamin' pie charts – it just ain't gonna happen.'

No-one's going to stick their head above the parapet, not on this one, not in this atmosphere, not in this climate of political correctness and senior officers being present; it'd be career suicide.

Obviously I'm not talking about what dirty old men pass off as banter, where he uses it as an excuse for a sexual assault – that's not banter, that's not banter at all – that's the 'banter' the do-gooders like to lump in with proper banter, where everyone is in on the joke (and can say when it goes too far) and the only thing that gets hurt are my ribs from laughing too much.

She or zie had manipulated the whole room. Dumb silence. So, she, oopsadaisy, zie continued, 'Of course it's never acceptable to have a laugh at someone else's expense.'

And I just sat there thinking, dofuckinwhat, that's all I ever do, if I can't do that, I wouldn't have anything to say. My life wouldn't be worth living without laughter. There'd be a massive void in my life. I could just imagine trying to have a conversation with Ash, there'd be a lot of twiddling of thumbs, rolling finger tapping, puffing out of cheeks, going to say something and thinking better of it, eyebrow flashes, curling our lips in, pursing of lips, biting of lips, tomteetomteetomteetoms .

What a thoroughly boring, dull, sterile, stifling, colourless, worthless world it would be without banter. My day wouldn't be complete without someone calling me a silly old twat. Seriously, seriously why don't these do-gooders know when someone's joking and when someone's being serious? There's a world of difference between the two, and they're supposed to react differently depending on whether the person is joking or being serious. I thought Li'lolPoddyMouth in the pub on The Blabber had bestowed on me the power to give everyone a sense of humour and to know what a joke is. How do they not know this? How do they not know what an amazing sound laughter is? And this bloody woman or whatever she is, is dictating to me how I'm supposed to think.

#Seriouslydon'ttakeyourselfsofuckingseriouslyseriously

Zie continues, 'It's not difficult to remember what someone's preferred pronoun is, you simply ask them what their preferred pronoun is and what their preferred name is and then put it into your mobile phone so when they phone it shows their preferred pronoun and their name. For example, my name is Kyle and my preferred pronoun is 'zie' so it'll come up on your phone as zie, Kyle. zie, Kyle. zie, Kyle. Does everyone get it?' I think it was at this point that I noticed zie had a tiny moustache; I hadn't noticed it before.

Yeah, yeah, I get it, my love, it was the best bit of banter I'd heard in years and burst out laughing and clapping my hands and stamping my feet, it was absolutely bloody brilliant. She'd been having a laugh at our expense, comedy genius, she'd been winding us all up. I laughed and clapped and stamped. And then I noticed I was the only one laughing and clapping and stamping.

Only zie hadn't been having a laugh at our expense, it wasn't comedy genius, and she hadn't been winding us all up. It took a lot of explaining – and I think I got myself in a bit of a pickle when I tried to explain the moustache thing.

And it's all in a day's work.

And we both minced away not respecting the others point of view at all. And that was the incredibly funny thing about it.

We had to go through all the non-gender specific pronouns, and we'd kicked the arse out of the nine strands of diversity. And when we'd finished kicking the arse out of each one, someone piped up, 'Crikey, there are more strands of diversity than Al has hairs on his head.' Bloody brilliant. Absolutely hilarious, and the room was full of people laughing and clapping and stamping.

#seriouslyordinarybantsseriouslyseriously

Now we've got safe spaces, what the hell are they all about? Are they places where it's safe to take a risk? Or a place where you can go not to be offended? If that's the case, then you can't go in there, because you think, and because you think, it has the fortunate side-effect of having an opinion, which has the very fortunate side-effect of offending people. So, safe spaces are places for people who glory in their identity of being a victim where they can go to not think.

Anyway, what do you do when you walk into a safe room and someone's already in there? You daren't smile, they might think you're cracking on to them and interpret it as sexual harassment. Alternatively, you might want to keep a straight face and because you didn't smile, they could take this as a microaggression. These safe places are fraught with danger, I'm going to give them a massive body swerve, I hope no-one's offended.

Some people are so bloody woke, they need to have a good night's sleep to give 'em a bit of a chance to assimilate some information.

Like, for instance, the information, that for most people, there hasn't been a box built big enough to accommodate the size of fuck I couldn't give about their fucking identity. Or that there will never be a box built small enough to accommodate the size of fuck most of us would give for them to understand that just because we don't give a fuck it doesn't mean we're anti anyone's identity, it just means we really don't give a fuck. And we love everyone all the same.

I know what you're thinking, you're thinking, why on earth is Al, a white, devilishly handsome, heterosexual male who occasionally likes to have his arse tickled getting so worked up about all this nonsense?

Because it's playing into this awful culture that everyone's a victim. I'd rather be a villain than a victim. What a truly pathetic identity to adopt, they should get over themselves and be empowered.

If we're not careful this is all police officers will be wasting their time with; hurt feelings. We should be dealing with hurt bodies, not hurt feelings.

I'm confident that you wonderful people are clever enough to know that the Zie Kyle story is satirical, it's based on the truth and I've embellished it, of course Kyle didn't have a moustache and she or zie didn't say Zie Kyle, of course, she or zie didn't.

It's a bloody joke, nothing to get your knickers in a knot about. We've mollycoddled some people to the point of uselessness. They love it, they can't get enough of it, wallowing and glorying in their identity of being a victim, what we need here, is for people to stop taking themselves quite so seriously. We're all fighting our own demons, my friend. Lighten up. Relax, and have a nice cuppa Yorkshire tea and dunk yer Bourbon. I want to go back to the good ol' days of fun and laughter, with everyone taking the piss out of each other. I want it so badly, I miss it so much, I want it back. I'm bursting for it.

But it's political correctness at all costs. It's cost this country its culture. Britain was built on piss-taking. It's deprived us of fun, and maybe that's the biggest crime of all.

Please look up on The Google the case of Harry Miller if you don't believe me.

I want so desperately to have some fun and laughter. And not that stifled laughter waiting for some wanker to call "challenge" – not even as a joke. I want a shirt button-poppin' belly laugh, one that comes from every corner of my being, through my heart and soul and explodes and tears through my whole body so much that my sides feel like they're going to be ripped apart, tears roll down my cheeks, and I lose control of my bodily functions and I wake up in the morning feeling like I've been in a car crash. I've been deprived of it for far too long. We've all been deprived of it.

Who do these people think they are, to tell us what we can say and do and laugh at?

You know me now, my motto is "live and let live, love and let love". I'm not about rules, and I'm certainly not harsh and vindictive, if anything, I don't like retribution, I'm a big softie really. But if anyone even thinks about calling "challenge" I think a fair and just punishment would be a little gentle wedgie – nothing too drastic, nothing too vindictive, I don't like the thought of anyone suffering, but if someone actually calls "challenge" I think it's only fair and just for them to be pinned down and have "cunt" tattooed right across their forehead.

I'm not really one for taking advice, I love learning the hard way, so I really shouldn't be giving any, but if I may be so bold to give just a tiny bit of advice; when you find yourself in the middle of that terribly awkward situation, when someone says "I'm offended."

Just say "Oh. Really. Good for you. I really don't give a fuck. Anyway, as I was saying…."

That's just a tiny bit of advice you can take it or leave it, it's up to you.

There were 120,000 hate crime incidents last year, being a victim has become a national obsession, and I, for one, am getting pretty fed up with it. Some people really need to learn to know what a joke is, they should obtain that superpower from L'ilOl'Poddymouth. I take the micky out of everyone, and I hope everyone takes the micky out of me. And anyway, if anyone was being truly vile towards anyone who considers themselves to be oppressed, I'm bloody sure that I'd do summut about it, while all these do gooders sit there shitting their pretty little pink pants.

And come on, let's be brutally honest, we all know that the only people who are discriminated against in the police are the white heterosexual males, who may or may not like to have their arse tickled. 'Ark at me, entering into identity politics.

This is all just another masterpiece of misdirection of which Derren Brown would be proud, while these people from GRT+Q community (or whatever they are) are waffling on about how oppressed they are, no-one has the opportunity to talk about the lack of cognitive diversity, because if they could, the people who make decisions would shit themselves.

World

Back in the highly ineffective and inefficient world of modern policing, a couple of PCSOs have been out and about, as they should, mixing it up with the crazy cats of Oxford and have stumbled across Kylie who has got back together with Jason.

Now, I love a happy ending as much as any man. The only problem is that last week Kylie had given a statement saying that Jason had hit her and chronicled the domestic abuse that she'd suffered. Not forgetting that during the two hour statement taking process, she couldn't possibly miss the opportunity to tell the police officer how fuckin' useless they are and if Jason didn't get arrested, she'd make a complaint.

The diligent PCSOs who can't arrest Jason called up for the assistance of someone who can. With it being close to 2200hrs meant that it was handover time. The duty sergeant informed the PCSOs that they didn't have anyone available and then looked on the computer to see if there were any other officers available. To their absolute shock and surprise, they stumble across a Neighbourhood Officer who'd been piloting a pretty mean Stealth Fighter and flown under the radar, and skilfully navigated any form of police work for seven hours and calls him up and requests for him to go. The Neighbourhood Officer is a wily old fox and has been in the game for a little while now, and he knows that he always has to have a job in their back pocket just for such emergencies and says that he's going to have to tidy up that job and will not be able to attend. That job, that he always has in his back pocket, never involves any responsibility or paperwork. He's a dab hand at avoiding police work, he's got away with it for years, he knows that no-one will ever be bothered to challenge him on his appalling behaviour. But someone does call up and orders him to go.

The brilliant officers of the Armed Response turned up and arrested Jason, but couldn't transport Jason (and rightly so), because they may have to redeploy to a firearms incident. Two officers from the oncoming shift turned up and transported Jason. The Neighbourhood Officer never quite got around to helping his colleagues and left the oncoming shift on the back foot, with two officers short, before the shift had even started.

Kylie, had a high ol' time telling all the officers how fuckin' useless they all were and she'll be putting in a complaint.

Ten-minute job

The police service has been reduced to an organisation that just records everything without the time or the inclination to actually do anything about it. No-one would ever get bollocked or lose their job for adding another layer of bureaucracy. Maybe they should.

There should be more reward for the reduction of bureaucracy. What a great PDR entry that would be: *I scrapped the Evil Twins and the PDR*. You'd be an absolute legend. Yeah, I guess there's a slight flaw in my plan there, if they'd scrapped the PDR they couldn't use it as a PDR entry, ah, yeah, correct, very good point.

'It's only a ten-minute job.' That's all I ever hear. I've got about twenty 'ten-minute jobs' at the beginning of the shift: racist incidents, domestic incidents, some crap about work-based assessments, updating sickness records, completing reports of officers crashing their cars and so on and so on. And I've had much the same at the end of the shift, reviewing the incidents the officers have attended, although how they manage to squeeze actually doing some police work for me to review is a modern miracle; the constant safeguarding, the adult and child protection crime-related incidents – all just so someone has somebody to blame when it all goes horribly wrong.

In a desperate bid to be fair to everyone, we end up being fair to no-one. Wasting a helluva lot of time and money along the way. If we're to have a cat in hells chance of surviving, people have to take responsibility for their own feelings and not pass their responsibility onto the police.

I've no burning desire to rush out with a fresh batch of 'oh, you poor thing' cream.

A day after Sara Thornton made her comment about misogyny, Cressida Dick, the Commissioner of the Metropolitan Police, but more importantly a former Detective Inspector at St Aldates, came out in support of her. I've no doubt that throughout their police career both Sara and Cressida have been subjected to a massive amount of misogyny. I know, because I was responsible for most of it.

I'm joking, I'm joking.

But they did make a lovely cup of tea.

I'm joking, I'm joking.

No, I absolutely bloody hate misogyny. Only the other day I was talking to some Old Sweat.

'Have you seen the calibre of the recruits recently, Al?' Old Sweat said to me.

'Yeah, great isn't it?' I said to Old Sweat.

'They're all small, young, girls,' Old Sweat said to me, 'what good are they going to be in a riot, Al?' Old Sweat continued. 'I mean, what are they going to do, Al? Get their tits out?' Old Sweat said to me. He was speaking, and I was listening.

'You can just imagine it, can't you, Al? Oh Tommy, Tommy ... Tommy, Tommy, Tommy, Tommy Robinson ... ooh, Tommy, Tommy .... Tommy, Tommy, Tommy, Tommy Robinson ... ooh fuck me, nice tits, fuck fuckin' Tommy fuckin' Robinson, I'm looking at these beauties. You can just imagine it can't you, Al?'

'Now you just listen to me, Old Sweat,' I said to Old Sweat. I was talking, and he was listening, and boy, did I make him listen.

'I don't ever want to hear you talk about females like that ever again,' I said to him, 'You're an absolute disgrace to the uniform. Bloody hell, Old Sweat, what bloody century are you in? I'm amazed you didn't call them 'knockers'. Jeez, you're not even last century, you're in the century before that.'

'Oh.'

'So, Ol' Bald Sweaty Sweat, I would really appreciate it if you could take your old vile, misogynistic disgusting views out of my office and never darken this door again,' I said to him.

'Okay, Al, sorry.'

Yeah, that's what I'm like.

#YouToo

I had to go to Headquarters South to get my warrant card renewed and I pulled up alongside Fanny in my Citroen DS3, he was just getting into his Land Rover Discovery.

'Lovely car, Sir.'

'Yes, well, you know what, Robert, if you work extremely hard, make a few sacrifices, tolerate cancelled rest days, and the never ending duty changes, keep getting those detections and filling in those risk assessments, Robert, you too, could just about be able to contribute to me being able to buy a new one by the end of the year. Or maybe even contribute to me getting a cheeky little knighthood off the back of all your collective suffering.'

I dunno.

Lord Condon (1993–2000)

Lord Stevens of Kirkwhelpington (2000–2005)

Lord Blair of Boughton (2005–2008)

Sir Paul Stephenson (2009–2011) and

Lord Hogan-Howe (2011–2017)

I think a knighthood is a bit low, if I were him, I'd be aiming for a peerage.

Anyway, dunt ma"er, in July, the five of 'em, have only gone and written a letter published in *The Times*, stating that British policing resources have been 'drained to dangerously low levels'.

All wonderful stuff, it'd been great if they'd been a bit more vociferous when they held the position, that really would've been worthy of a peerage.

It's all too easy to pass this off as a broken system, failing to acknowledge that a broken system means broken officers. Broken people, with broken families, and broken lives. All because of this Emperor's New Clothes mentality.

Lynne Owens

While we're fannying around with a pot o' pink paint, we've got East European slave traffickers, Russians trying to pop off the Skripals, billions of pounds being laundered, an incredible rise in knife crime and drugs lines and Aaron Banks trying to pull some stunt with Brexit.

There are close to 5,000 drugs gangs in Britain and over 30,000 professional gangstas, and our response in Oxford is best described as a token effort. The criminals would just piss themselves if they ever found out. And we fiff and fart around with a model of policing that should've been killed off years ago. And it just gets worse and worse.

We need someone with real vision to bring us into the twenty-first century. To get us to chuck away our paint brushes and take the fight to the criminals. The country is in a helluva state and we're more interested in filling in some meaningless form. We're in our little comfort zone. There's real police work to be done.

Well, not for much longer, there is a light at the end of the tunnel, I only hope it's not coming from the oncoming gravy train being driven by that Special Kinda Guy. Some horrible person would say "The only fuckin' train left running after he fucked up Railtrack." I hate it when some horrible people say such horrible things. No, the light at the end of the tunnel comes in the form of the director-general of the National Crime Agency, Lynne Owens.

Lynne Owens has described the consequences of us not focusing on the important stuff. If we don't, she says, 'We are going to be left behind. We need to move.'

Desperate times call for desperate measures, the pot o' pink paint is just going to have to go to waste. Someone needs to fire a few fucks into the politicians and chief constables. Owens needs to put together a coherent and radical vision of the future of policing, this is not a time for piddling around and tweaking.

Owens has repeatedly stated, 'This is a shift not a spike.'

She says that 'the service's current structure and funding lacks cohesion and is wholly out of date.'

Ain't that the truth.

Lynne also uses the term 'a two-way handshake'. I call it a cycle of respect, but 'a two-way handshake' is almost as good.

Going to Amsterdam

You're not going to believe this, but the folk in the Resource Management Department have told the great people on Party 3 that we won't be going to Amsterdam because we need to do some training/learning on one of the days. But, but, but we've all been looking forward to it for so long we've had to put up with everything that Resource Management and everyone else has chucked at us, all the leave embargoes, duty changes, rest days cancelled, working long hours without a break, getting in to work early, going home late, etc, etc, because we knew that we could all go and have a great time in Amsterdam. It's just cruel. Why does this organisation allow their Officers to be treated like this? Where's that fucker, with his fuckin' formula for fuckin' fairness when you fuckin' need him?

Ash had organised it all, we were to go on our rest days. Resource Management have said that if we wanted to go away on our rest days, we needed to protect our rest days. We were all devastated and demoralised.

My throat

Oh, my fuck, what are we getting treated to here? Ash and I are having a nice little bimble along St Aldates when my attention is drawn to smoke and a goddamn awful smell. As the smoke clears, I am treated to the sight of someone in a frock, cycling towards McCoys. The silly bugger had only put their saddlebags on the back wheel without fitting a rack. They were making really hard work of it.

'Ah hello ... oh it's you,' I said, as the penny dropped.

'Oh hello, sergeant,' All Frock and Bollocks replied.

I had great difficulty in getting my head around the enormity of the situation.

'Are you all right?' he enquired.

'Yep, yep, I'm fine, thank you, thank you ever so much for asking.' As my mind scrambled to make sense of the situation.

'I think that, er, you've got your, erm… Your grollocks are snagged in your back wheel, there, er, my friend. You know it's no big deal or anything, just making you aware.' As the smell of scorched ball sack and singed pubic hair scorched the back of my throat.

'Oh yeah, I thought it was a bit harder than usual, I thought it was because I was going uphill.'

'No, no it wasn't, it was because you had your, er, grollocks snagged in your, er, back wheel.'

'Thanks, sergeant.'

'Good ol' boy… Shit… Ash, please just drive away.'

Ash was absolutely furious. 'Al, I told you before, I'm not going to let you get away with your transphobia. I'm going to sit here until you apologise.'

'Please, Ash, please just drive on. I promise. I haven't got a transphobic bone in my body, you know that. Please, Ash, please go. I'm sorry, it'll never happen again, please.'

'Al, apologise.' He was absolutely fuming, he wasn't going to move, he was going to teach me a lesson I'll never forget.

Sheepishly I wound down the window and muttered, 'Sorry.' Without any eye contact and so quiet that even I didn't hear it. And wound the window back up. Ash, just sat there, him and his fury, glaring.

The window went back down. 'Sorry.'

'What about?'

'I said "good ol' boy", sorry.'

'Oh, don't worry about that, I've been called a lot worse. Anyway, if it makes you laugh it doesn't bother me. Laughing at me or with me, the end result's the same.'

'That's just brilliant, absolutely brilliant, take good care of yourself, bruv.'

'I will, you too.'

'And stick a pair of pants on, please.'

Ash was beside himself with anger.

We didn't speak to each other for about half an hour; eventually I broke the silence.

'To tell you the truth, Ash, I'm getting a bit fed up with you being my grollocks, you slow me up at every opportunity.'

Ash pissed himself.

Sticky beak

At 2100hrs on Wednesday 21 November 2018, our wonderful Chief Constable was enjoying a good ol' Livechat session, when KT asked, 'How many officers do you have patrolling each shift, in say, for example, Milton Keynes?'

He replied, 'Hi, due to operational reasons we wouldn't disclose officer numbers but there is a resource in place to police every area of the Thames Valley.'

Oh, nicely handled, Sir, I wouldn't have been so dignified. I would've told him or her exactly where to get off.

'Hi, KT, I can see what you're trying to do, you're being sneaky, you're trying to trick me into telling you how many officers I've got working in say, for example, Milton Keynes. Don't be such a nosy bloody parker. Mind your own bloody beeswax. You just stick to paying your taxes and I'll stick to spending them; who on earth do you think you are? I don't have to tell you that there are only seven officers on the response team, in Milton Keynes. On occasions you've got more concrete cows than officers.'

I'd've been even more livid than a senior officer, who, having sold his soul (and granny) to instigate some meaningless bureaucracy and then finds themselves passed over for promotion, I really have no idea how he kept so cool.

'So, stop sticking your sticky beak into where it's not wanted. I mean, you'll be asking me how many officers, do I have on duty in say, for example, all of Thames Valley at the moment, next. Less than a hundred, not that it's any concern of yours, Mr KT from Milton Keynes; so, if you don't mind going to build some more roundabouts, you lot are good at that kind of thing. I'll continue to avoid answering your questions.'

Through the bloke's legs

Following a press release to identify someone responsible for a racist incident, someone called in to say they had seen the offender, wearing his distinctive glasses on the Woodstock Road. By the time Ash and I got there, the suspect was on the Wolvercote bridge. We swooped in, he didn't stand a chance.

I thought it would be funny to git around a bit and make Ash laugh, so I put his glasses on. They were like those goofy contraptions that Ali G wore. But on steroids. I was stunned by how they turned everything orange, and then I was stunned by how tight they were to my head, and then I was stunned because they were airtight. They'd make excellent spunk goggles. I was obsessed by them, I saw a business idea, I could see a market for them at every The Academic and The Consultant speech. I could make an absolute fortune.

'How much did you pay for them?' 'Where did you buy them?' 'Will I get a discount if I bought them in bulk?'

I was very excited, I missed Ash letting out a bit of tinkle when he caught a glimpse of me peering at him through the bloke's legs. Ash is very unprofessional at times like these. I told him to pull himself together. It was all very, very funny until I realised the damn things had become part of me. I wasn't wearing them they were wearing me. I was like Jim Carrey when he put the mask on. I couldn't get the ruddy things off. Because of the suction I felt my eyeballs coming out of their sockets when I tried to remove them. I was panicking. I decided to front it out and walked our suspect past all the people in their cars. By this time Wolvercote was in total gridlock. I was all happy and smiling but inside I was panicking, I was beginning to imagine having to adjust to life in an orange world.

Eventually I had the bright idea of breaking the suction at the side of my head and managed to prise the confounded things off.

Unless this bloke has a deep dislike of Oompa Loompas or Tom Mason (Tom is an officer who likes to go on the sunbed – a lot–and is a great bloke), he's almost certainly not a racist.

Gotta Love Lawrence Lawrence

Lawrence Lawrence (every time I saw him, I'd ask him what his middle name was – he didn't get it – he went 'uh'), arsehole of the parish and all-round wanker, got his comeuppance.

Lawrence Lawrence thought it would be a really good laugh to nick a car and drive like an absolute twat up and down the Cowley Road on a Wednesday night, which is Fishes night (used to be known as Fuzzy Ducks) so it was packed with great bright young people.

That was until he came up against PC Roffy, who thought it would be a really good laugh to put a stop to this madness and rammed him by the Manzil Way Surgery. Not satisfied with that, the twat carried on, across the recreational ground, nearly knocking over lovely folk, that was until he came up against APS Jon Lewis, who thought it would be a really good laugh to put a stop to this madness and rammed the fucker so hard he had to stop.

Inevitably I had to complete all the bureaucracy and fill in a report as to who was to blame for the collision; obviously, I put all the blame fairly and squarely on APS Jon Lewis. I recommended that he should be 'stuck on' – whatever that is. I mean, I've never been one to bear a grudge, but he really, really shouldn't have nicked me Bourbons, because I was really, really looking forward to dunking them.

I hope I get another opportunity to do another bit of police work before I leave, and that's the point. And it does ma"er because me and Party 3 wunt be going to Amsterdam in December. Gutted.

It's not hey ho one month to go. I'm devastated.

DECEMBER

Goodbye and the Real Househusbands

Wow, well done, you've nearly made it, thank you so much for sticking with me, Al, on my adventures in Policeland, it's greatly appreciated. I know I'm hard work on occasions, everybody tells me. I'm sure we fell out somewhere along the way, but you persevered and I'm grateful. Hopefully, you had a bit of a giggle and learned a bit along the way.

So, this is how it has come to this.

1. Far too few officers (that's a big one, that is). It's BACOOMA time all the time. We are policeless.

2. Looking after people who have no sense of personal responsibility (that's a huge one, that is). We need Mr Bugarov to sort it out.

3. The unfair distribution of work across the Departments, far too much is dealt with by response officers (that's a hulking one, that is). Mr Bugarov would sort it out, it's a doddle.

4. Decisions being made by consultants and academics (that's a vast one, that is). The Consultant and The Academic can bugger off. Let change be made by those affected by it, who know what they're doing, and care deeply.

5. We're too bogged down in safeguarding (that's an enormous one, that is). I'm tired of taking the initiative where other public services should be taking the lead.

6. We place too much emphasis on meaningless statistics (that's a gigantic one, that is). Leave that to PieChartMan, he's good at that sort of thing. I'm more interested in using my judgement, common sense and discretion, to arrive at a solution that is good for everyone and not a solution that is good only for politicians, and a lazy media, hungry for an easy soundbite.

7. Too many Accelerated Promotion Schemes and Direct Entry to senior rank schemes. (that's an elephantine one, that is). Having to work through the ranks and get promoted on one's own merit worked for years. It gave officers an understanding of the idiosyncrasies and nuances of what is involved in policing in the lower ranks. People who are on these schemes are too easily manipulated. Erm, I'm beginning to have a bit of a rethink on this one.

8. Officers on the frontline are treated appallingly (that's a massive one, that is). No-one wants to be a frontline officer because they are treated so badly, most notably by Resource Management and Control Room staff, and almost everyone else. There needs to be a massive change in culture, (oops, there it is) that ensures the frontline officer is the most important role and everyone else is there to support them. And this is born out of the absolute predilection of blaming and criticising the poor sod of an officer who has to make a spur of the moment judgement. Instead of putting an arm around them and caring for them.

9. Far too much irrelevant drivel (that's a colossal one, that is). Get rid of the PDR, 360 Reviews, Work-Based Assessment, they serve no useful purpose, and prevent us from policing. These are the very things that prevent us challenging the hierarchy, which is where the lack of fairness lies. Just have some straightforward honest talking, tempered with a bit of love. Employ a team of people who are completely independent of the police to ensure that there is fairness in the grievance procedure, promotions, appointments to departments etc. To put an end to all the arse-licking and power trips.

10. Too many officers don't wear their radios and spend too long in meetings (that's gargantuan, that is). Come on guys, there's police work to be done. Which leads me nicely on to…

11. The Senior Officers are too detached (that's a monstrous one, that is). Come on guys, police work has to be done in the evening and night and weekend, please join in. Let's get our *esprit de corps* back and stop all this ring-fencing. Which leads me to...

12. There's no focus (that's a substantial one, that is). We exist to stop and fight crime, we are here for hurt bodies, not hurt feelings. We need to stop the emphasis on domestic incidents and other similar initiatives. All crime is important. We need to stop saying 'yes' to things we shouldn't be involved in, these are incidents we need to police less, which leads nicely into...

13. Too many 'yes' people get promoted (that's a mammoth one, that is). Promote people who question the narrative coming from above, healthy discussion and debate never hurt anyone. Surround yourself with people who challenge you. Disagreement is the starting point of discussion, not the end.

14. Fluttering Senior Officers and Home Secretaries (that's megalithic one, that is). Stop their bloody fluttering and make them accountable. Which leads me nicely onto...

15. Everything is too myopic (that's a Brobdingnagian one, that is). Because everyone is fluttering around, there is no vision or long-term plan. They're too busy firefighting to look at the bigger picture, which I think is a little bit different to ...

16. There's no leadership (there is no word big enough, there isn't). Wherever possible we should be apolitical. We're about as strategic as a cork bobbing on the high seas. We give in to every whim and fancy of the politicians – what do they know about policing? Look at what has happened due to the scrutiny of stop and search. The PCCs are political – this has to stop. Maybe Lynne Owens is the person for the job, but we have become irrelevant, and we need someone with a real vision of what policing should be and let them get on with it without any political interference.

17. We're too wrapped up with risk assessments and detection rates (they're a bugger, they are). We can't get to where we want to be because of these buggers, the Evil twins, the Devil's Work and the Spawn of Satan. It should be the very last resort to arrest someone and no-one should have to be Nostrafuckindamus. In that regard we need to police less.

18. The Police Act 1996. The biggest one of all.

And why it works is:

1. The great ol' girls and boys in the lower ranks make it work.

And that's the point.

360 Review

My old mate Bally – all round great bloke and a sergeant on another shift – has got himself in a bit of a pickle.

He has only gone and challenged one of his officers for spending too much time on social media or summut like that. I'm really not too sure what they've allegedly been getting up to, and I really wouldn't like to speculate, I really wouldn't. But anyway, it dunt ma''er but it must've been summut bad for it to've upset good ol' Bally.

And what does he get for doing all this? In fairness, he's been given the opportunity and taken it, to a move to another shift.

And, as a cruel and unusual punishment, a 360-degree review is sent out. A 360-degree review is a something that is sent out to officers requesting that they rate how an officer is performing, in this case my old mate Bally.

I don't mean it's a cruel and unusual punishment to Bally. No, it's a cruel and unusual punishment for anyone unfortunate enough to be chosen to fill in the wretched thing. In this case, me.

Usually when I receive a bit of this corporate shit, I'd treat it with as much contempt as a young drug dealer does politics. They don't even acknowledge its existence, not even to the point of, ignore it and it'll go away, that's too good for it, they treat it with so much disdain that it doesn't even not exist. It's treated with as much disdain as the Middle Floor Massive have for their police radios. Whenever I heard any corporate nonsense I knew it was a waste of time to argue with it, nobody above the rank of inspector wanted to hear what I had to say (or anyone else, for that matter), it would just irritate them, the only way I could cope with it was to drift off to The Maldives, the water was so warm.

Anyway, Bally is a mate, and he's bailed me out many, many times, and quite frankly, some things in life are far more important than me making my pissy little points.

So, I opened up this 360-review shit, and am overwhelmed by the sheer scale of the corporate bollocks. I have to rate Bally on such bizarre drivel such as:

'Transparency'

'Public service'

'Integrity'

'Impartiality'

'Emotional awareness'. Oh, watching the magnificent manta ray glide under our hut on the Maldives, was just wonderful.

I didn't really speak the lingo so he got top marks on all of those, if only the police service acted the same way we wouldn't be in this mess.

And then it went into a parallel universe where all the walls were painted pink.

'We take ownership' asked me to grade Bally on six or seven statements and asked me for my comments. I didn't have a Scooby Doo what they were on about, so I wrote *Yep, he does that*. Oh, my Goodness the waiter, in the Maldives was just great, he went out of his way to make our stay so memorable.

'We are collaborative', this is a very secret code to say other hard-pressed public servants can dump their responsibility onto the police, with six or seven even more banal comments and asked me for my comments. I just wrote, *And that*.

'We deliver, support, and inspire' followed by a weird comment about 'internal and external environments'. Oh no, it was all going so well, I just had to be honest – *But not that, I don't think Bally knows what internal and external environments are, I'm not sure if anyone does. I don't. Maybe someone in HR does.* Oh, the food in The Maldives, was just magnificent.

'We analyse critically'. I'm not sure who, when and where we're supposed to critically analyse and no-one would listen or even acknowledge if Bally analysed anything, so I just wrote, *Yep, I'll give him a full house on that one.*

'We are innovative and open pots o' pink paint'. No, sorry, I got a bit carried away there. 'We are innovative and open-minded', ha, who are they trying to kid? Nobody'd listen to Bally if he had any form of innovation (this is incredibly debilitating for all officers); this is the reserve and preserve of the academics and consultants and we're forced to be open-minded about their latest hare-brained diktat. So, I thought, now, this is really where Bally lets himself, his colleagues, and the organisation down and I would really like to see a marked improvement. *Nah, probably not, Bally would struggle a bit with this. He's probably far too busy being a good old boy and police officer to concern himself with this drivel.*

I treated it with the same amount of contempt it had treated me.

'Al, have you done Bally's 360 review?' asked the boss.

'Never heard of it. What's one of them then?'

And just in the nick of time the person in charge of training, the wonderful Jamie C has stepped in and told us that the training that had been arranged for when we should be in Amsterdam can be rearranged. So, me and Party 3 are off to Amsterdam!!

You know yer onions

One of the city's many colourful characters who's got a bit of a particular penchant for getting drunk, getting his wanger out, being rather lewd around the young ladies at St Clement's and has got an Anti-social Behaviour Order or a Community Behaviour Order or a Just Fucking Well Don't Do It Order or Whatever They Call It Order against him doing it, has got drunk and got his wanger out and has been rather lewd towards the young ladies at St Clement's.

Obviously, he was arrested and taken to Abingdon Custody and because he had warnings for concealing drugs, he was strip searched and found to have, for reasons best known to himself (and I'm sure there are many great reasons, but I can't think of one off the top my head), an onion up his arse. I kid you not, a bloody onion up his arse.

And it had rooted.

The poor old searching officer asked him, 'Is that it?'

'Have another look.'

And blow me if there wasn't another one. And out it popped. A bit smaller than the first.

'Now is that the lot?'

'Have another look.'

And fuck me sideways, there was another one. And out it popped. A bit smaller than the second.

'Please say that's the lot.'

'That's it, my friend. That's shallot.'

We had a great time in Amsterdam!!!!!

Microcosm

'I need the police here, now, my son has gone mad and he's run out of the house with the kitchen knife.'

Not a problem, Emma and Oz are on their way, this is why we get our massive salary.

Fortunately, we also had an armed response unit in the area, so at least it looked like we could be bothered. For half an hour I was worried sick about what the lad was going to do, I was even more worried about what his useless father wasn't going to do. He had seen his son and ignored him and opted to phone the police to sort his shit out.

So, inevitably Oz and Emma had to put their lives on the line when the lad returned to the home and had to arrest him.

There was not an ounce of appreciation from either the mother or father. In fact, there was the complete opposite.

'So, what's going to happen when he gets released?' they asked.

'You're going to act like parents,' they got told.

'If he goes missing, if he plays up, if he throws things around, I will be right on the phone to you.' Useless parents.

Oh no, there you go.

And in that tiny microcosm of everyday life is the problem. Everything is the police's problem, and everything is the police's fault, it couldn't possibly be piss-poor parenting.

And now that I'm on a roll. Maggie Oliver is an incredible person. She told the truth. She had the courage to say that the Child Sexual Exploitation (CSE) was the failing of Senior Officers who were too busy being politically correct to deal with what it actually was/is: Muslim men taking advantage of vulnerable young girls

And that is the true perils and pitfalls of the hierarchy within the police. It's particularly sinister that it's happened in so many Constabularies that none of the Senior Officers had the courage to call it out.

Poor ol' Mrs R had an extremely angry man shaking his copy of the Oxford Mail at her as she walked down the Cowley Road, because of this failing.

All I've ever received from Muslim people is love and kindness.

The wonderful Professor Sir Simon Wesseley has been pottering around with the Mental Health Bill because he thinks that the police cell (pink or not) and a police car is not the right place for someone with mental health issues.

Isn't that what I've been saying?

He wants an overhaul of the Mental Health Act to stop the police being used to fill the gap for the underfunding of mental health services. The £20bn the Tories promised for the NHS in the budget won't touch the sides. On the day that this was in the news, 5 December 2018, there was a very poorly man in Abingdon who had to be taken to the JR2. It took the NHS over five hours to cobble together the three mental health professionals to section him. On this occasion a police officer had to look after him for over five hours. The police have taken up the slack for far too long.

Hastily put together

Friday night is Nightsafe night and far more importantly, my last full Nightsafe night.

Oh no, what are we getting treated to here? There appeared to be a hastily put together creature which very vaguely resembled a human being flicking the V-signs at me with both hands. What have I done to deserve this? I'm just doing my job. Away from Mrs R. I could be out having a really good time, or in, having an even better one with her. How rude.

'Grow up before it's too late,' I told him.

'What are you going to do about it, you fucking cunt?' he said, walking into PC TeeTee.

'Arrest you,' I said, showing tremendous restraint by denying myself the initial rush of pleasure I would've undoubtedly have felt if I could've just added, 'You fucking xkclunt.' A brilliant but massive bit of restraint.

PC TeeTee arrested him for being drunk and disorderly. And the hastily put together fucking xkclunt tried to make out that he wasn't calling me that vile and disgusting word, he was saying it to his mate. Standard. Of course, you were, you hastily put together fucking xkclunt, so I placed the hastily put together fucking xkclunt in the back of the police transit.

Bothersome vagina. Probably a really nice bloke when he's sober, but when he's drunk, he's a bothersome vagina.

The general plan was to take him and his girlfriend to her home in Marston and let him out, but he just couldn't help himself, he just kept on being abusive and gurnin' like a good 'un. The wind'll change and it'd stick like that, and by the looks of things you've already been caught out a couple of times. The girlfriend got out of the van and apologised for his behaviour. So, the hastily put together creature that very vaguely resembled a human being was taken to Newbury custody (because there weren't cells available at Abingdon). In the morning he was given a fine and then put in a complaint. Standard. Wasting thousands of pounds of taxpayers' money. Standard.

A lot of people are arrested for drunken behaviour, and I feel sorry for them and they are enormously apologetic in the morning, particularly with their behaviour towards officers. Sometimes they are shown the Body Worn Video (BWV) footage and they are ashamed. If we weren't so hung up on our bloody silly detection rate, I think it would do the offender and the officer a helluva lot more good if there was an option for them to shake hands and discuss what happened, and forget the pointless detection.

All the hard work of educating people about how they should behave goes out the window the moment that alcohol is involved. Nearly all criminality is caused by drink and/or drugs.

32-point turn

All I wanted to do was go for a bimble but as we were going over Magdalen Bridge we were flagged down.

'There was a girl who was going to jump off the bridge. She's just gone down there,' said the panic-stricken person.

In my haste to break out of the bimble and actually inject a little bit of urgency into the proceedings, I got the Transit stuck in Rose Lane and had to perform a 32-point turn. Tomtetomtetomtetom. Hopefully she will have grown a beard and pissed off by the time I get around to where I should be. No. We were flagged down again, she had gone under the bridge and was swimming towards the punts.

Not satisfied with drowning in her misery and putting her own life in danger she had to put two officers' lives in danger, so Kelly and Sophie had to get in the water to try to stop her suffering. She had to pull people into her misery. She swam away and then looped around into a side stream next to Magdalen School, where I'd pushed the boundaries of my athletic prowess by straddling a three-foot high gate. Kelly had got herself out of the water and was encouraging her to swim towards us, but she just yelled that she was running out of breath and forced herself under the water. Kelly jumped in, got her around the chin and spun her on her back and dragged her out of the water. She feigned passing out. It just wasn't on. She was sectioned and taken to hospital.

The police family sprang into action. The custody staff at Abingdon were amazing and looked after Sophie and Kelly. It's this part of the job that I will miss tremendously.

It's the part of the job that senior officers do not understand because they're never there, because they don't want to be there, they don't want to contribute, they don't have the shared experiences that bring the lower ranks together, the commonality. They just want to sit in judgement so the bonds can't form, and the detachment grows, and incredibly stupid decisions are made, and it goes around and around and on and on.

While in Abingdon Custody I popped in to have a look at the pink cell and under the lights it looked purple.

Cinderellas

'Good evening, Thames Valley Police, Laura speaking, how can I help?'

'Oh hi, yeah, well, yeah, the bloke across the road keeps staring at me. He always does it when I finish work, just after midnight.'

'I'm really sorry, I think I may have misheard you there, I thought you said, "staring at you".'

'Yeah, he keeps staring at me.'

'Oh really, hang on let me see if there's anyone in here who could care a tiny bit... hey, listen up' (Laura shouts to the rest of the Control Room), 'I've got someone who is telling me that their neighbour keep staring at him ...no.' Turns back to the caller. 'No, everyone is just shrugging their shoulders and turning the corners of their mouths down, no-one is overly interested ... hang on, the sergeant has just walked in... sergeant, I have someone who has a neighbour who keeps staring at him... Hahahahaha, he's just pinched his nose and pulled an imaginary chain, I think it's quite safe to say that he doesn't care too much.

'I would ask the Neighbourhood Team (it's the same Neighbourhood Team that worked so incredibly hard at getting out of doing Nightsafe, I'm sure they wouldn't've done it if they knew that they were causing me so much stress and anxiety) to have a word, but we call them the Cinderellas, they don't work past midnight. They're not so much scared that they'll turn into a pumpkin, but they're frit shitless that they may turn into something that remotely resembles a police officer. I think that they think they're engagement officers or something like that, they've forgotten that they're police officers. They shouldn't because they have 'police' on their shirt sleeves and on their stab vests, and they definitely are police officers, but all they want to do is engage with people who know only too well how to contact the police about crap about their neighbours staring at them. You've more chance of shitting a diamond than you have of finding someone from that Neighbourhood Team who could give a flying flapping flamingo. But this is the precise reason why you never see a police officer, because they're dealing with this type of twoddle.

'Why don't you do what any normal civilised person would do under these circumstances? You know, just give him the wanker sign, or stick your middle finger up, or tell him to fuck off or all three. How about taking responsibility for the situation? Ask him if there's a problem. If people actually took responsibility for themselves, there would be little need for the police. Go on, give it a go, I think you'll surprise yourself, take good care of yourself.'

Real Househusbands

On my last day, the Boss gave a wonderful speech saying that he will remember me for three things: my honesty, my sense of humour, and that I was a father figure to the other officers. That is precisely how I'd want to be remembered I couldn't ask for anymore.

The Occy Health referral had never materialised – I may have had a phone call consultation with someone. I really can't remember but they're miles too busy, with far too few employees, they must be incredibly stressed.

'Good morning, Sergeants Office Cowley, soon to be retired police sergeant Al Robinson speaking, how can I help?'

'Good morning, Al, I'm Laura from Contact Management. I have Leon Wolf from the Real Househusbands of Hockmore Tower on the line and he's wondering what is going on about his harassment case? Apparently, he's been arrested for harassing his neighbour and he wants to know why his neighbours haven't been arrested.'

This sorta shit is what we have to deal with at least fifty per cent of our time.

'For fuck's sake, this is exactly what I didn't want on my last day, put the twat through.'

'Ha, thank you, here he comes.'

'Good morning, Big Bad Wolf. Well, you're big and bad, and I'm not afraid of you, not one little bit. Police Constable Sergeant soon to be retired Al Robinson here.

'So, Mr Wolf, today it's the police's turn to have their time wasted by your petty drivel, tomorrow it will be some other poorly resourced public service, but today it's the police's lucky day. The problem is your actual talent of being an arsehole is surpassed only by your imagined skill of being intelligent.

'What inconsequential bit of shit, shit that the rest of the population cannot be bothered to give brain space to, let alone bother the police with, are you going to bore me with today, Mr Wolf? I'm all ears, and don't give me any old bollocks that you are a victim of crime, because you're not, you're a victim of your own stupidity. In fact, your whole problem is that you're unwilling to take responsibility for your own life, and that is the biggest crime that I've had to deal with throughout my career.

'What do you do all day? What's the time, Mr Wolf? Oh, wow, it's wank o'clock. It's always bloody wank o'clock. Leave the poor little thing alone, it's worn out, give it a break, let it up for air every now and then, let it catch its breath, it's gasping for oxygen. I think you misheard your psychologist when she told you to be more grateful and thank at every opportunity. The only break it gets is when you phone me, or some other poor sod of a public servant, and give them shit or get off your stupid face on drugs.'

'I only phoned to wish you a merry Christmas.'

'Yeah, you too.'

'And you may be listening to too much Jordan Peterson,' he said.

'No-one could ever listen to too much Jordan Peterson. It's impossible. Take good care of yourself. Bye,' I stated.

Porridge Bowls

I get up and walk into the report-writing room and hope the officers don't mind if I tidy up their porridge bowls (again) which have been kicking around for a week or so (again) and their teacups (again). The radio just keeps going, the silly little cunt just down the hill from the police station is being a silly little cunt just down the hill from the police station, some fucker is wanting to kill themselves, some fucker is dealing drugs, some fucker is stealing, and so it goes on.

I've absolutely no doubt that we may have had to move to Phase 2 with the Operating Model, but someone will come up with something even more ludicrous, they'll be more subtle with its implementation, but they just can't stop meddling. How it should work is that a constable should report to their sergeant that things aren't working (and, probably, how things could be made better) and the sergeant reports it to their inspector. It's there that there's a blockage, because it would be career suicide for the inspector to say that things aren't working, because the chief inspector doesn't want any problems to deal with; all they want to hear is that everything in the garden is coming up roses, so nobody in the lower ranks can implement change. And it's not like anyone in the Chief Constable's Management Team will spend six months on the frontline to experience just how awful it is – so they never get to find out what the problems are.

I couldn't help thinking that Mr Wolf wasn't too dissimilar to the police service, the academics and consultants and people who've never done a moment's police work need to leave the poor little thing alone, it's worn out, give it a break, let it up for air every now and then, let it catch its breath, it's gasping for oxygen.

And that's the point. And that's how it has come to this.

Some people asked what job I was going to when I leave. I told them, 'I've got quite a promising career as a poet if I could just force my way past a rhyming couplet, and if that doesn't come off, I could offer my services as a dog walker up on the Hill of Roses, all those puppies born after the mating frenzy after Mrs WBAA let out her high pitched screech aint gonna walk themselves you know.'

Well, that's what I told people, but what I'm actually going to do is be an adviser (I couldn't possibly become a consultant) to the people who make those TV police dramas like *Lewis* and *Vera*. The attention to detail in these dramas is appalling, I mean, who's ever heard of a DI leaving the comfort of their office to talk to a witness? I mean, that ain't ever gonna happen, ever. Somebody really ought to tell these people and that somebody should be me.

I was overwhelmed by the love everyone had for me.

I had my day.

I was in the Sergeants Office telling someone about All Frock and Bollocks. 'They must've been the hugest pair of nuts the world has ever seen...' when Paddy came rushing into the office, doing that strange pulling down the corners of mouth using his neck muscles thing, while using his thumb to point behind him. 'So, I got the most massive wrench I could get my hands on and gave them an almighty anti-clockwise turn, and those taps have never leaked since. Ah, Sir, thank you so much for coming to see me.'

The superintendent had made a special journey to come and see me. As always, he was great and gracious.

All the notes about the high risk mispers and the mind maps I'd scrawled to find them, that I'd diligently chucked in a tray in the cabinet I scrumpled them all together and bunged in the confidential waste. They were a massive thing in my life at one point. They'd just come and go, they'd come and gooooo, just like everything else.

Just like me.

Ain't life like that in so many ways?

Brocky broke open the finest malt whisky and cut up my warrant card. I was absolutely elated. I was no longer restricted by all the policies and procedures, no more Evil Twins, no more pie-charts, no more priorities, no more DMMs, no more doing no police work. I could have banter again; I could be me again. I was free again. I was euphoric.

I went to St Aldates where they'd all gathered. Paddy produced a wonderful book of memories. Ash gave a great speech. As I looked over the sea of faces, my sadness at not being able to work with these wonderful people was eclipsed by the euphoria of not having to put myself through it anymore.

They are incredible people doing an incredible job – I love them and miss them terribly.

I savoured the moment. This hastily put together shambles of a group of people who vaguely resemble a police service is all that stands between lawlessness and some tiny semblance of order. These are the most amazing people that you will ever meet. They are heroes.

These are the kind of people who get called racist at every opportunity, these are the kind of people who never get any appreciation, these are the kind of people who are the tiniest thread that keep the fabric of society sewn together. These are the kind of people who run towards danger when everyone else is running away, these are the kind of people who put their lives on the line when someone is on a mad one, these are my kind of people.

I've nothing but love and admiration for every single one of them.

For all their love, I was so relieved it was all over. I was beside myself with joy.

Driving home, I had a breakdown, not my car, me. I was sobbing my heart out.

I could've done so much more. I should've stood up to the wankers who've reduced the job to taking responsibility for other people's lives. How dare they, how fucking dare they? I was in a hell of a state,

I had to pull over. What the fuck have they done to this magnificent organisation? What are they doing to those incredible people? Why the fuck didn't I do so much more? I'm as bad as them, I shouldn't've kept drifting over to the Maldives. I was crying uncontrollably. I'm crying writing this. It's painful, it hurts. I shouldn't've let them treat me like that, I shouldn't've trusted them, I should've had more fight, I should've had more spirit, I failed in my obligation. Sometimes it just gets inside me, and it comes out in ways I don't foresee, all the anger, sadness, and frustration. I was hysterical. You fucking bastards. How fucking dare they fuck over these amazing people.

Love the police. Please just love them.

Just One More Thing

Hokey cokey, any man of a certain age knows exactly what the Columbo Moment is. You've finished, its all tucked away, all nice and safe and sound and comfy, and you're just about to walk away from the urinal but he has other ideas, he's yelling 'just one more thing.'

And there is just one more thing.

The good people at the Managing the Public to Access Information About Joints Unit or whatever they call themselves have stated that:-

Between 01/01/2015 and 01/01/2020, there were 1459 Police Officer Joiners via various entry routes (Student officers, Police Now, Transfers in, Rejoiners, Direct Entry, Secondees in). Between 01/01/2015 and 01/01/2020 there were 1627 Police Officer leavers (retired, resigned, transferred out etc)

That's a deficit of 168, at the very time that we should be recruiting more officers we've lost 168. We've gone past the tipping point.

Hopefully, I'll still be around on 1st January 2026, but if I'm not, I'd be grateful if one of you could get in touch with the good people at the Joints! Accessing, Managing and Informing the Public Unit (yep, I know, I've kicked the arse out of that joke) or whatever they call themselves, to find out how many of the bright eyed and bushy tailed officers that joined between 1st January 2020 to 31st December 2020 (the Boris Bobbies) have stayed in for five years. My prediction is at least fifty per cent will've metamorphosised from Tigger into Eeyore.

Of course, you'll get some officers who fully understand Da Rules of Da Game and sell their soul to get to wherever they want to be. You'll get some that are completely useless and will be mollycoddled throughout their career. But, more than half will be great, caring, kind, compassionate and loving people. These wonderful people will sneak a sneaky peak around the creeky door of the police service and think 'WTFuckfuckityfuckballs in the name of all that is Holy is this shit show? I thought I was going to be serving the public by showing love and compassion and understanding to those I serve, but all I do is go through soulless procedures. I'm fucking off before this job takes me down. Tafuckinta.'

It doesn't take too long to realise that because they care passionately about serving the public, their every move will be analysed and they will be held accountable for every little thing that they do.

Unlike those who've worked out Da Rules of Da Game who are acutely aware that the system is so convoluted that the higher up they get, they can have all the power without any of the accountability.

Political correctness will come at a massive cost, and that massive cost will be your police service (and society) it's a dragon that will eat its own tail, until all that is left is the gormless grinning face of narcissism. Narcissism has been mistaken for political correctness.

And that's what it's all about.

GLOSSARY

APS – Acting Police Sergeant

The Blabber – Blackbird Leys; a housing estate on the outskirts of East Oxford in the 1950s and 60s. Until a few years ago it was the largest council estate in England.

CCMT – Chief Constable's Management Team.

CCTV – Closed Circuit TV monitoring.

CMM – Conflict Management Model, sometimes referred to as the CRM – Conflict Resolution Model – I love it.

DMM – Ha, I call it the Daily Morning Meeting, but it isn't, it's the Daily Management Meeting, anyway, it's where I went to get my nuts slow-roasted.

Dunning Kruger effect – When people over-estimate their ability.

Exigency of Duty – Words in Police Regulations that is a cover-all for just about anything to shaft an officer to change their duty.

Headquarters South – Thames Valley Police has two Headquarters in Kidlington, a few miles North of Oxford City Centre. One is in the North of Kidlington and that is called Headquarters North, the other is in the South of Kidlington, and I hope it doesn't come as a shock to you, when I say, that is called Headquarters South.

IHub – Investigation Hub.

Immediate incident – and incident that requires police attendance in, I think, 20 minutes, I'm not sure, I just got there as quickly as I could.

Littlemore – although it's a village on the outskirts of Oxford, in the book I am referring to Mental Health Facility.

LPA – Local Police Area.

Misper – Missing person.

NDM – National Decision-making Model – it's my meth.

NOM – New Operating Model – or if you prefer – The Ferkin Merkin.

NTE – Night-Time Economy.

On the Fizzer – Being the subject of an internal disciplinary Investigation.

OST – Officer Safety Training.

PSU – Police Support Unit. A group of 'ordinary' officers who are specially trained to resolve Public Order incidents.

Resource Management Department – A Team of who use computer algorithms to determine the number of officers required on duty at any specific hour of the day.

SMT – Senior Management Team.

St Aldates – Police Station in the centre of Oxford, apart from response officers, it also accommodates administration staff and the SMT for the Oxford LPA.

ACKNOWLEDGEMENTS

The Wonderful Little Thing, Carol Robinson, I know I'm a bit difficult on occasions.

My incredible Mum, who sadly is no longer with us, who gave me the courage to do it.

And my lovely Dad, who thankfully is still very much with us, who gave me the belief to do it.

They both knew that I was always perfect. I think that's where the problem lies.

My brother John and Les (who did the front cover artwork) for all their love and support, and think that I'm perfect, obviously.

The amazing Tim Parker for the back cover and his poem. And the quite brilliant Steve Fisher, whose attention to detail is second to none.

All the superb officers I had the good fortune to serve alongside, and all the ones I didn't, I love you all. I know I was a bit difficult on occasions.

The wonderful Mike Ellis, he was there in my darkest hour, I'll never be able to repay him, can't wait for you to publish your book.

The incredible Mark Gauld, when I turned up with the body, you just grabbed a shovel, forever in your debt. And you gave me all the best one-liners.

Duncs, such an amazingly kind soul.

The amazing Keely, Nick Gilbert, Gordy K, Dex, Andy B, Gareth H, Pricey, Smilo Milo and Hayley, Russ Mizon, Slynchie and Phil G, when I was out for the count, you got me back on my feet, I am so incredibly lucky to have you in my corner. And I'll hit back harder.

And of course, 5RB, my incredible barristers, who worked so hard to keep me out of trouble.

Lastly, and every bit as importantly, the great Chrissy Cradock, who is everything a great friend should be.

You are all always in my thoughts.

Take a few risks.

Don't go along with anything for an easy life.

If you've got something to say, say it, and live with the consequences.

Thank you all so much for giving me such an incredible life.

I don't have money, but what I do have are a very particular set of skills, skills I have acquired over a very long career. Skills that make me a nightmare for people like you. When this all blows over, I will look for you, I will find you, and I will hug you, right arm up, left arm down, it's the only way.

Printed in Great Britain
by Amazon